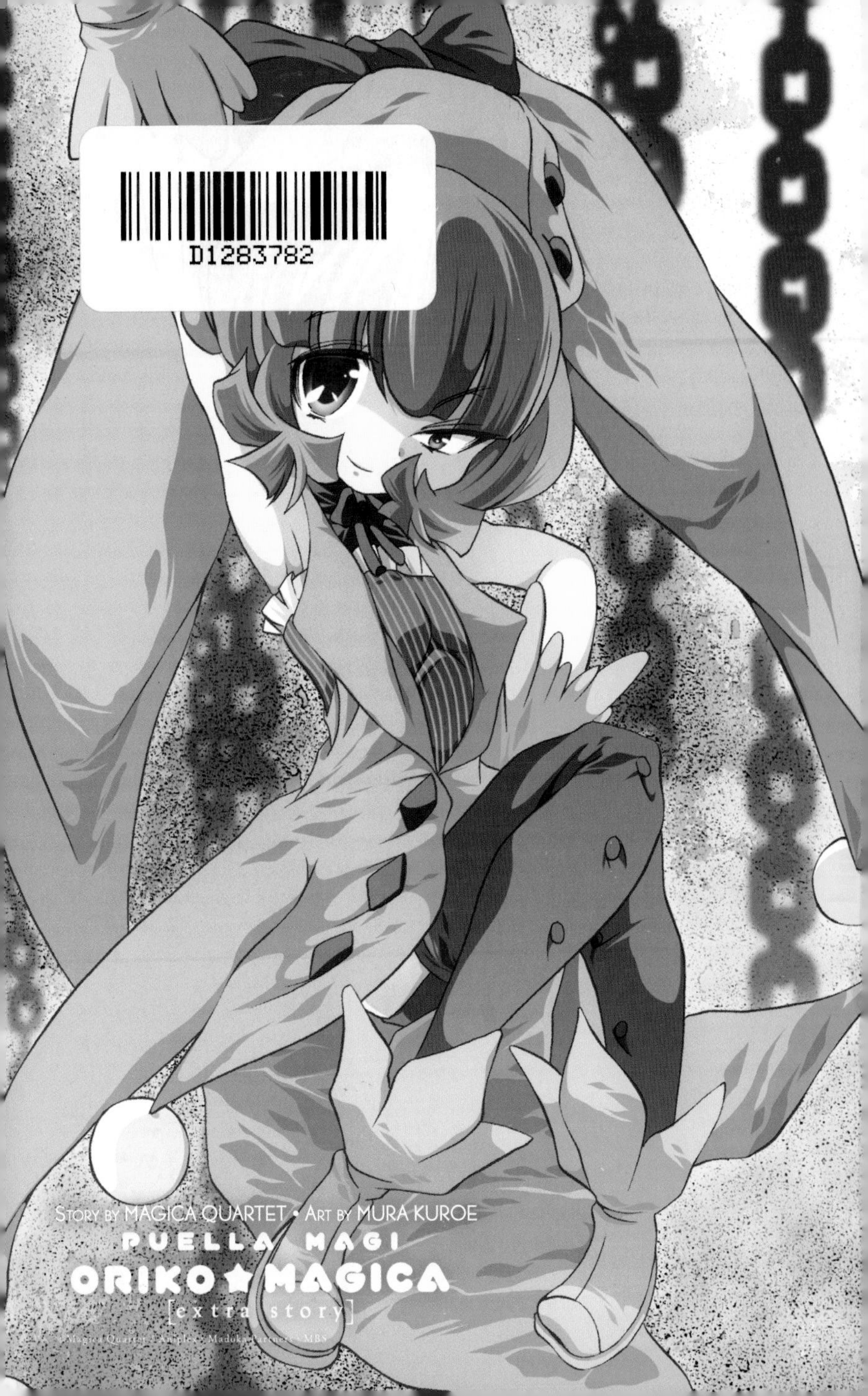
STORY BY MAGICA QUARTET • ART BY MURA KUROE
PUELLA MAGI
ORIKO☆MAGICA
[extra story]

PUELLA MAGI
ORIKO MAGICA

WHICH WOULD BE AN INCIDENT THAT WOULD CHANGE HER DESTINY—
WHICH WOULD BE THE BEGINNING OF A WHOLE OTHER MAGICAL GIRL TALE—

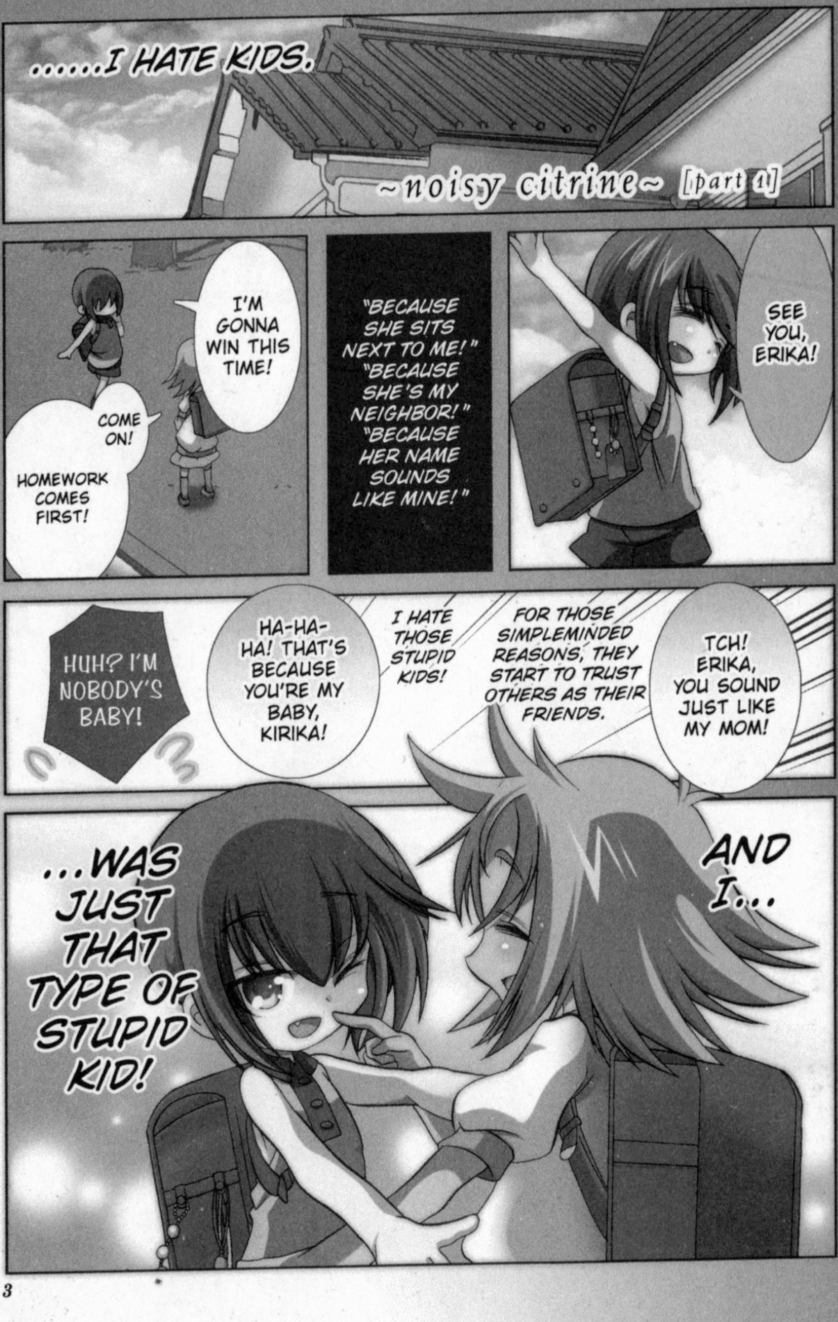
......I HATE KIDS.
~noisy citrine~ [part 1]
SEE YOU, ERIKA!
"BECAUSE SHE SITS NEXT TO ME!" "BECAUSE SHE'S MY NEIGHBOR!" "BECAUSE HER NAME SOUNDS LIKE MINE!"
I'M GONNA WIN THIS TIME!
COME ON!
HOMEWORK COMES FIRST!
TCH! ERIKA, YOU SOUND JUST LIKE MY MOM!
FOR THOSE SIMPLEMINDED REASONS, THEY START TO TRUST OTHERS AS THEIR FRIENDS.
I HATE THOSE STUPID KIDS!
HA-HA-HA! THAT'S BECAUSE YOU'RE MY BABY, KIRIKA!
HUH? I'M NOBODY'S BABY!
AND I...
...WAS JUST THAT TYPE OF STUPID KID!

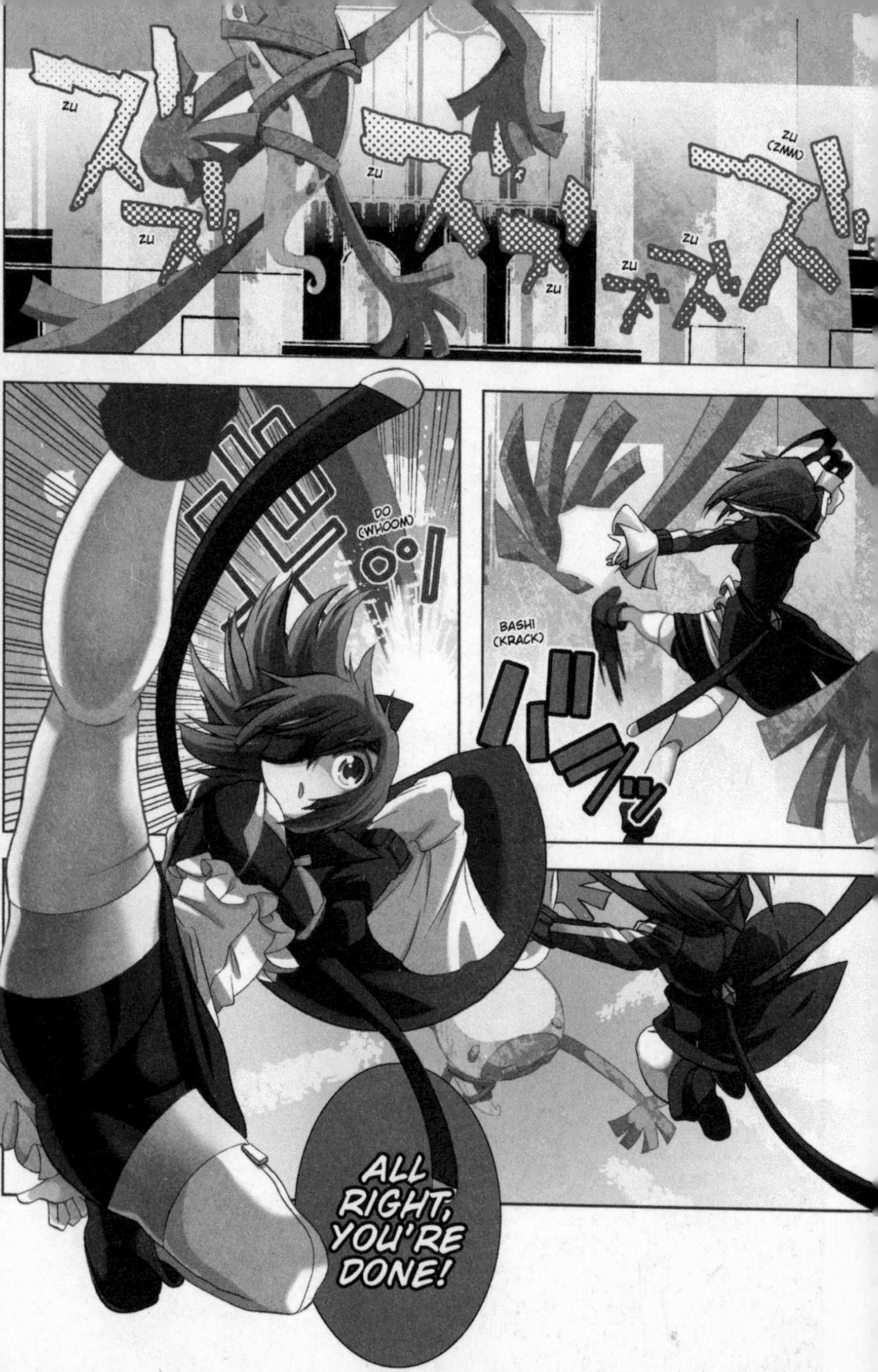
ZU (ZMM)
ZU
ZU
ZU
ZU
ZU
ZU
BASHI (KRACK)
DO (WHOOM)
ALL RIGHT, YOU'RE DONE!

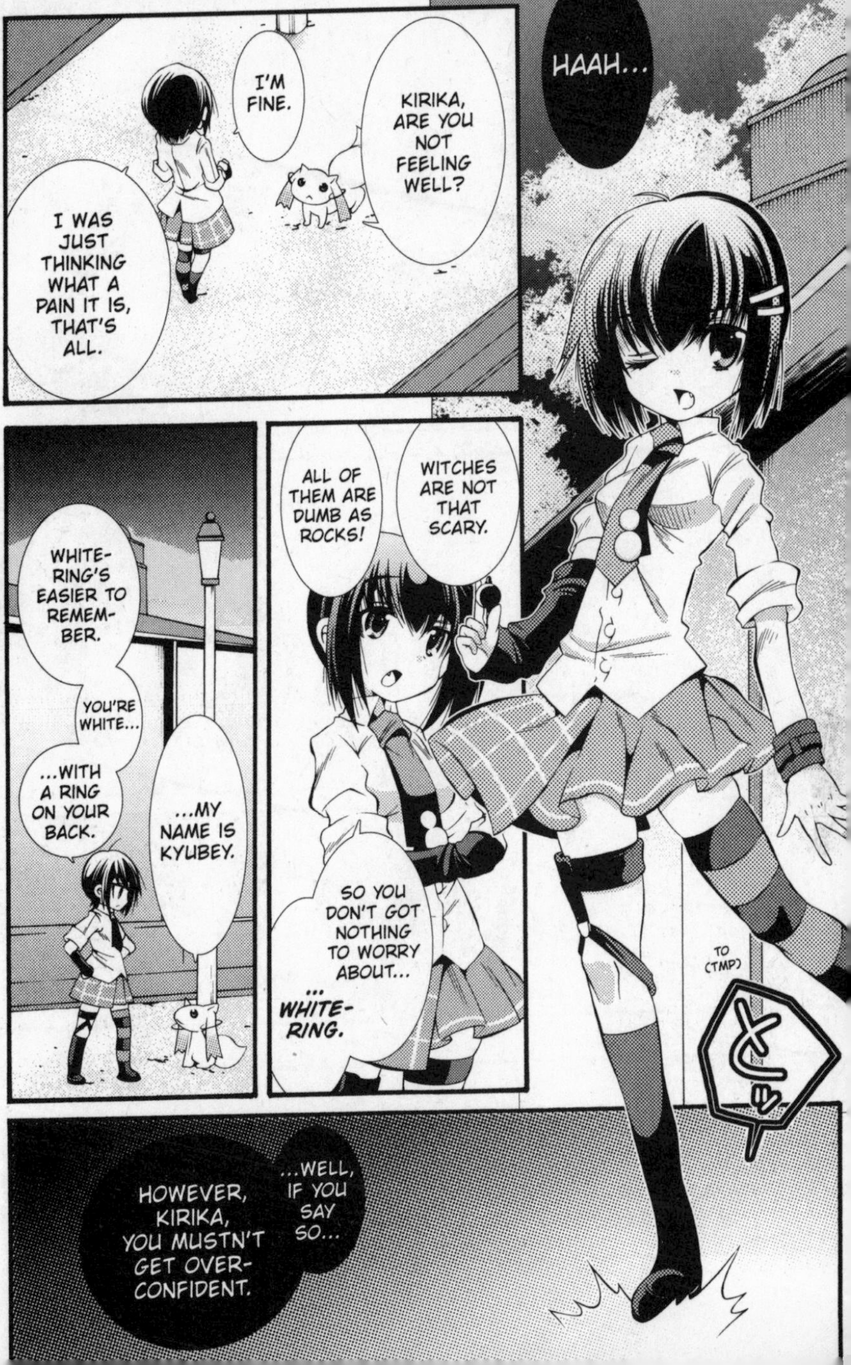
HAAH...
KIRIKA, ARE YOU NOT FEELING WELL?
I'M FINE.
I WAS JUST THINKING WHAT A PAIN IT IS, THAT'S ALL.
WITCHES ARE NOT THAT SCARY.
ALL OF THEM ARE DUMB AS ROCKS!
SO YOU DON'T GOT NOTHING TO WORRY ABOUT...
...WHITE-RING.
...MY NAME IS KYUBEY.
YOU'RE WHITE...
...WITH A RING ON YOUR BACK.
WHITE-RING'S EASIER TO REMEMBER.
TO (TMP)
...WELL, IF YOU SAY SO...
HOWEVER, KIRIKA, YOU MUSTN'T GET OVER-CONFIDENT.

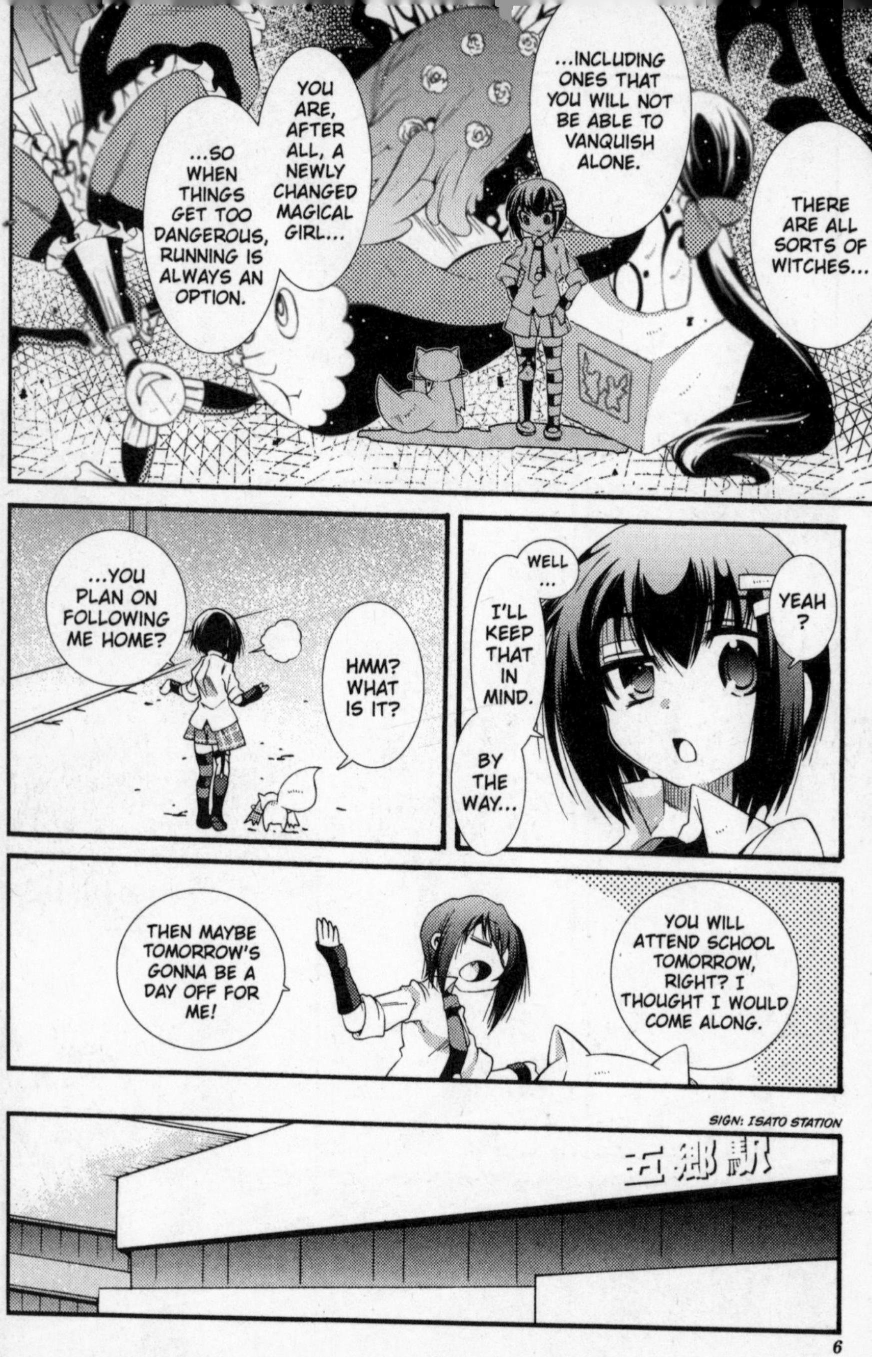
THERE ARE ALL SORTS OF WITCHES...
...INCLUDING ONES THAT YOU WILL NOT BE ABLE TO VANQUISH ALONE.
YOU ARE, AFTER ALL, A NEWLY CHANGED MAGICAL GIRL...
...SO WHEN THINGS GET TOO DANGEROUS, RUNNING IS ALWAYS AN OPTION.
YEAH?
WELL... I'LL KEEP THAT IN MIND.
BY THE WAY...
HMM? WHAT IS IT?
...YOU PLAN ON FOLLOWING ME HOME?
YOU WILL ATTEND SCHOOL TOMORROW, RIGHT? I THOUGHT I WOULD COME ALONG.
THEN MAYBE TOMORROW'S GONNA BE A DAY OFF FOR ME!
SIGN: ISATO STATION
五郷駅

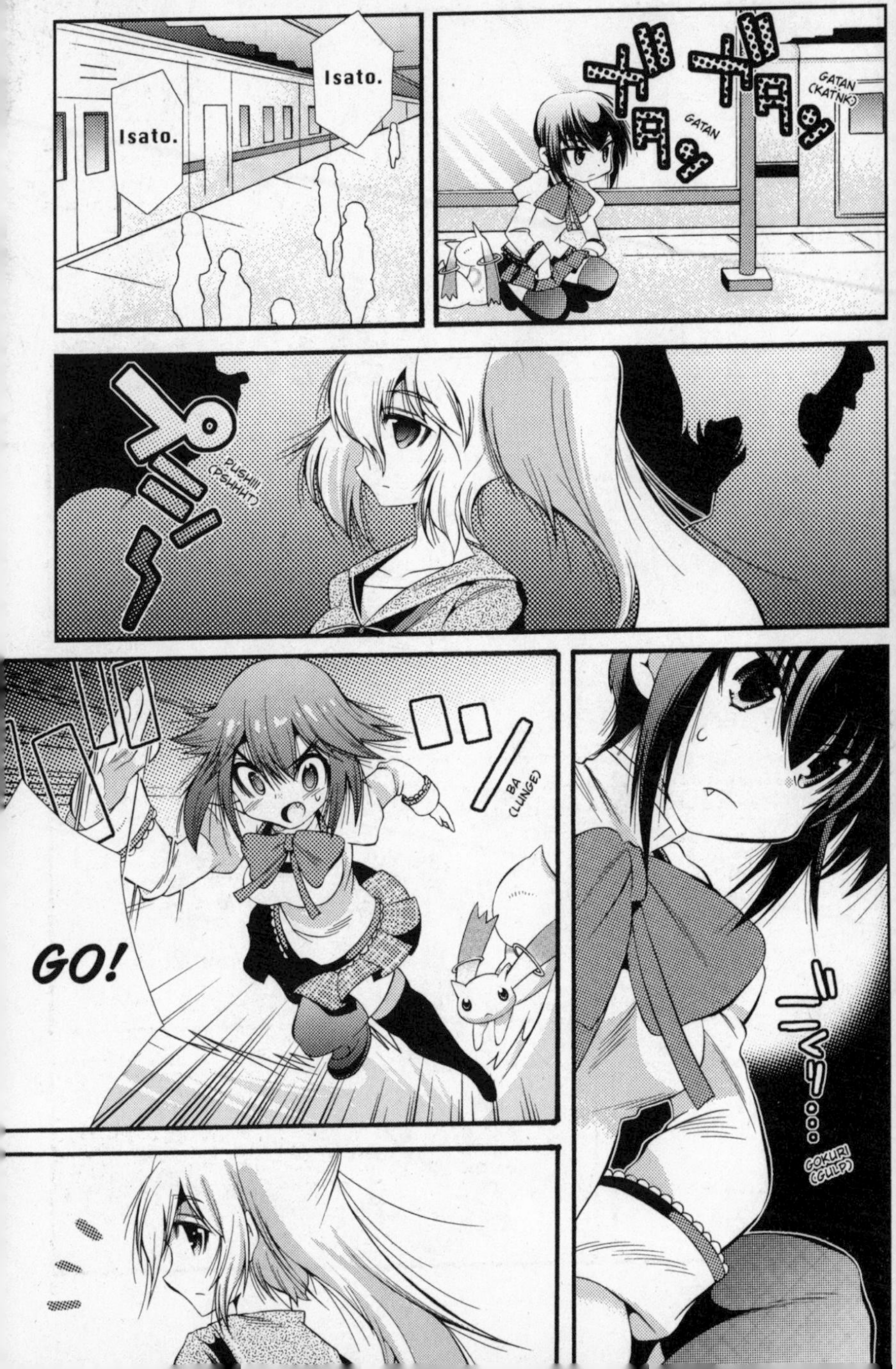
GATAN (KATNK)
GATAN
Isato.
Isato.
PUSHII (PSHHHT)
GOKURI (GULP)
BA (LUNGE)
GO!

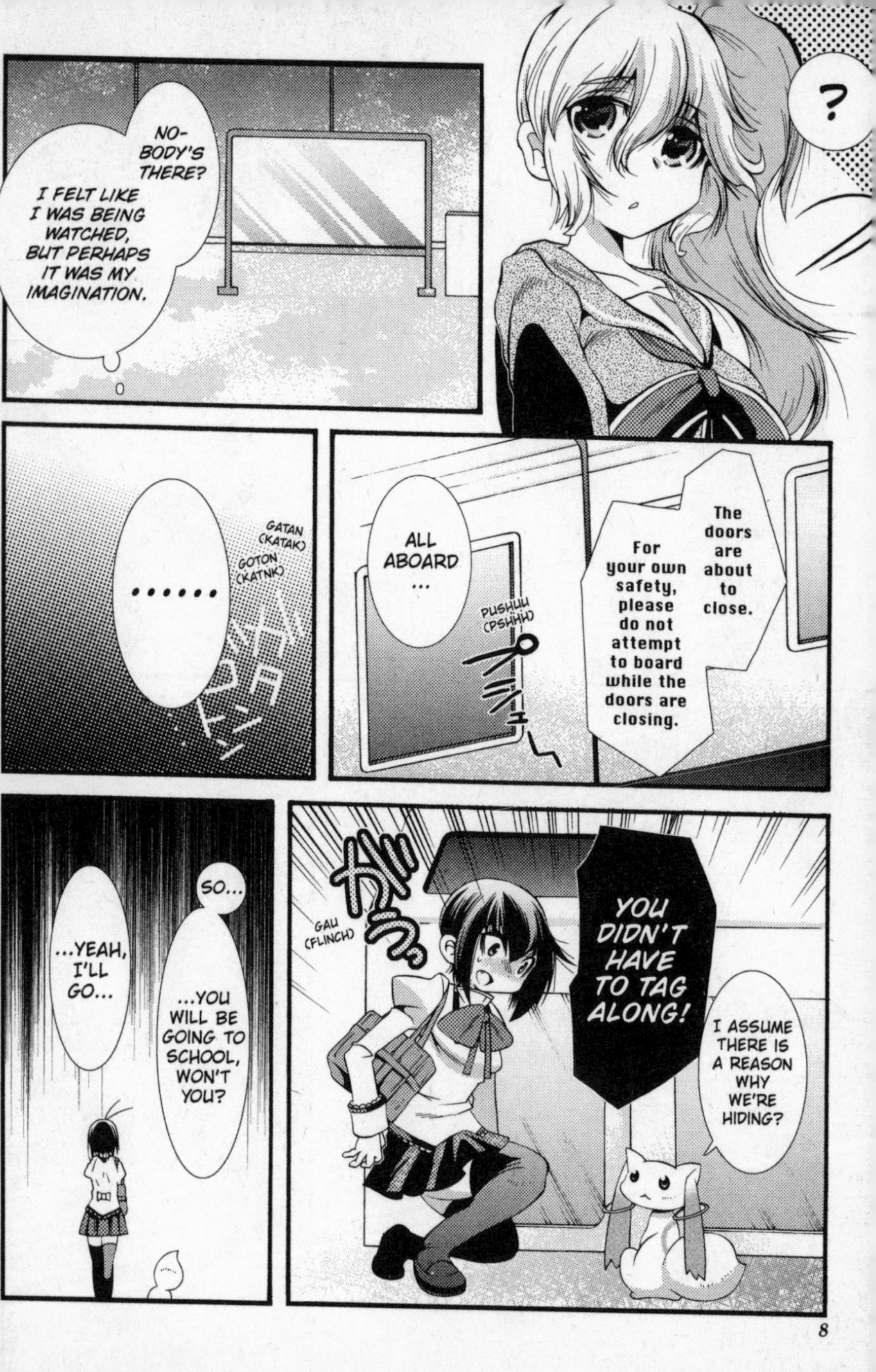
?
NO-BODY'S THERE?
I FELT LIKE I WAS BEING WATCHED, BUT PERHAPS IT WAS MY IMAGINATION.
The doors are about to close.
For your own safety, please do not attempt to board while the doors are closing.
ALL ABOARD ...
PUSHUU (PSHHH)
GATAN (KATAK)
GOTON (KATNK)
......
I ASSUME THERE IS A REASON WHY WE'RE HIDING?
YOU DIDN'T HAVE TO TAG ALONG!
GAU (FLINCH)
SO...
...YOU WILL BE GOING TO SCHOOL, WON'T YOU?
...YEAH, I'LL GO...

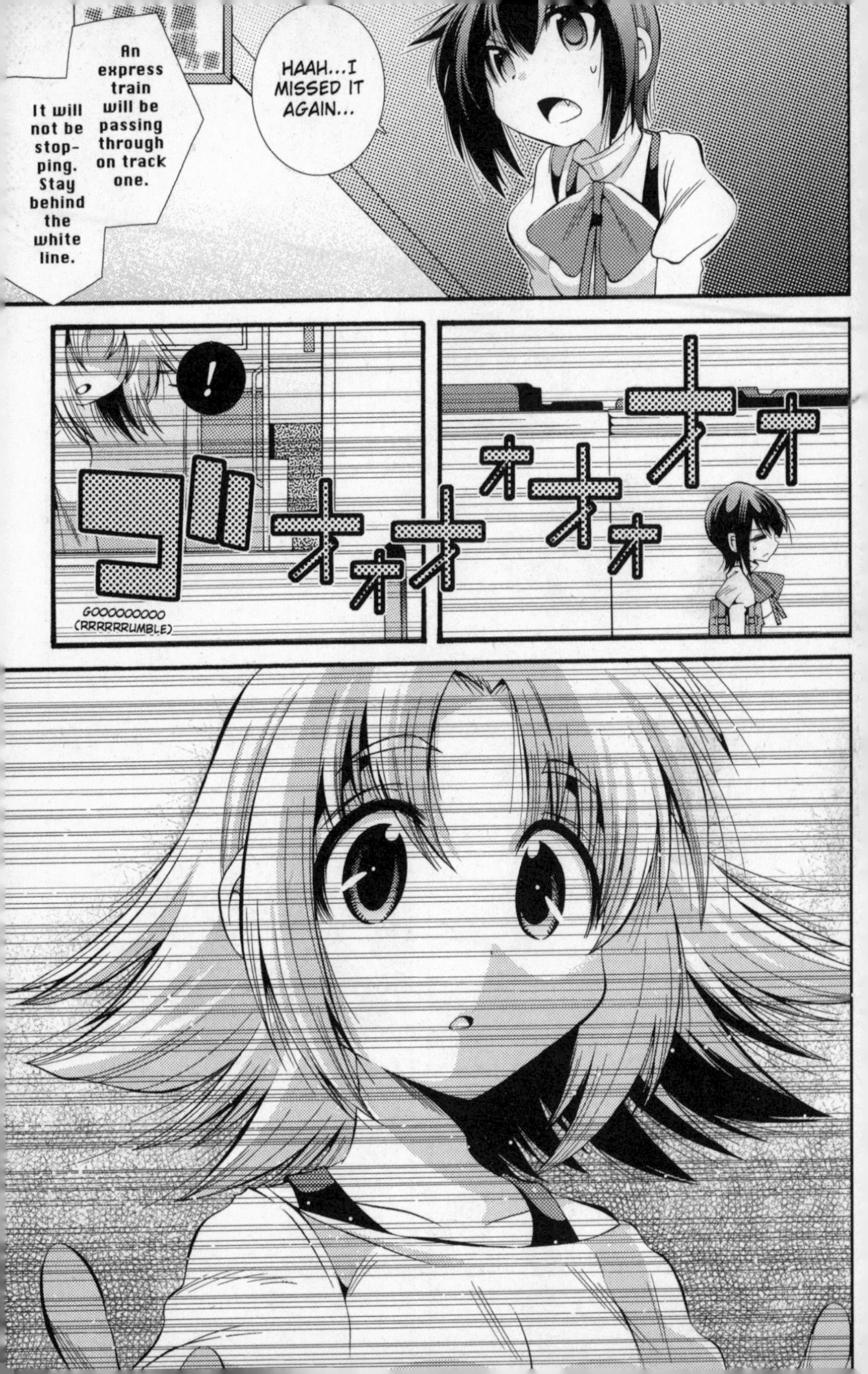
HAAH...I MISSED IT AGAIN...
An express train will be passing through on track one.
It will not be stopping. Stay behind the white line.
!
GOOOOOOOOO (RRRRRRUMBLE)

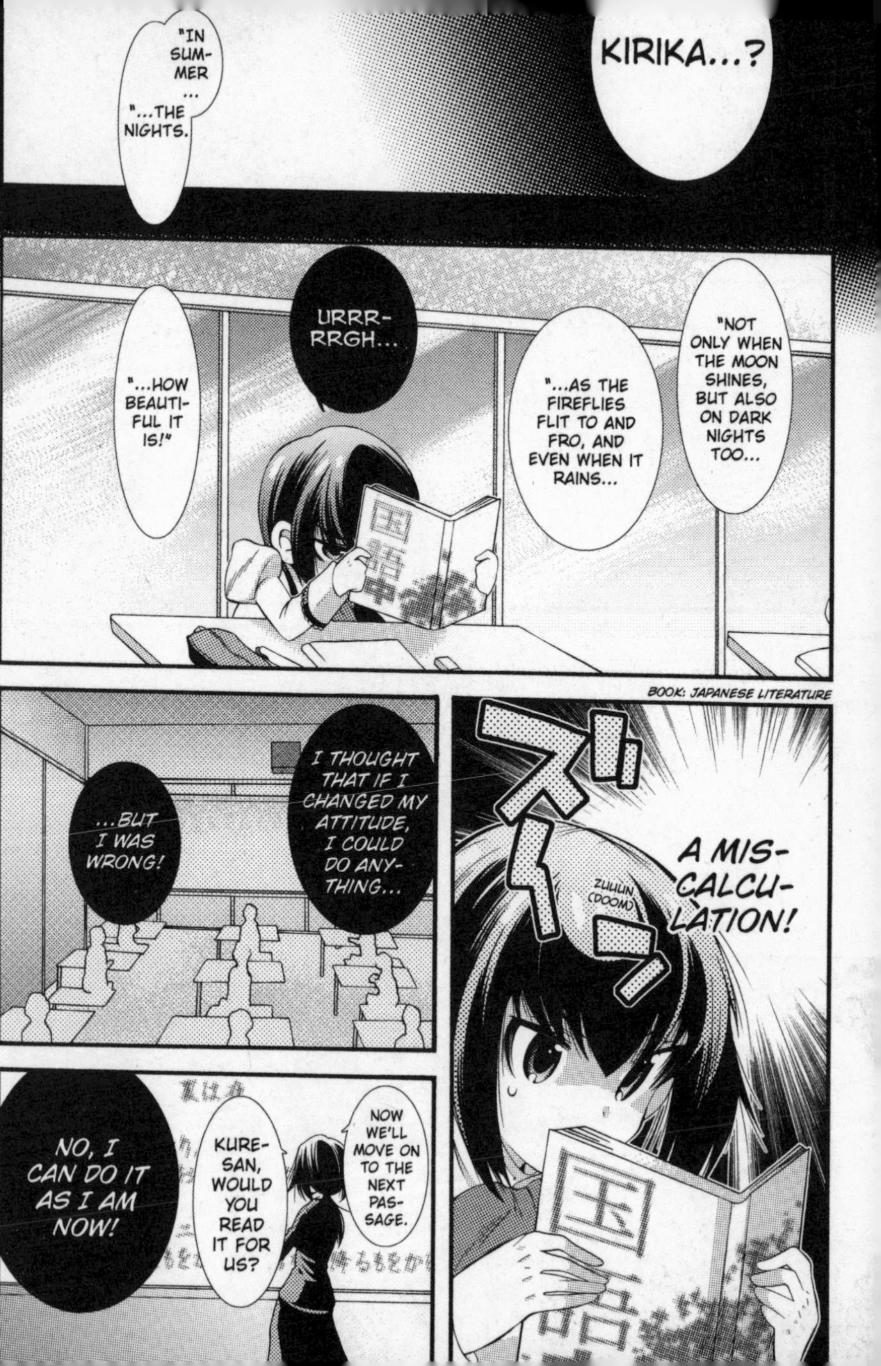
KIRIKA...?
"IN SUMMER... "...THE NIGHTS.
"NOT ONLY WHEN THE MOON SHINES, BUT ALSO ON DARK NIGHTS TOO...
"...AS THE FIREFLIES FLIT TO AND FRO, AND EVEN WHEN IT RAINS...
URRRRRGH...
"...HOW BEAUTIFUL IT IS!"
BOOK: JAPANESE LITERATURE
ZUUUN (DOOM)
A MIS-CALCULATION!
I THOUGHT THAT IF I CHANGED MY ATTITUDE, I COULD DO ANYTHING...
...BUT I WAS WRONG!
NOW WE'LL MOVE ON TO THE NEXT PASSAGE.
KURE-SAN, WOULD YOU READ IT FOR US?
NO, I CAN DO IT AS I AM NOW!

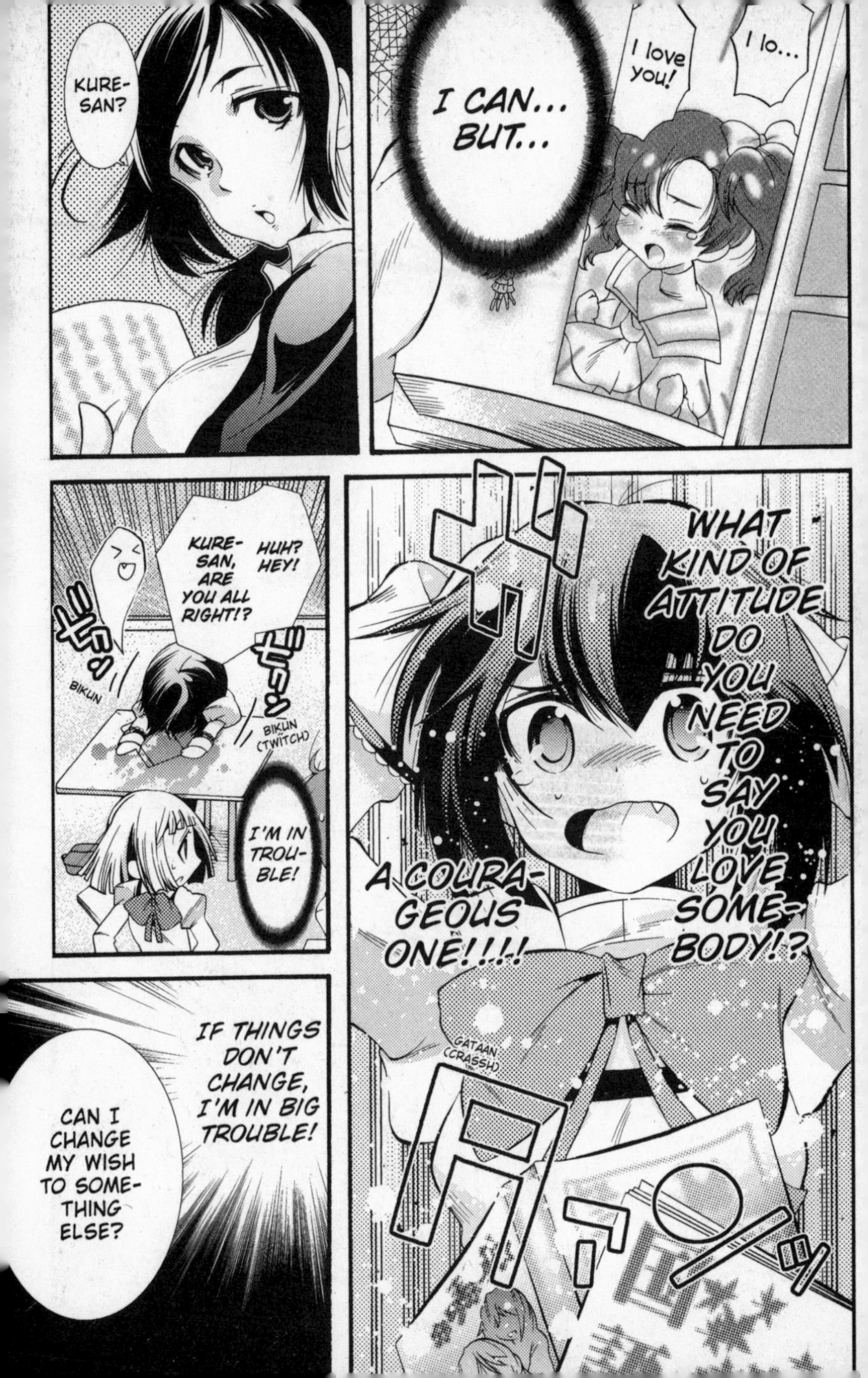
I lo...
I love you!
I CAN... BUT...
KURE-SAN?
WHAT KIND OF ATTITUDE DO YOU NEED TO SAY YOU LOVE SOMEBODY!?
A COURAGEOUS ONE!!!!
GATAAN (CRASSH)
HUH? HEY!
KURE-SAN, ARE YOU ALL RIGHT!?
BIKUN (TWITCH)
BIKUN
I'M IN TROUBLE!
IF THINGS DON'T CHANGE, I'M IN BIG TROUBLE!
CAN I CHANGE MY WISH TO SOMETHING ELSE?

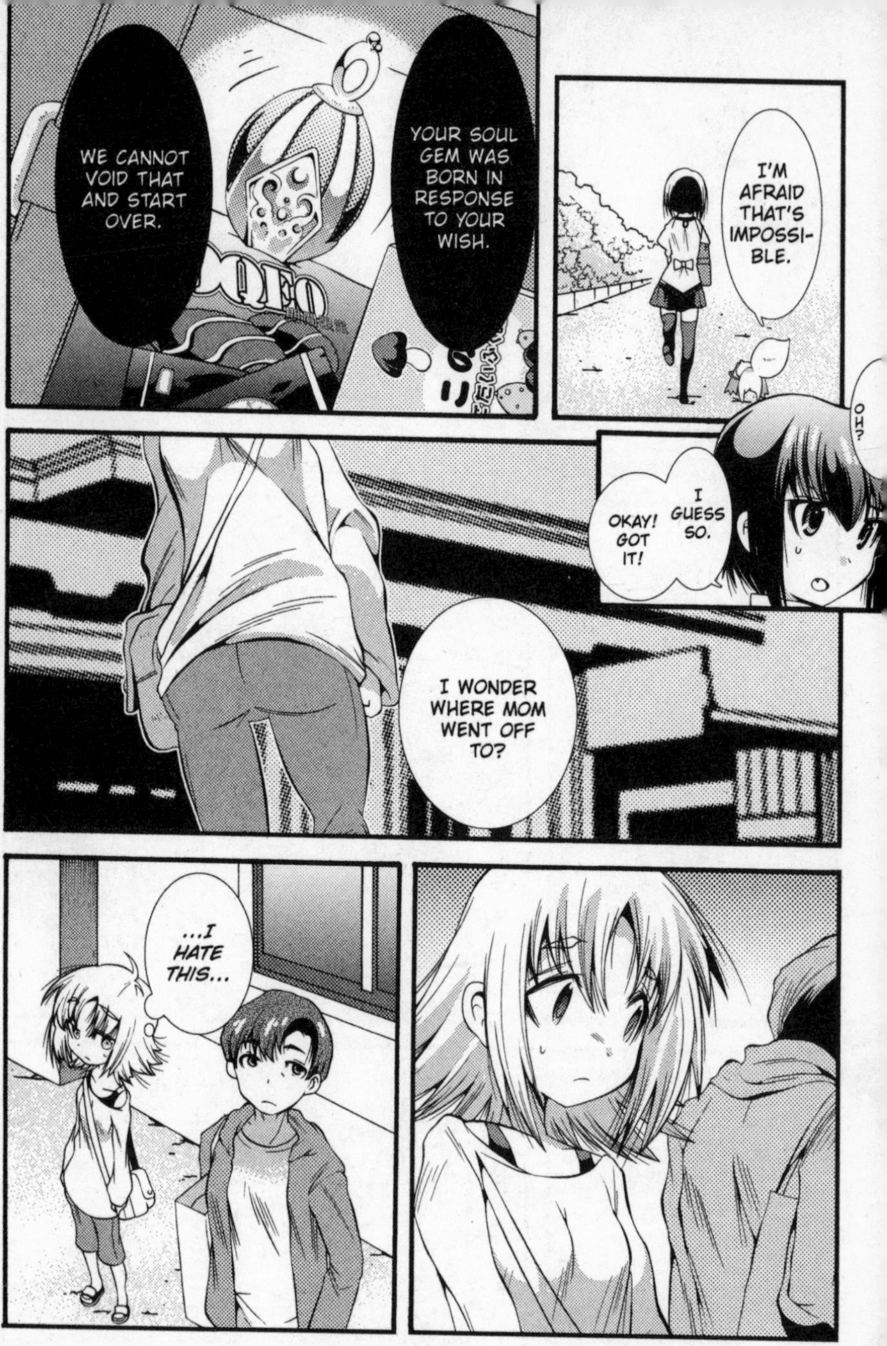
I'M AFRAID THAT'S IMPOSSI-BLE.
YOUR SOUL GEM WAS BORN IN RESPONSE TO YOUR WISH.
WE CANNOT VOID THAT AND START OVER.
OH?
I GUESS SO.
OKAY! GOT IT!
I WONDER WHERE MOM WENT OFF TO?
...I HATE THIS...

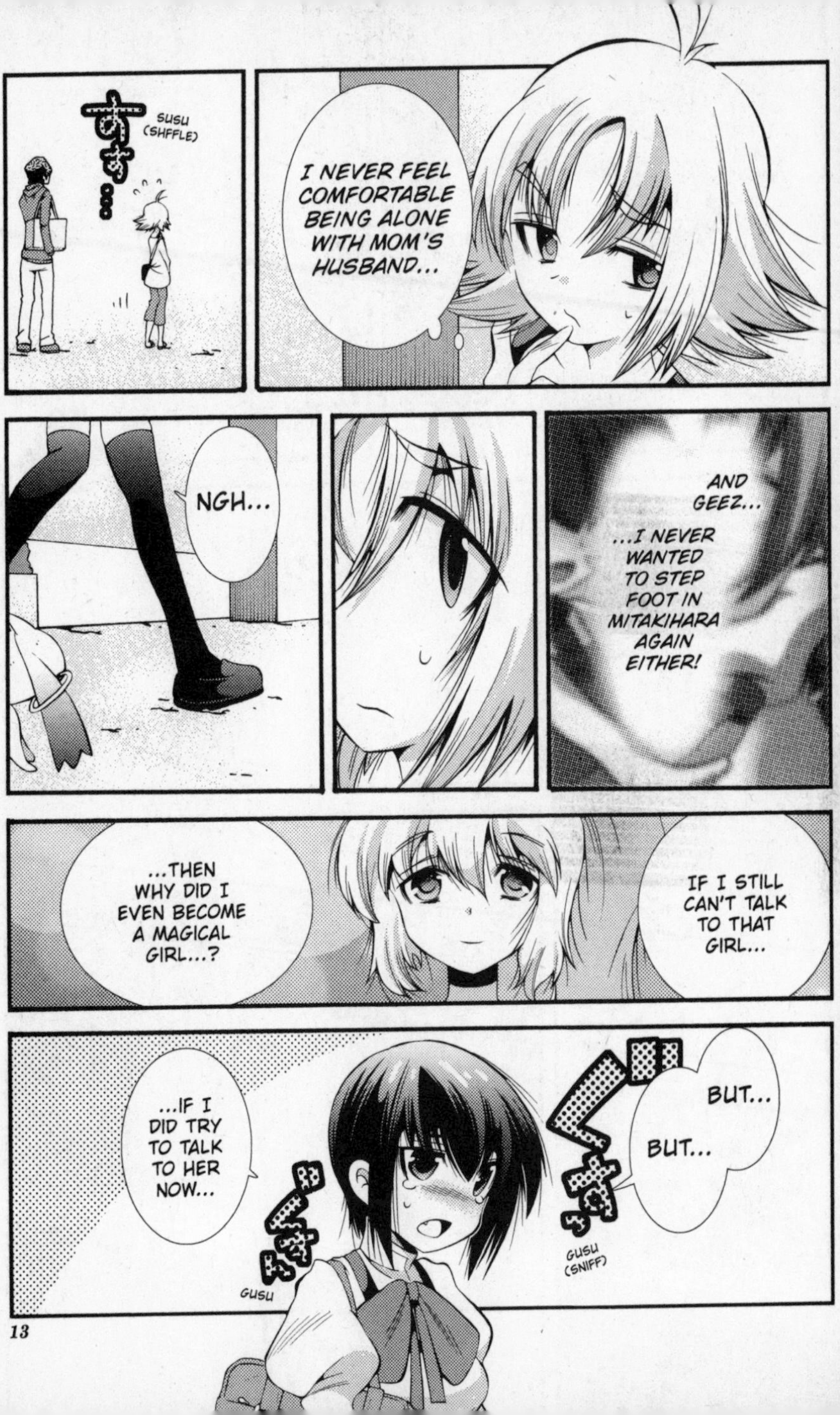
I NEVER FEEL COMFORTABLE BEING ALONE WITH MOM'S HUSBAND...
すす...
SUSU (SHFFLE)
AND GEEZ...
...I NEVER WANTED TO STEP FOOT IN MITAKIHARA AGAIN EITHER!
NGH...
IF I STILL CAN'T TALK TO THAT GIRL...
...THEN WHY DID I EVEN BECOME A MAGICAL GIRL...?
BUT...
BUT...
GUSU (SNIFF)
...IF I DID TRY TO TALK TO HER NOW...
GUSU

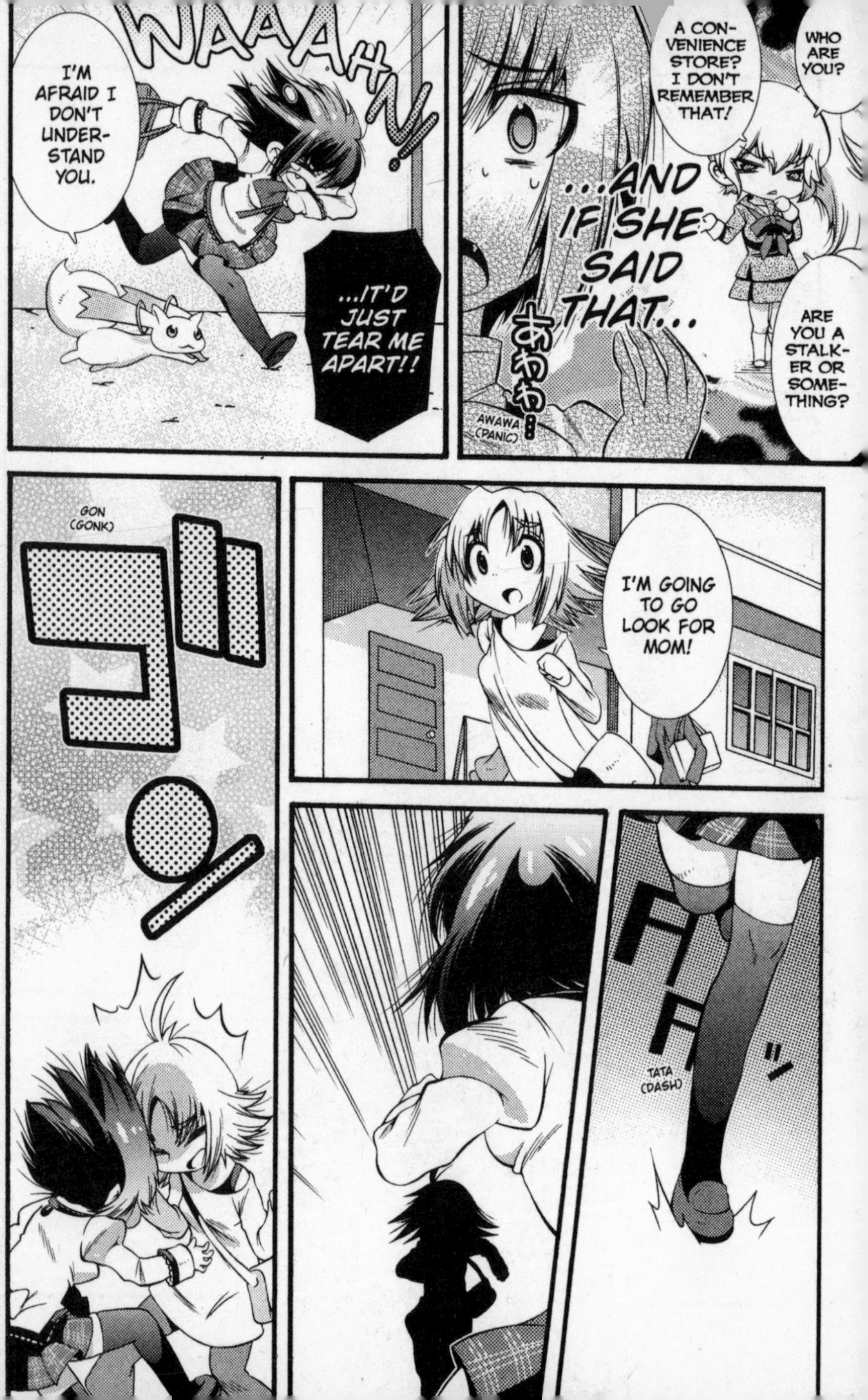
WHO ARE YOU?
A CON-VENIENCE STORE? I DON'T REMEMBER THAT!
ARE YOU A STALK-ER OR SOME-THING?
...AND IF SHE SAID THAT...
あわわ
AWAWA (PANIC)
...IT'D JUST TEAR ME APART!!
WAAAAHN!!
I'M AFRAID I DON'T UNDER-STAND YOU.
I'M GOING TO GO LOOK FOR MOM!
TATA (DASH)
GON (GONK)

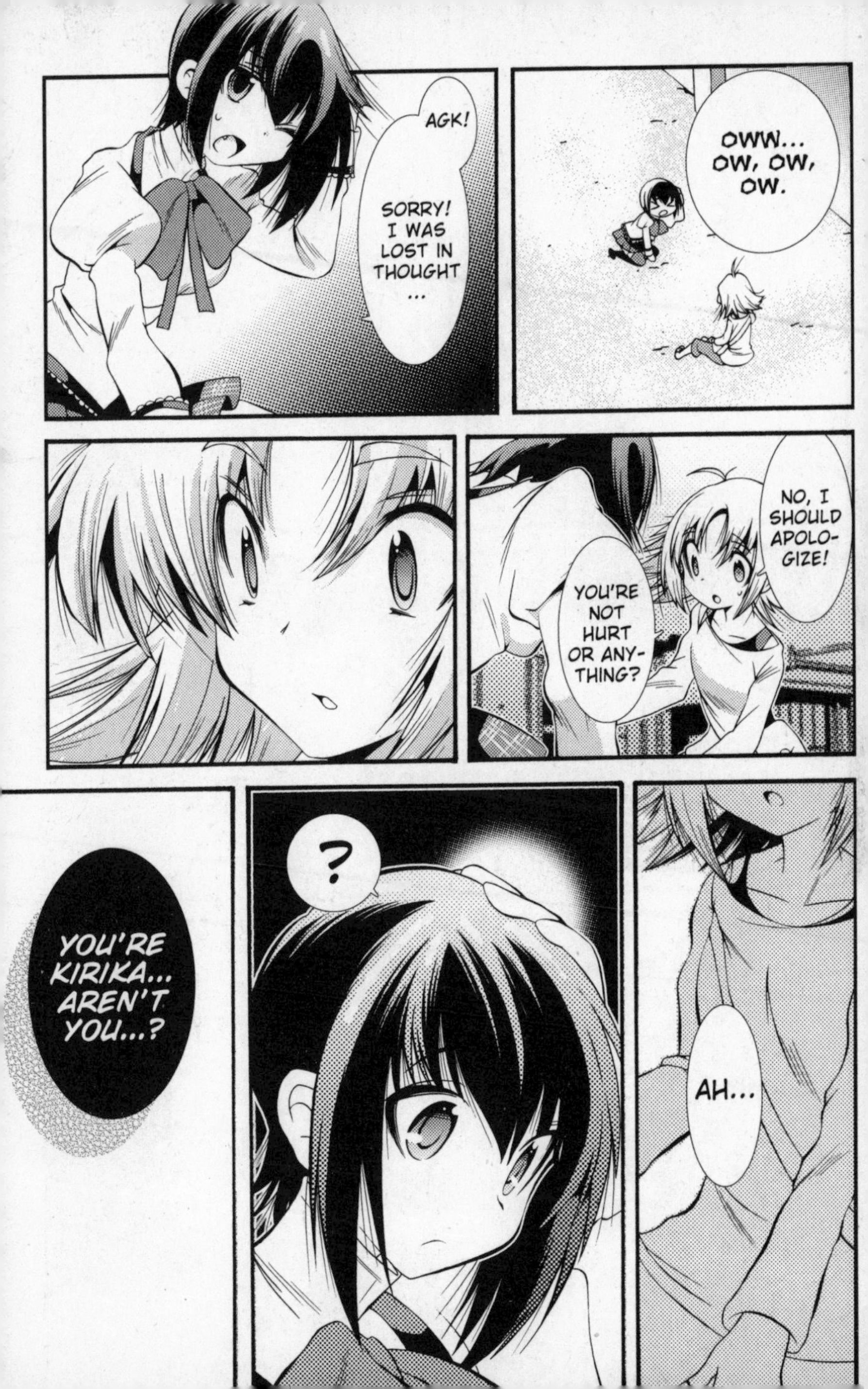
OWW... OW, OW, OW.
AGK!
SORRY! I WAS LOST IN THOUGHT...
NO, I SHOULD APOLO-GIZE!
YOU'RE NOT HURT OR ANY-THING?
AH...
?
YOU'RE KIRIKA... AREN'T YOU...?

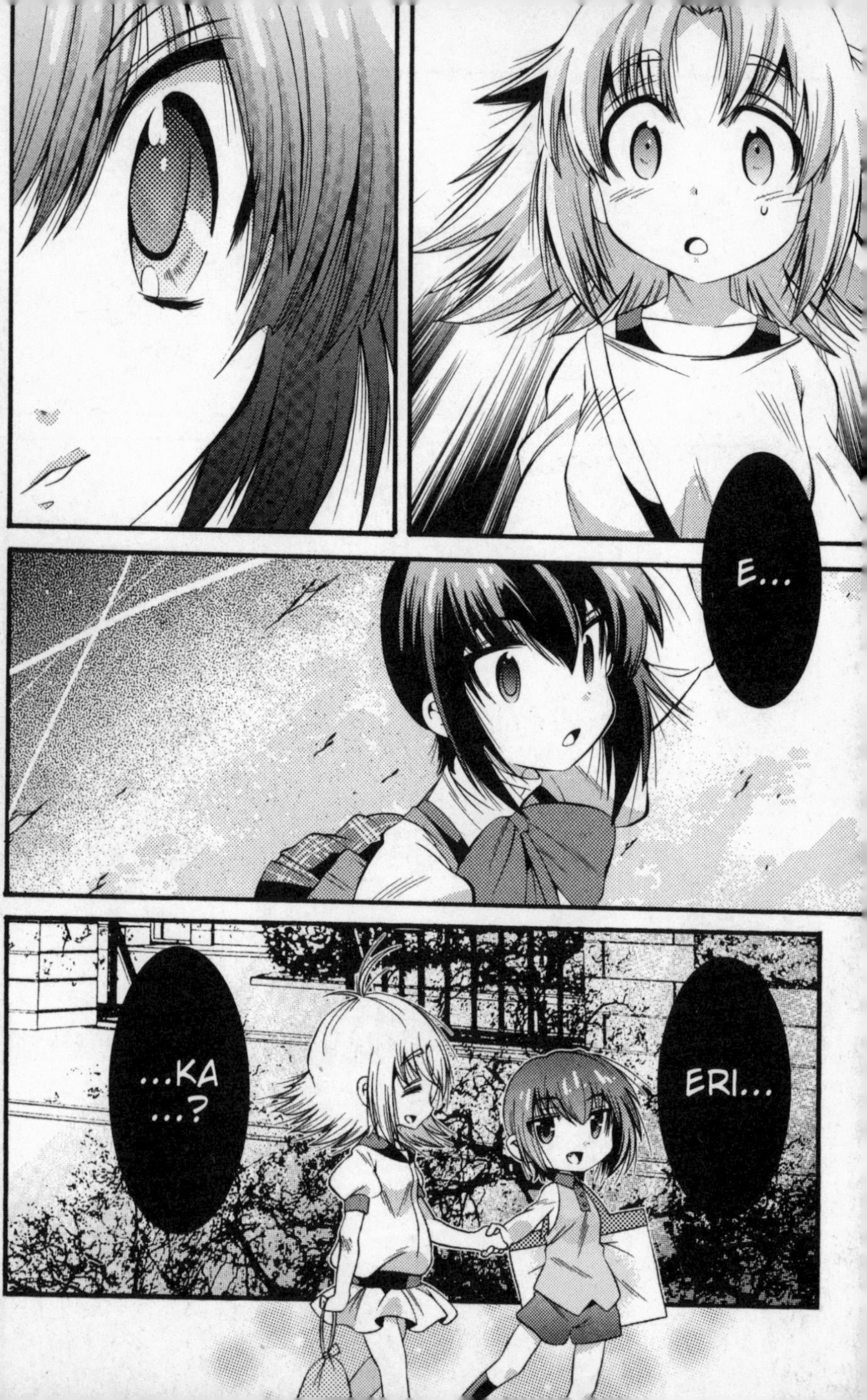
E...
ERI...
...KA ...?

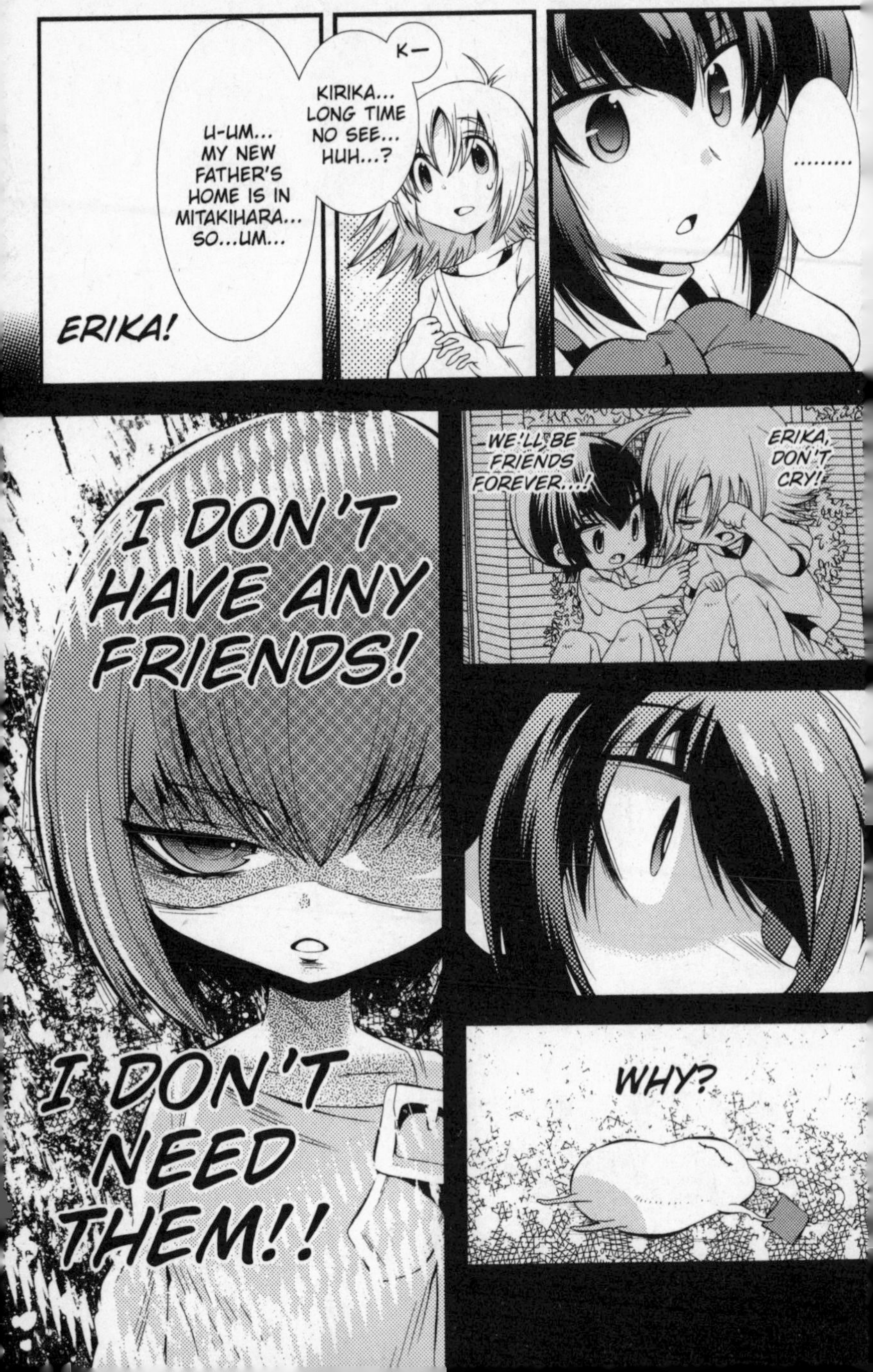
....
K—
KIRIKA... LONG TIME NO SEE... HUH...?
U-UM... MY NEW FATHER'S HOME IS IN MITAKIHARA... SO...UM...
ERIKA!
ERIKA, DON'T CRY!
—WE'LL BE FRIENDS FOREVER...!
WHY?
....
I DON'T HAVE ANY FRIENDS!
I DON'T NEED THEM!!

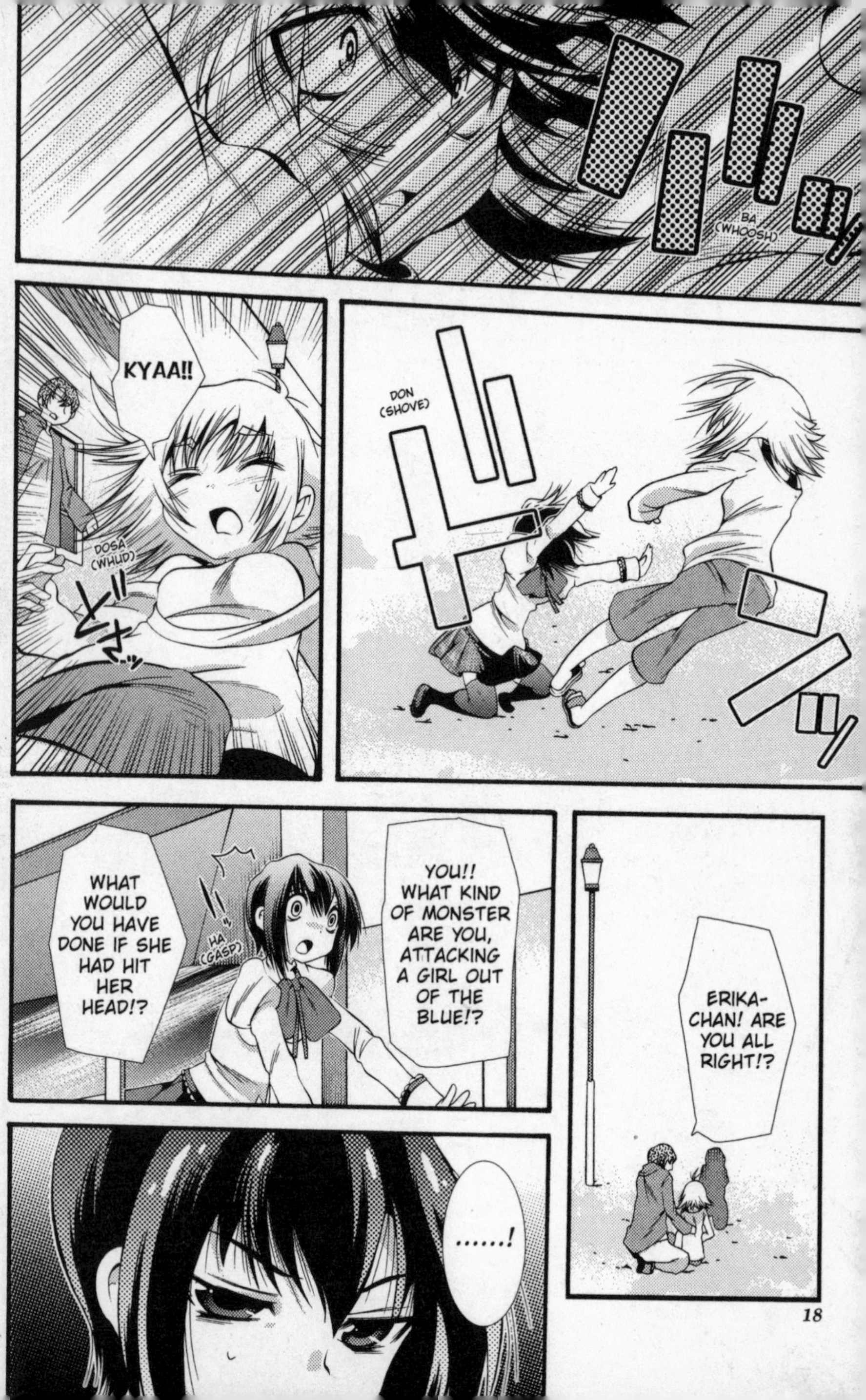
BA (WHOOSH)
DON (SHOVE)
KYAA!!
DOSA (WHUD)
ERIKA-CHAN! ARE YOU ALL RIGHT!?
YOU!! WHAT KIND OF MONSTER ARE YOU, ATTACKING A GIRL OUT OF THE BLUE!?
HA (GASP)
WHAT WOULD YOU HAVE DONE IF SHE HAD HIT HER HEAD!?
......!

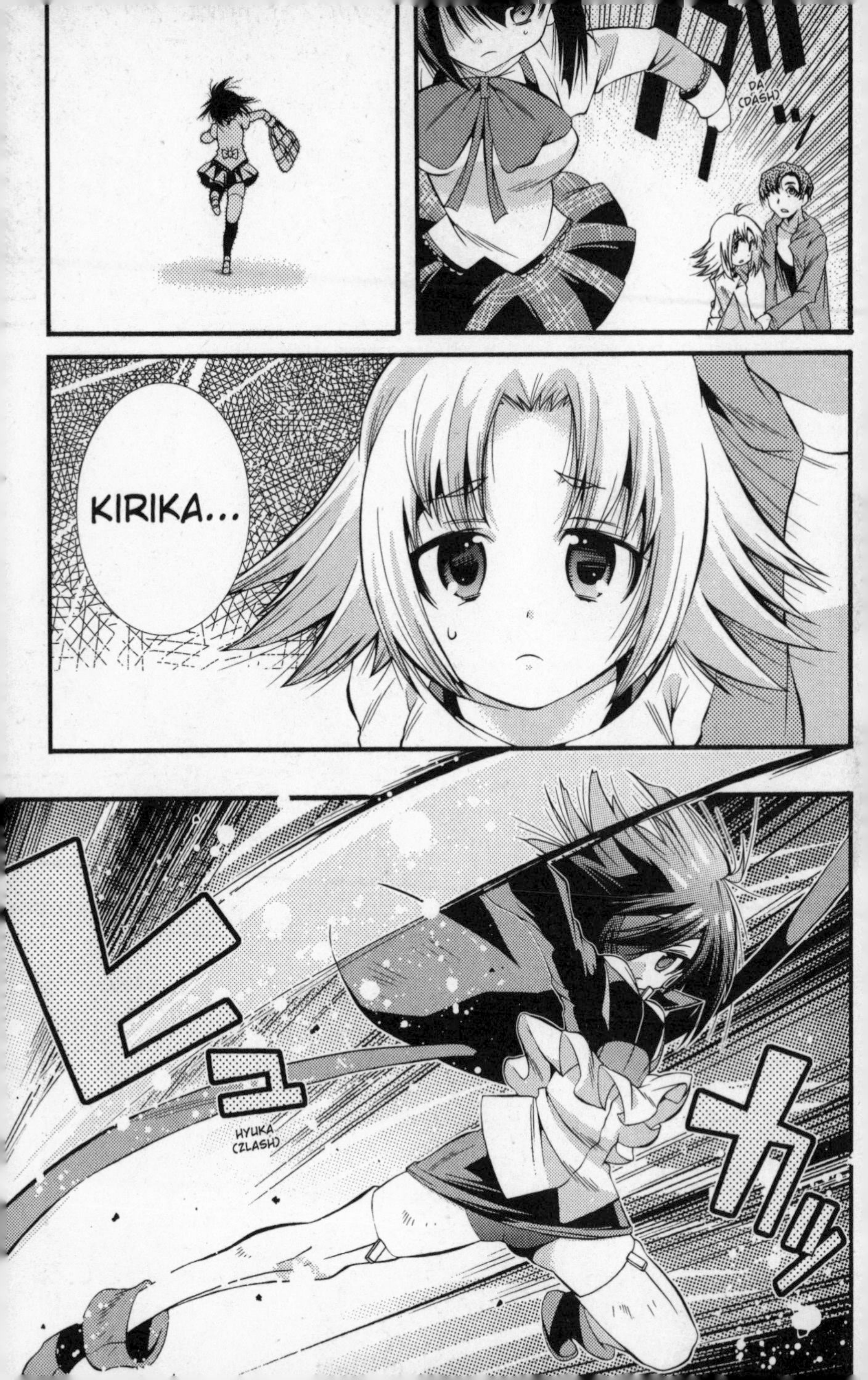
DA
(DASH)
KIRIKA...
HYUKA
(ZLASH)

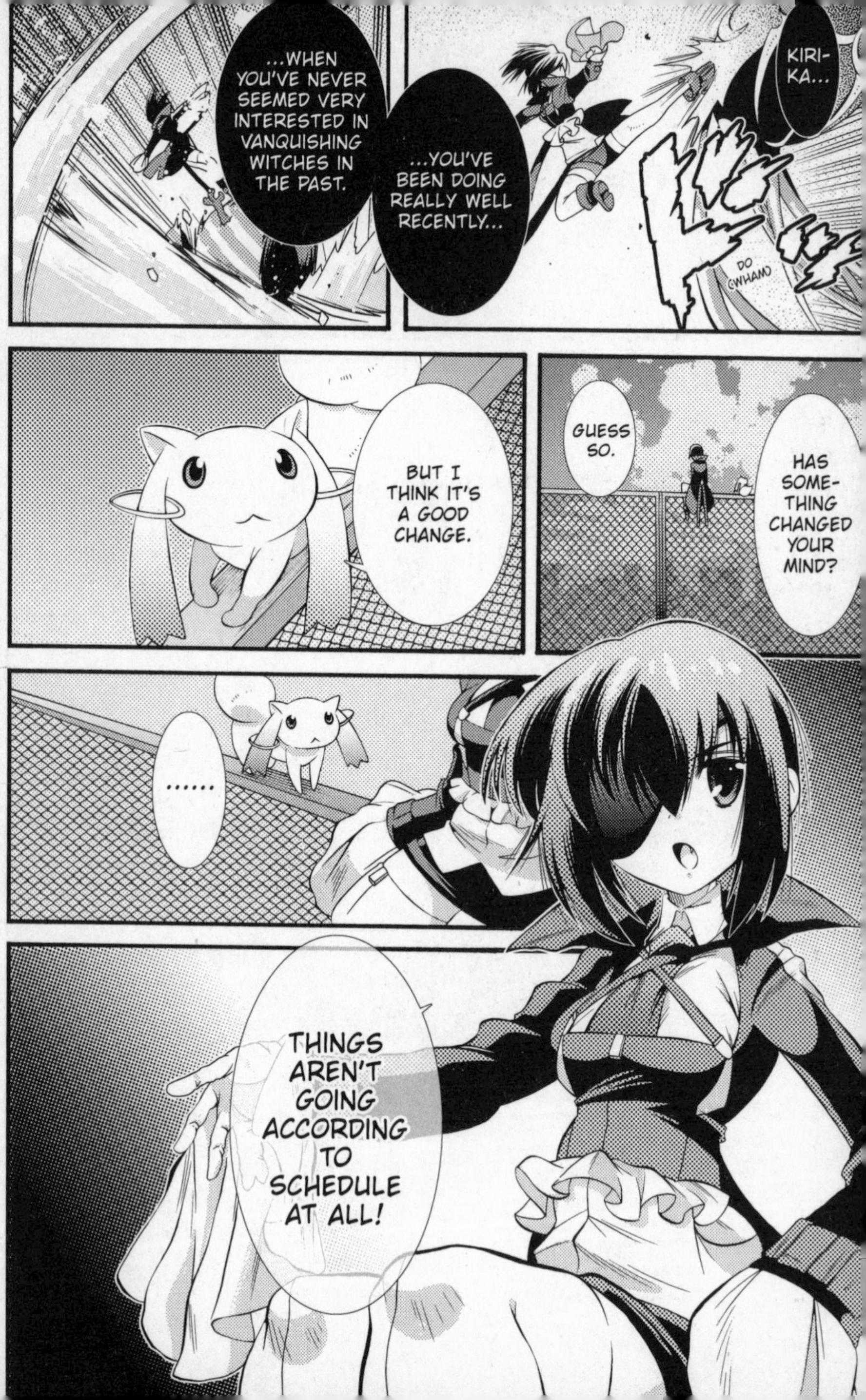
KIRI-KA...
DO (WHAM)
...YOU'VE BEEN DOING REALLY WELL RECENTLY...
...WHEN YOU'VE NEVER SEEMED VERY INTERESTED IN VANQUISHING WITCHES IN THE PAST.
HAS SOME-THING CHANGED YOUR MIND?
GUESS SO.
BUT I THINK IT'S A GOOD CHANGE.
......
THINGS AREN'T GOING ACCORDING TO SCHEDULE AT ALL!

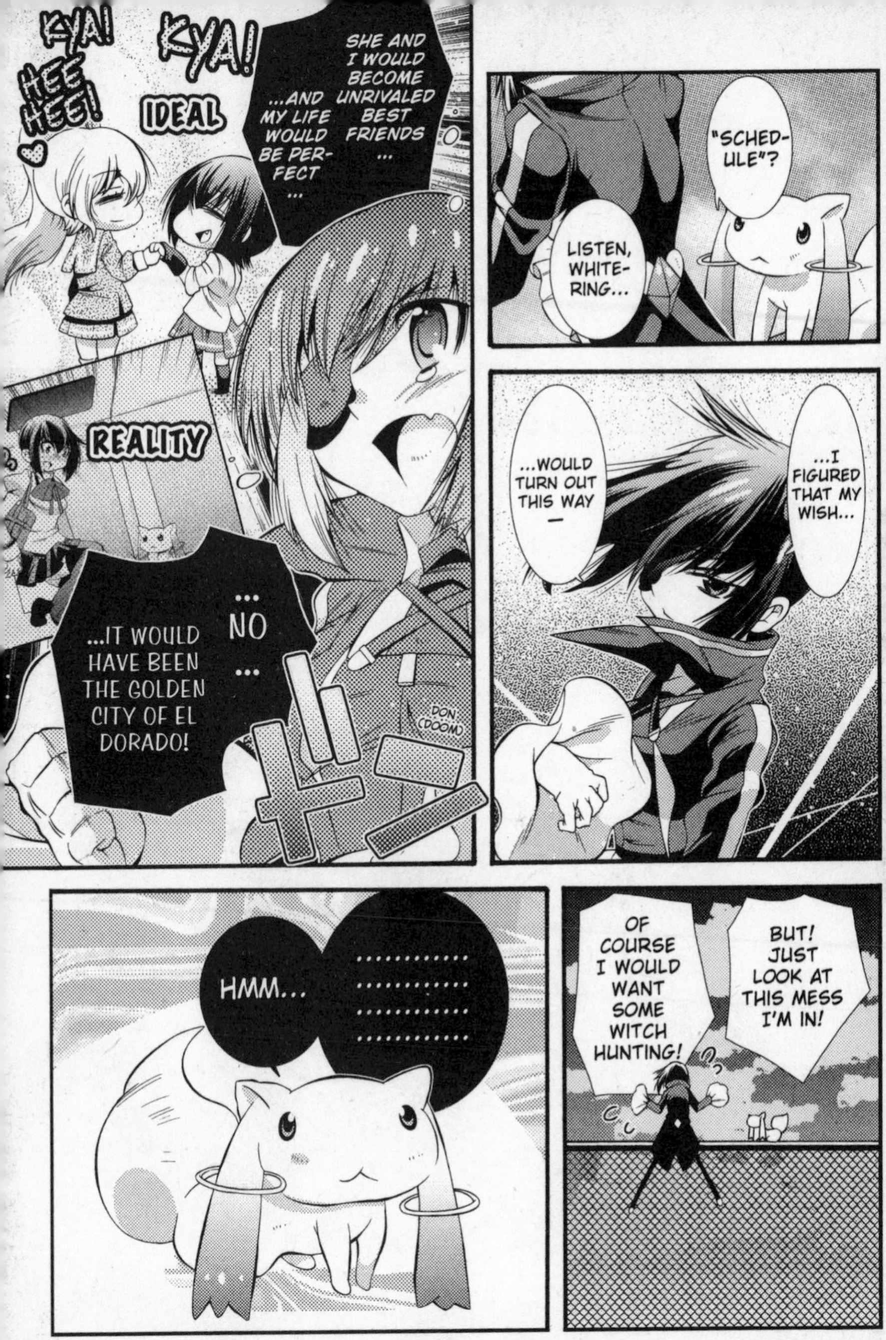
"SCHED-ULE"?
LISTEN, WHITE-RING...
...I FIGURED THAT MY WISH...
...WOULD TURN OUT THIS WAY —
SHE AND I WOULD BECOME UNRIVALED BEST FRIENDS...
...AND MY LIFE WOULD BE PERFECT...
KYA!
KYA!
HEE HEE!
IDEAL
REALITY
...NO...
...IT WOULD HAVE BEEN THE GOLDEN CITY OF EL DORADO!
DON (DOOM)
BUT! JUST LOOK AT THIS MESS I'M IN!
OF COURSE I WOULD WANT SOME WITCH HUNTING!
....
HMM...

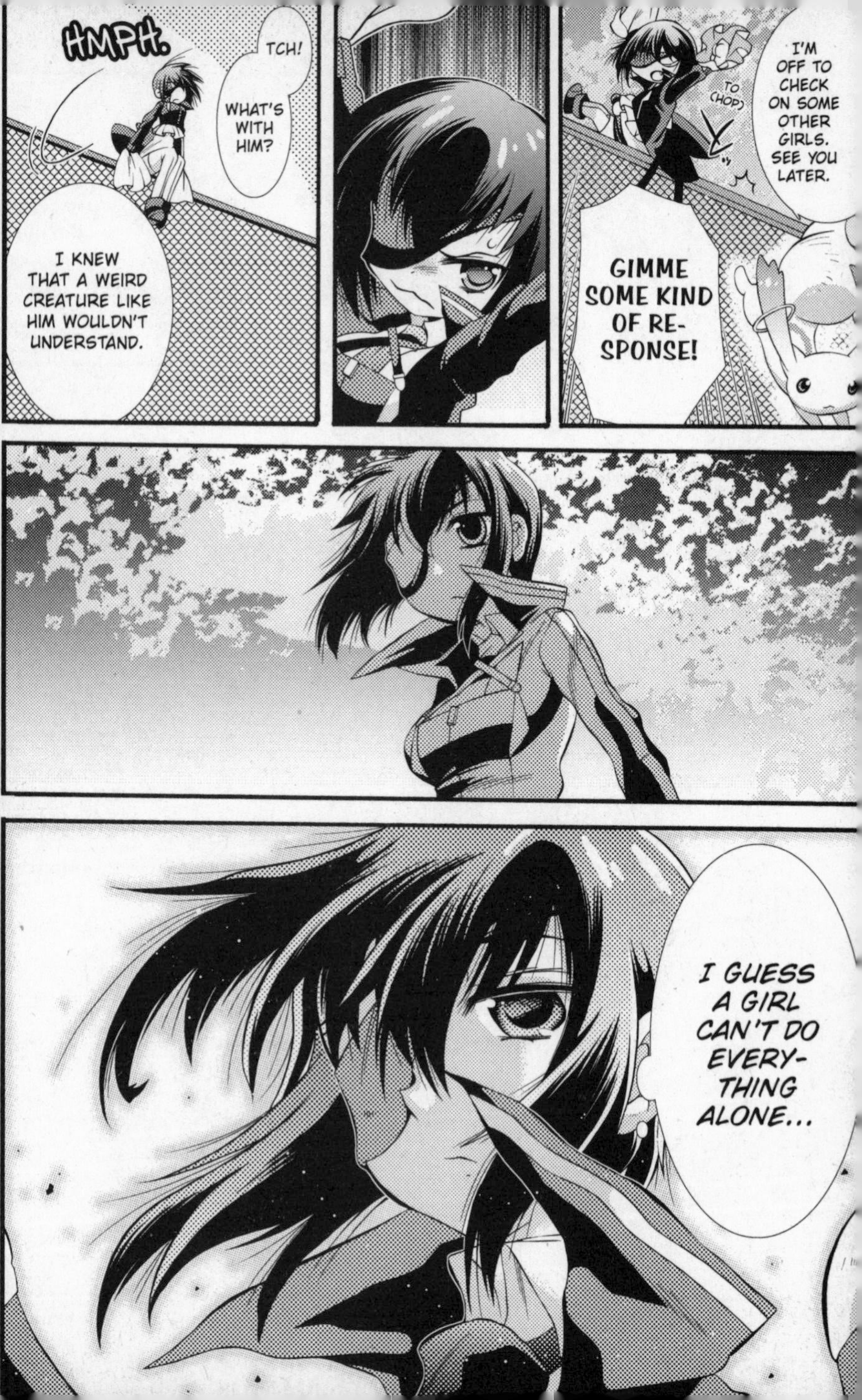
I'M OFF TO CHECK ON SOME OTHER GIRLS. SEE YOU LATER.
TO (HOP)
GIMME SOME KIND OF RE-SPONSE!
TCH!
WHAT'S WITH HIM?
HMPH.
I KNEW THAT A WEIRD CREATURE LIKE HIM WOULDN'T UNDERSTAND.
I GUESS A GIRL CAN'T DO EVERY-THING ALONE...

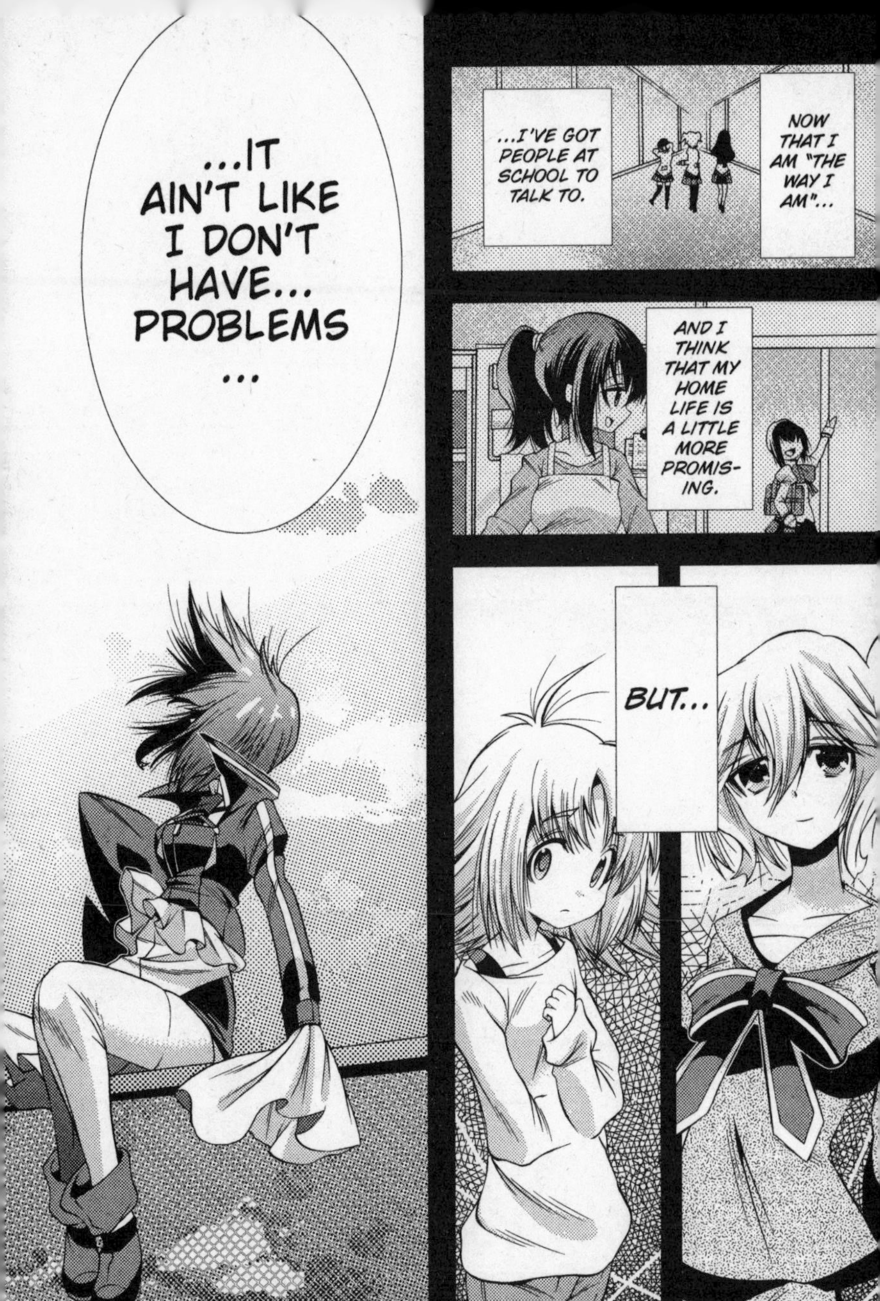
NOW THAT I AM "THE WAY I AM"...
...I'VE GOT PEOPLE AT SCHOOL TO TALK TO.
AND I THINK THAT MY HOME LIFE IS A LITTLE MORE PROMIS-ING.
BUT...
...IT AIN'T LIKE I DON'T HAVE... PROBLEMS ...

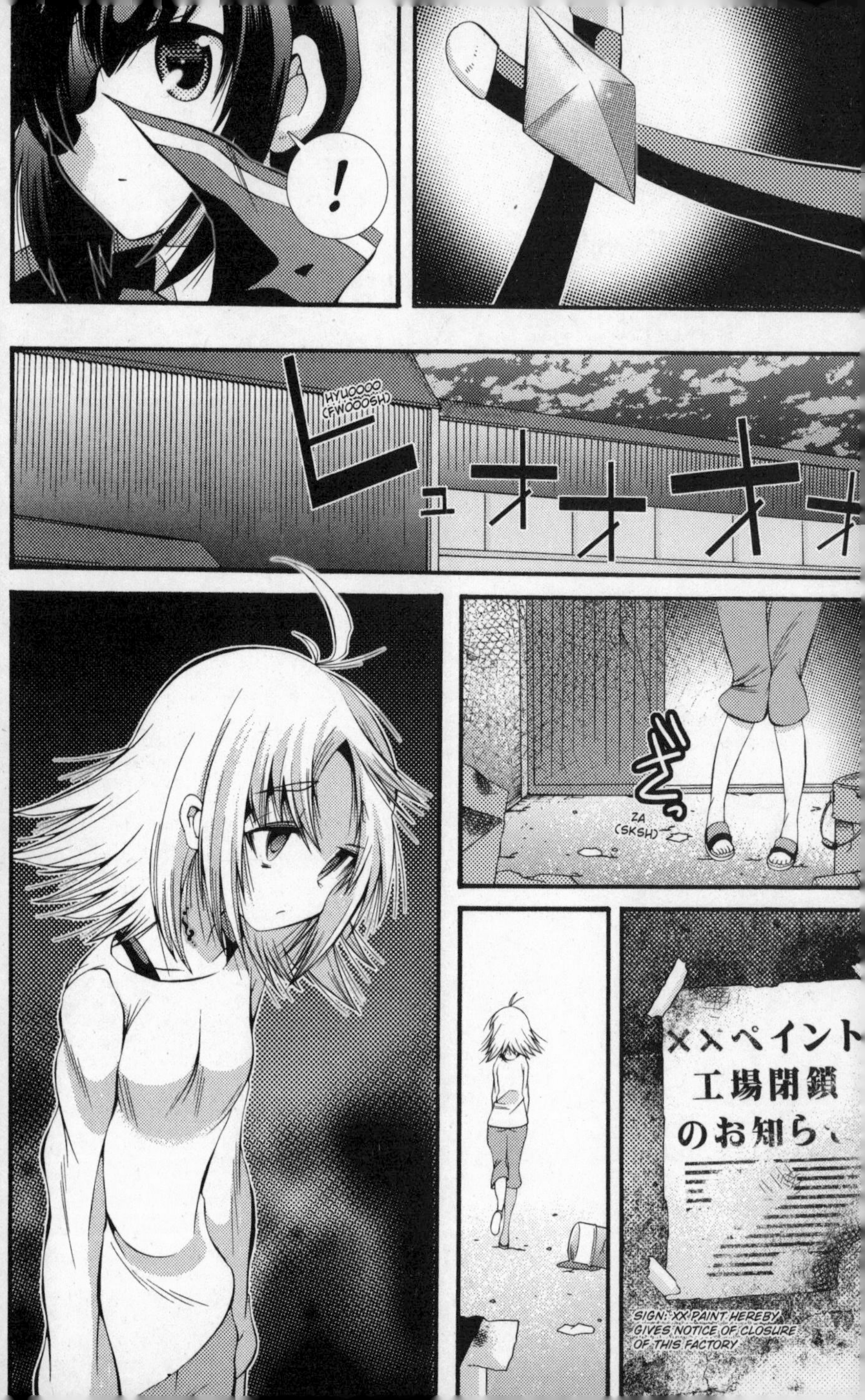
!
ヒュオオオオ
HYUOOOO (FWOOOSH)
ザッ
ZA (SKSH)
××ペイント
工場閉鎖
のお知ら
SIGN: XX PAINT HEREBY GIVES NOTICE OF CLOSURE OF THIS FACTORY

PUELLA MAGI
ORIKO ☆ MAGICA
[extra story]

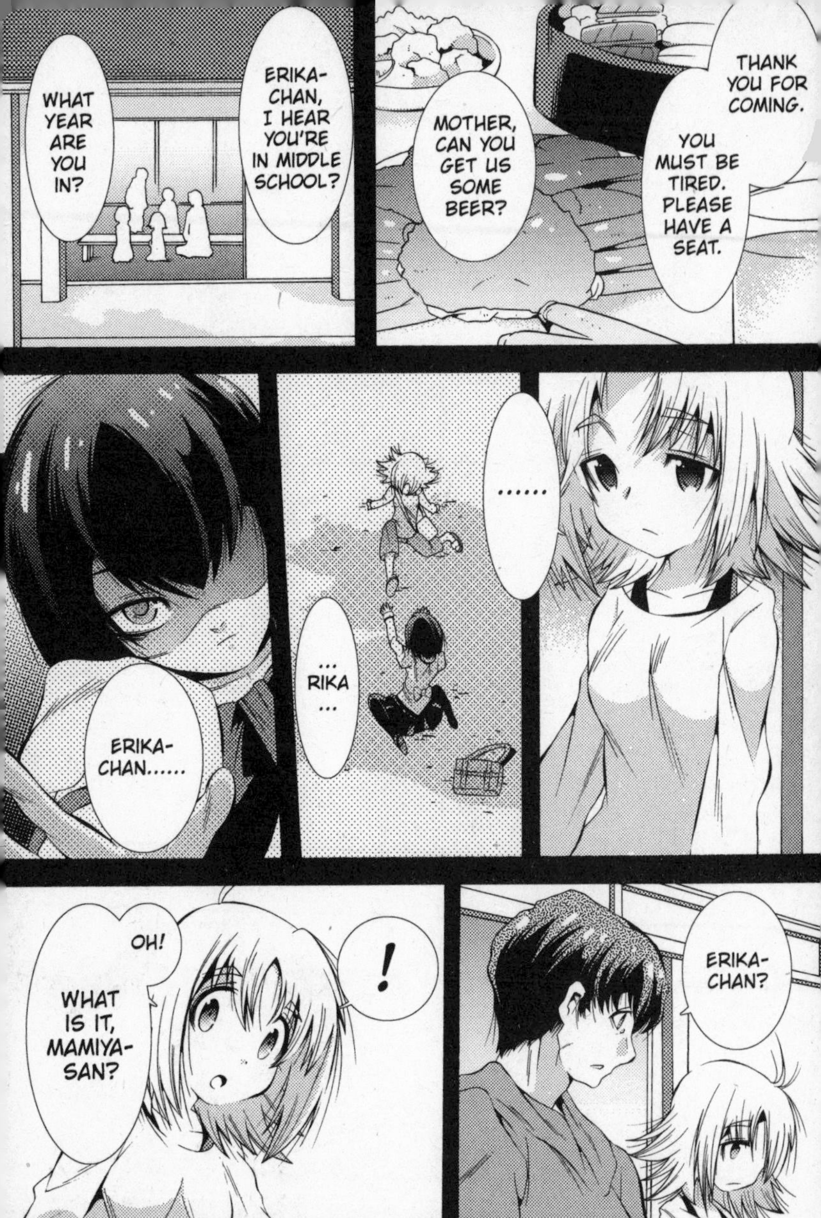
THANK YOU FOR COMING.
YOU MUST BE TIRED. PLEASE HAVE A SEAT.
MOTHER, CAN YOU GET US SOME BEER?
ERIKA-CHAN, I HEAR YOU'RE IN MIDDLE SCHOOL?
WHAT YEAR ARE YOU IN?
......
... RIKA ...
ERIKA-CHAN......
ERIKA-CHAN?
!
OH!
WHAT IS IT, MAMIYA-SAN?

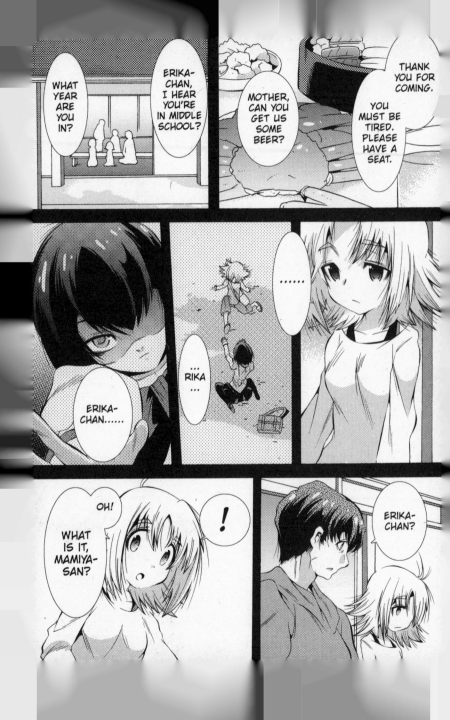

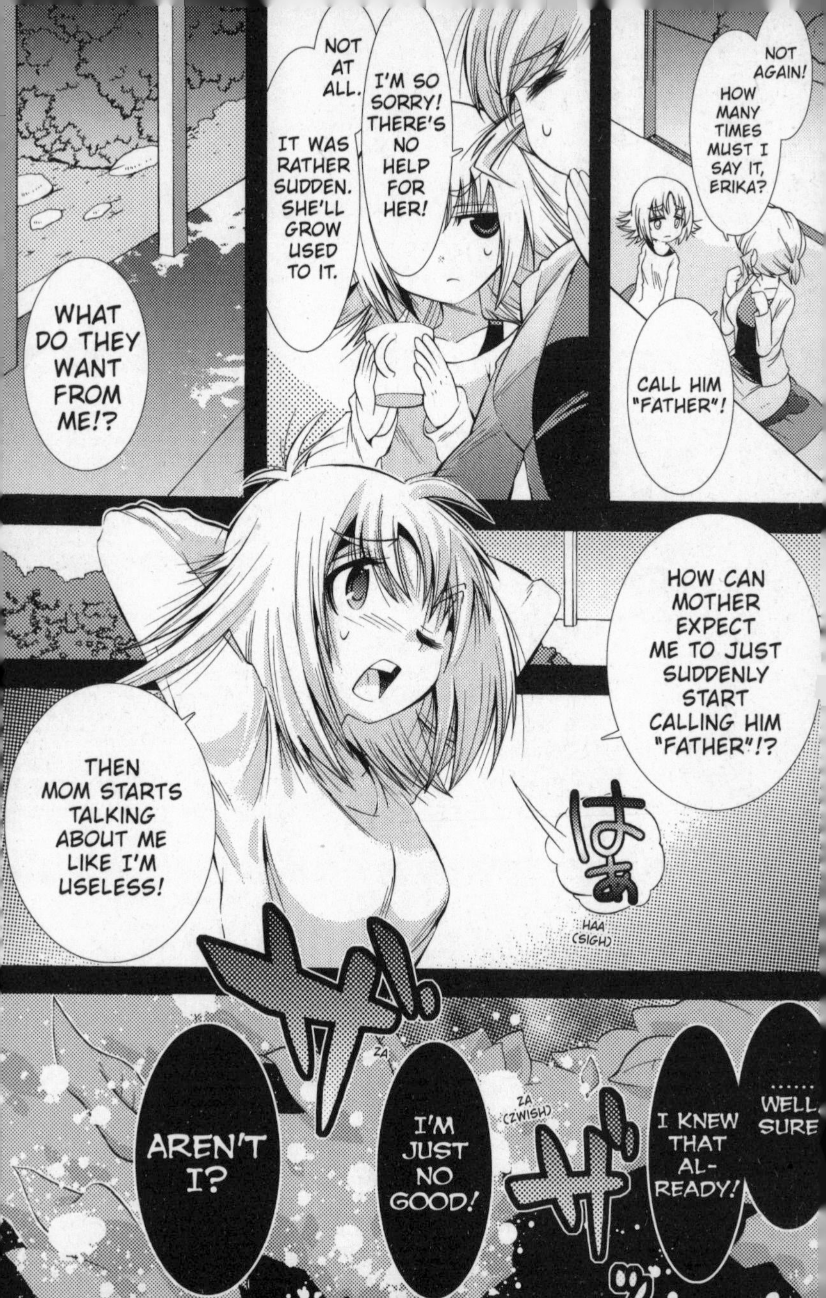
NOT AGAIN! HOW MANY TIMES MUST I SAY IT, ERIKA?
CALL HIM "FATHER"!
I'M SO SORRY! THERE'S NO HELP FOR HER!
NOT AT ALL.
IT WAS RATHER SUDDEN. SHE'LL GROW USED TO IT.
WHAT DO THEY WANT FROM ME!?
HOW CAN MOTHER EXPECT ME TO JUST SUDDENLY START CALLING HIM "FATHER"!?
はぁ
HAA (SIGH)
THEN MOM STARTS TALKING ABOUT ME LIKE I'M USELESS!
......WELL, SURE
I KNEW THAT AL-READY!
ZA (ZWISH)
I'M JUST NO GOOD!
ZA
AREN'T I?

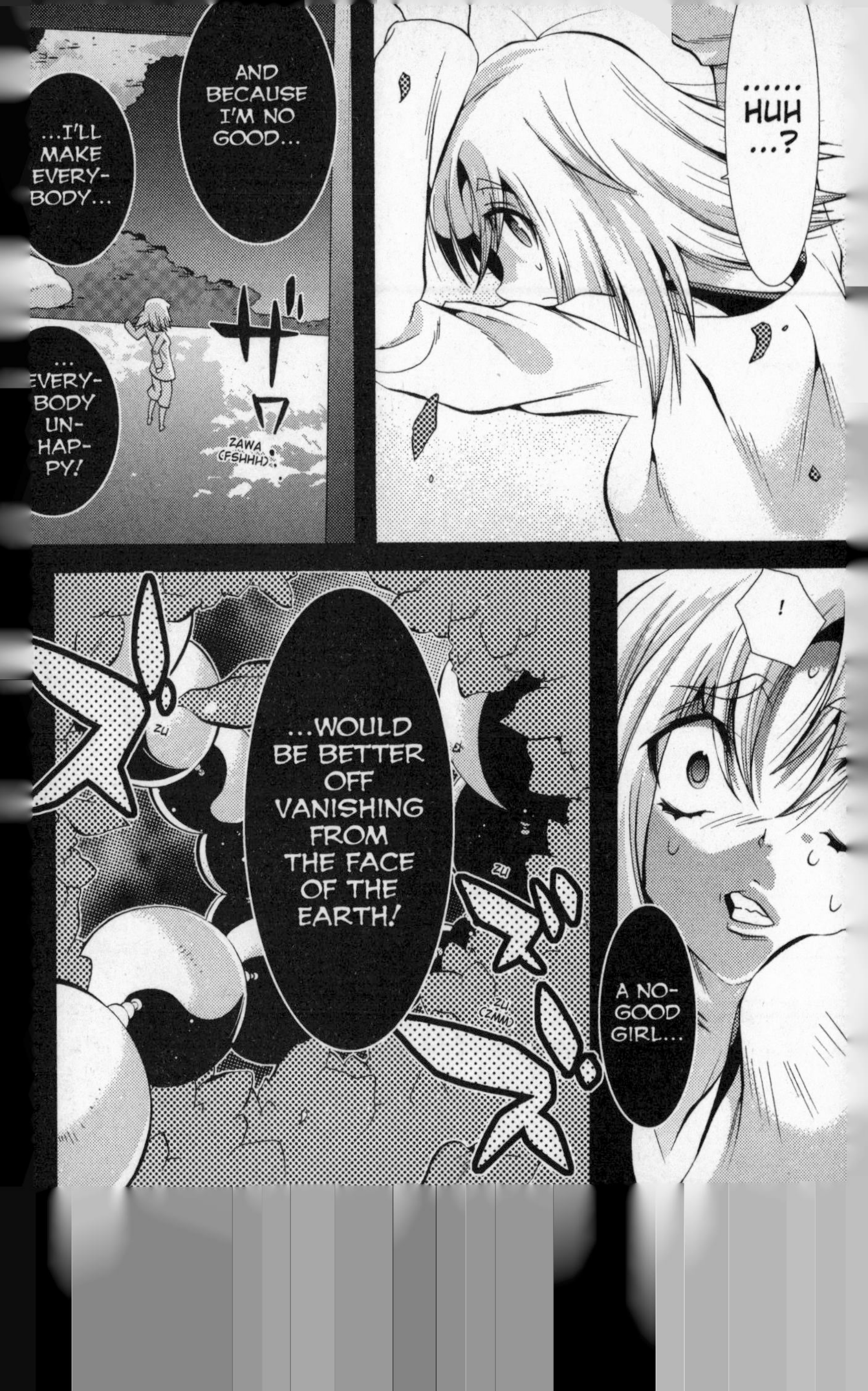
......HUH ...?
AND BECAUSE I'M NO GOOD...
...I'LL MAKE EVERYBODY...
ZAWA (FSHHH)
...EVERYBODY UNHAPPY!
!
A NO-GOOD GIRL...
ZU
...WOULD BE BETTER OFF VANISHING FROM THE FACE OF THE EARTH!
ZU
ZU (ZMM)

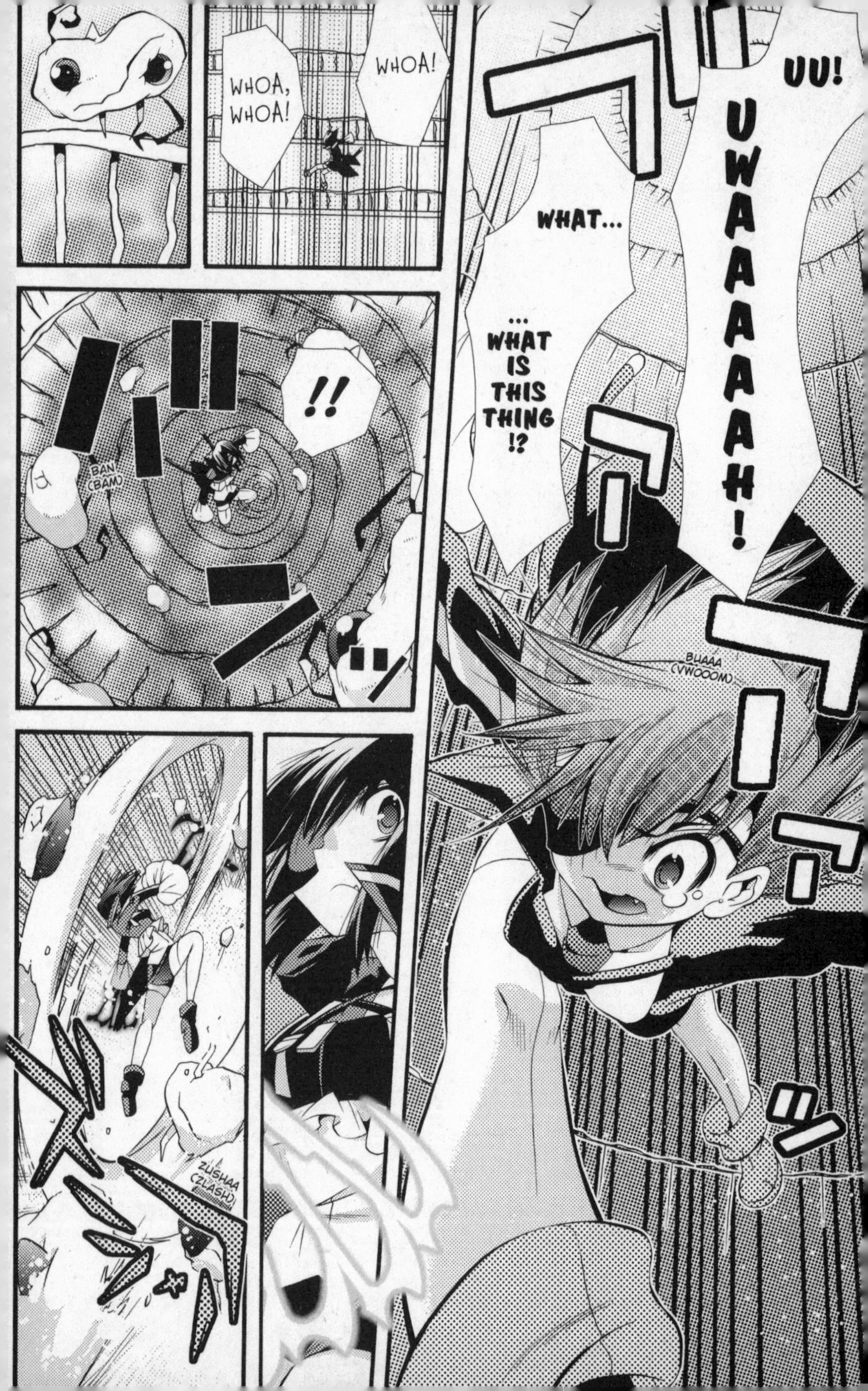
UU!
UWAAAAAH!
WHAT...
...WHAT IS THIS THING!?
BUAAA (VWOOOM)
WHOA!
WHOA, WHOA!
!!
BAN (BAM)
ZUSHAA (ZLASH)

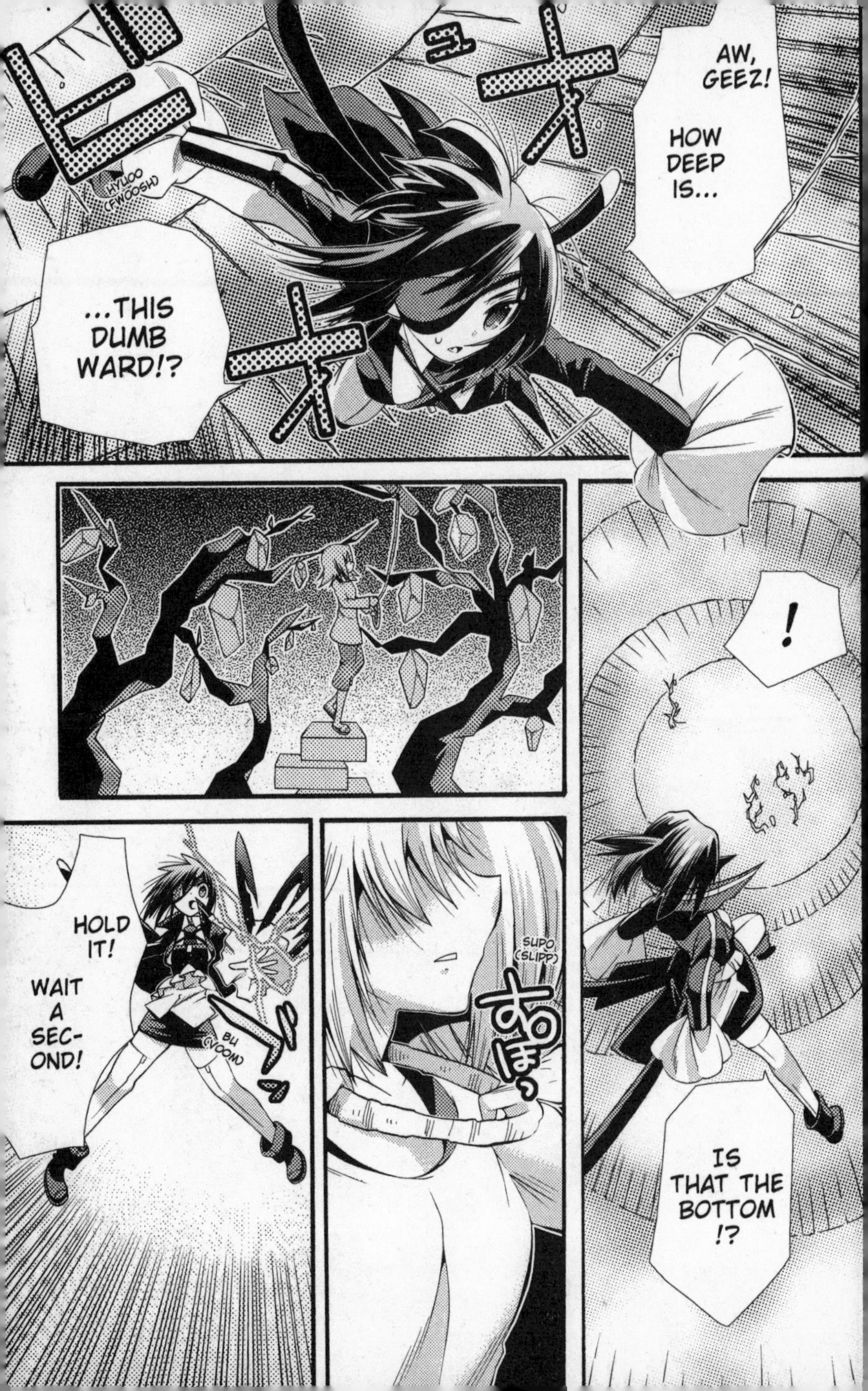
AW, GEEZ!
HOW DEEP IS...
HYUOO (FWOOSH)
...THIS DUMB WARD!?
!
IS THAT THE BOTTOM !?
SUPO (SLIPP)
HOLD IT!
WAIT A SEC-OND!
BU (VOOM)

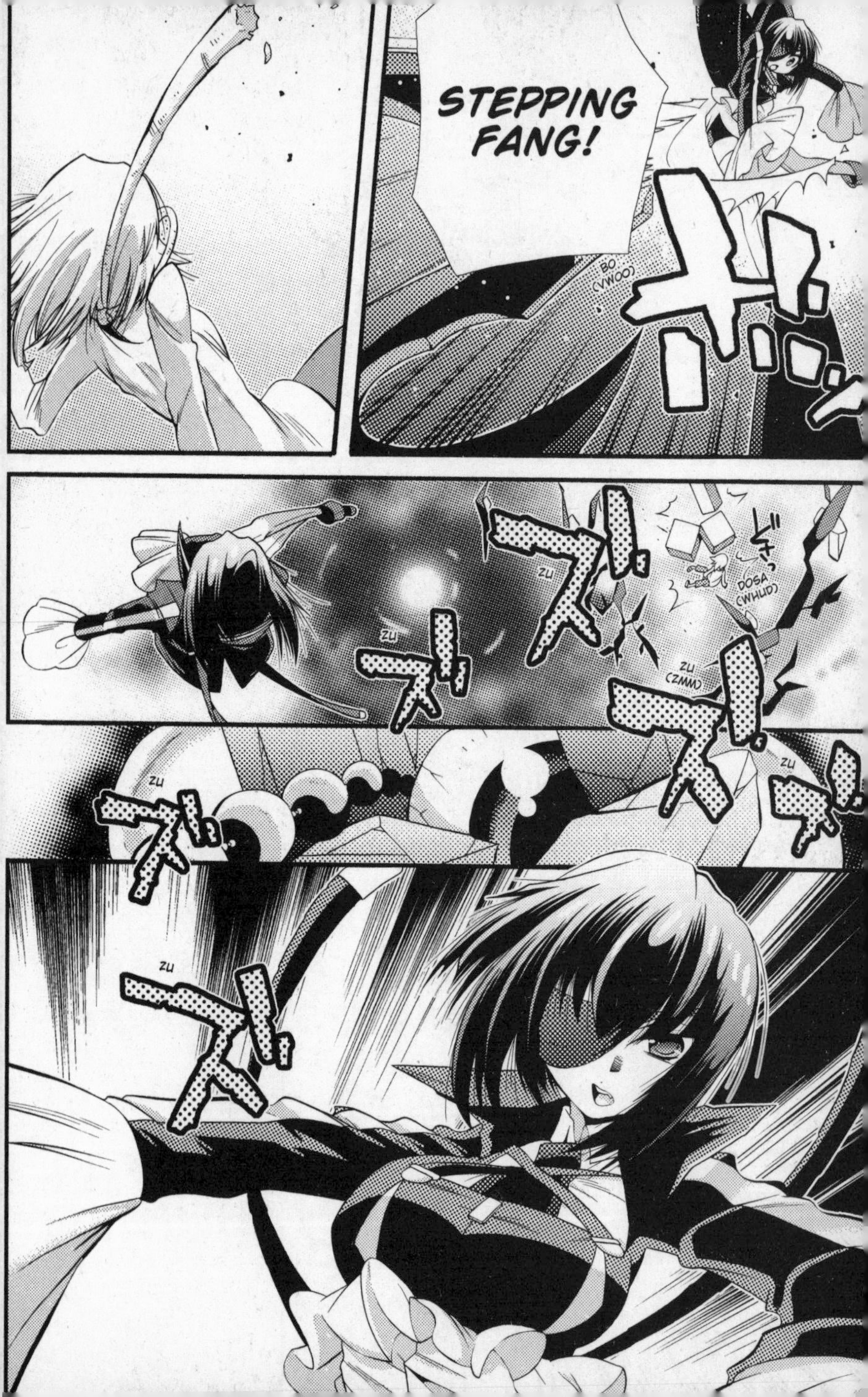
STEPPING FANG!
BO (VWOO)
DOSA (WHUD)
ZU
ZU (ZMM)
ZU
ZU
ZU
ZU

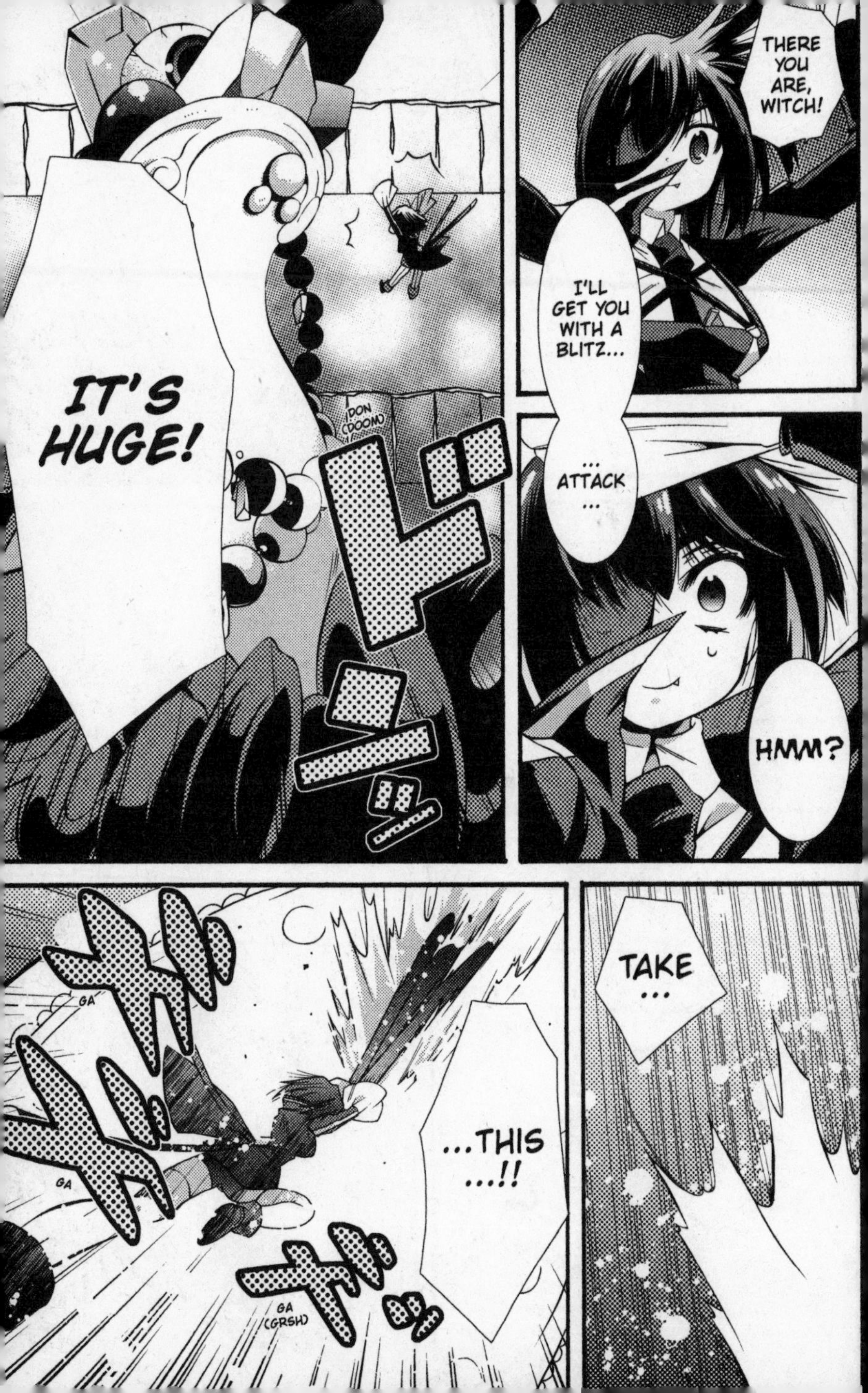
THERE YOU ARE, WITCH!
I'LL GET YOU WITH A BLITZ...
... ATTACK ...
HMM?
IT'S HUGE!
DON (DOOM)
TAKE ...
...THIS ...!!
GA
GA
GA (GRSH)

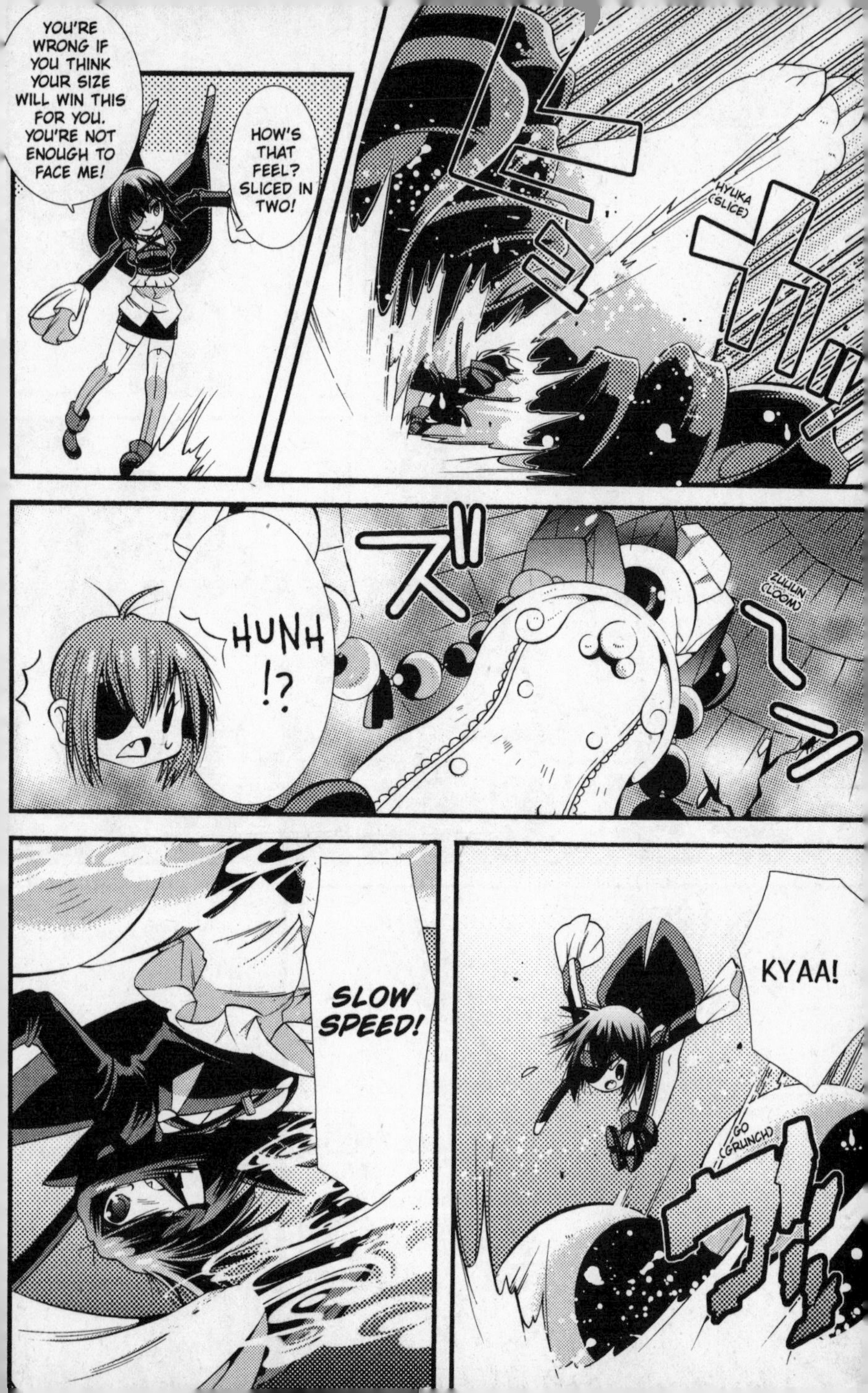
HYUKA (SLICE)
HOW'S THAT FEEL? SLICED IN TWO!
YOU'RE WRONG IF YOU THINK YOUR SIZE WILL WIN THIS FOR YOU. YOU'RE NOT ENOUGH TO FACE ME!
ZUUUN (LOOM)
HUNH !?
KYAA!
GO (GRUNCH)
SLOW SPEED!

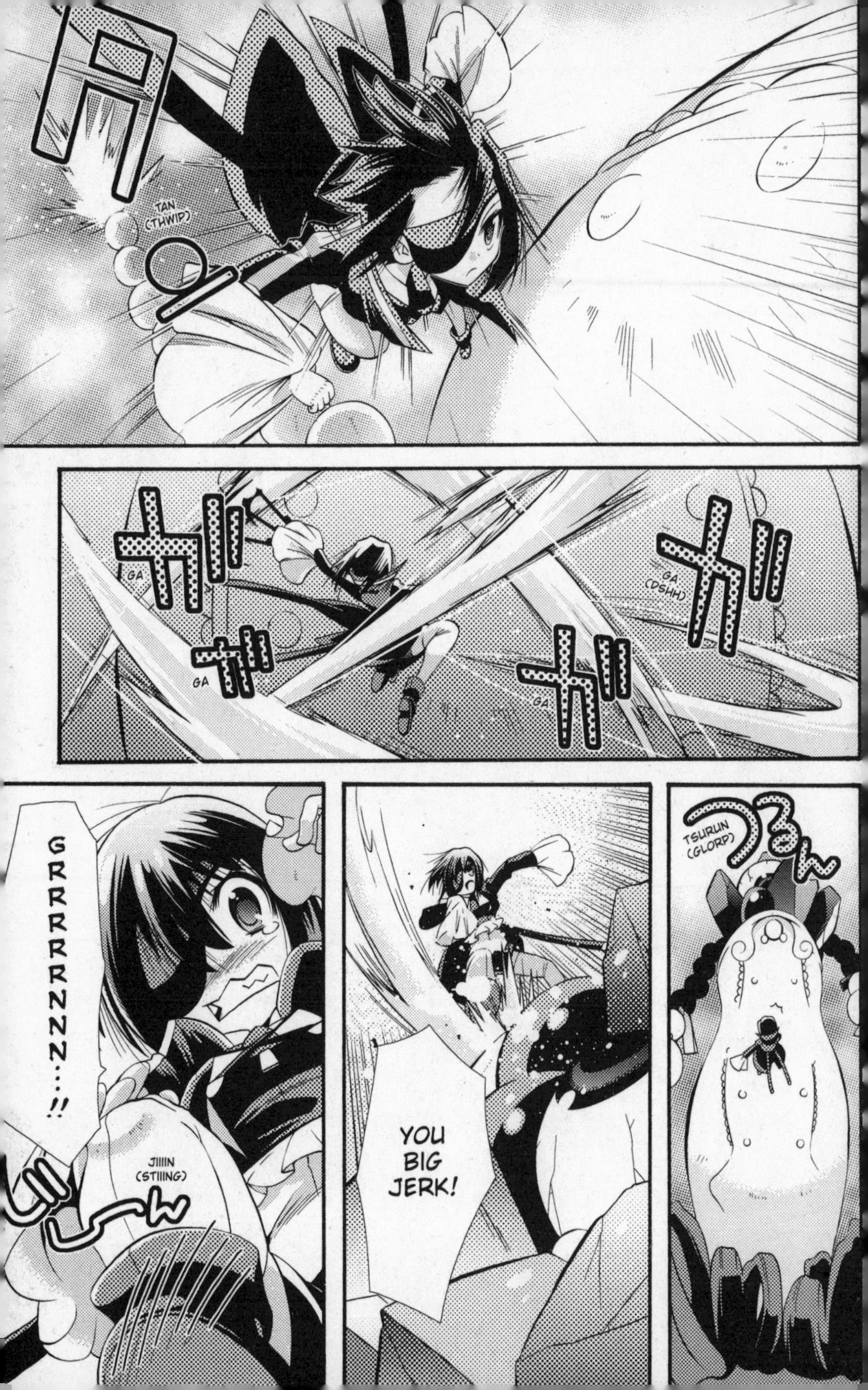

TAN (THWIP)
GA (DSHH)
GA
GA
GA
TSURUN (GLORP)
YOU BIG JERK!
GRRRRRNNN...!!
JIIIIN (STIIING)

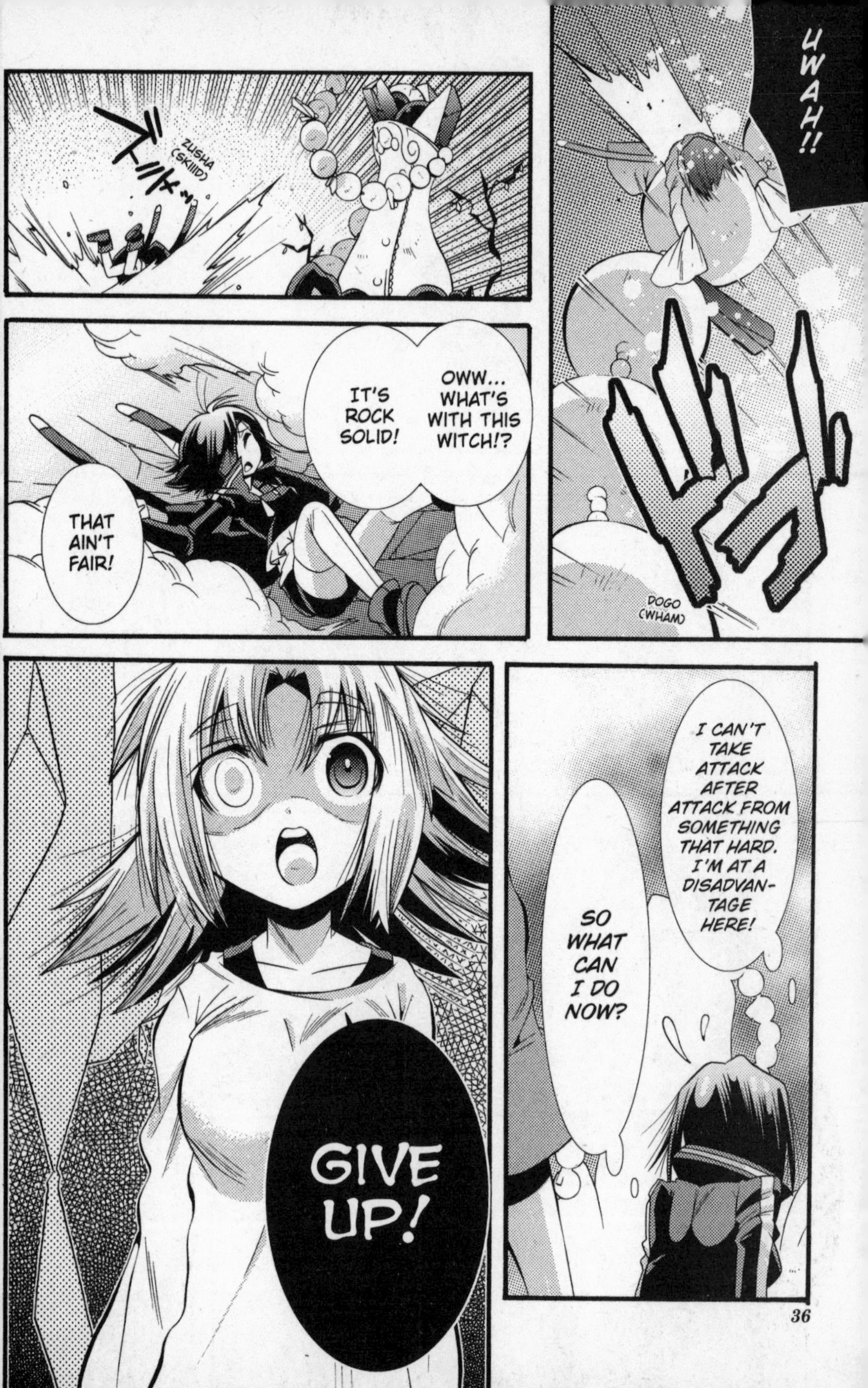
UWAH!!
DOGO (WHAM)
ZUSHA (SKIIID)
OWW... WHAT'S WITH THIS WITCH!?
IT'S ROCK SOLID!
THAT AIN'T FAIR!
I CAN'T TAKE ATTACK AFTER ATTACK FROM SOMETHING THAT HARD. I'M AT A DISADVAN-TAGE HERE!
SO WHAT CAN I DO NOW?
GIVE UP!

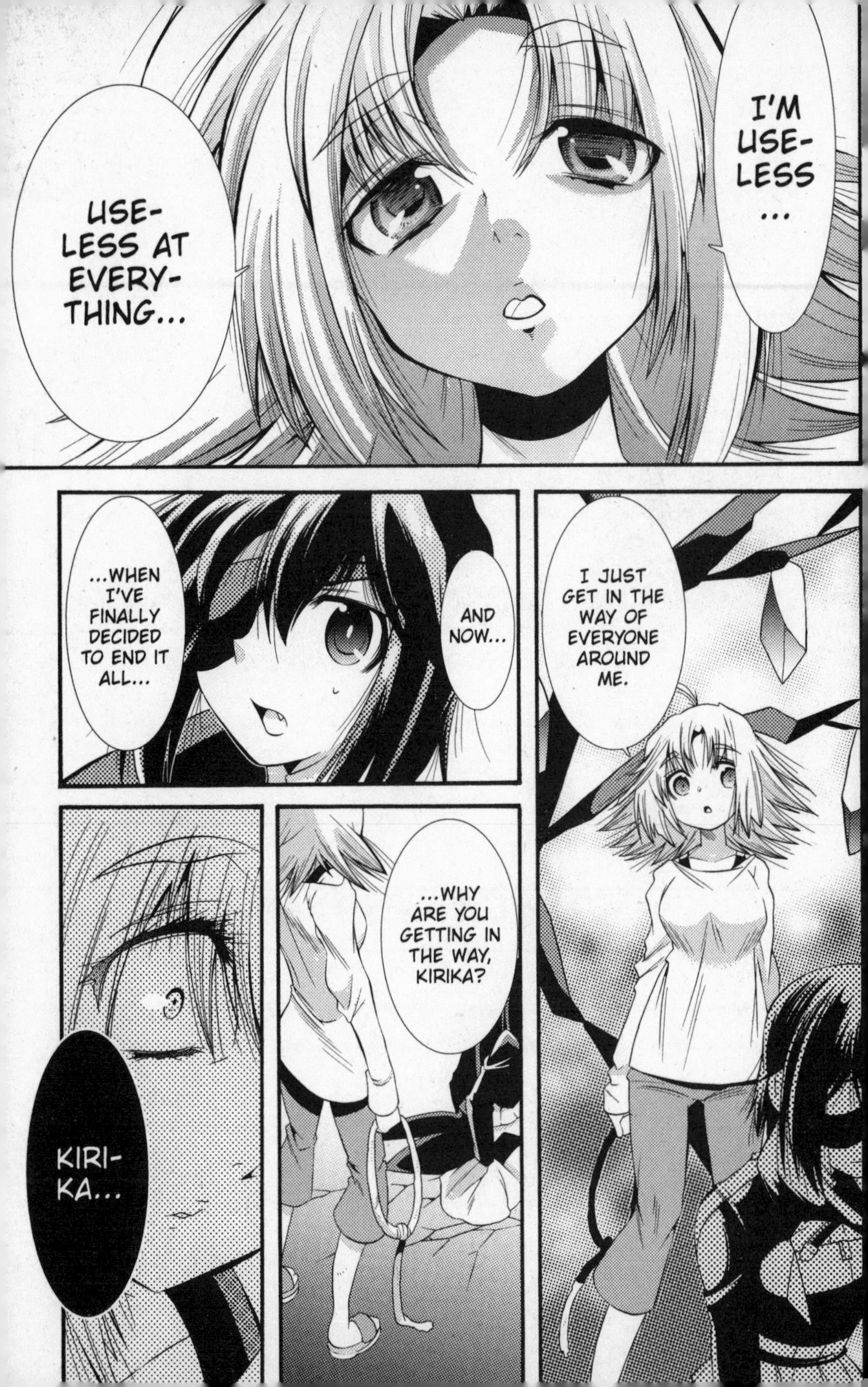
I'M USE-LESS...
USE-LESS AT EVERY-THING...
I JUST GET IN THE WAY OF EVERYONE AROUND ME.
AND NOW...
...WHEN I'VE FINALLY DECIDED TO END IT ALL...
...WHY ARE YOU GETTING IN THE WAY, KIRIKA?
KIRI-KA...

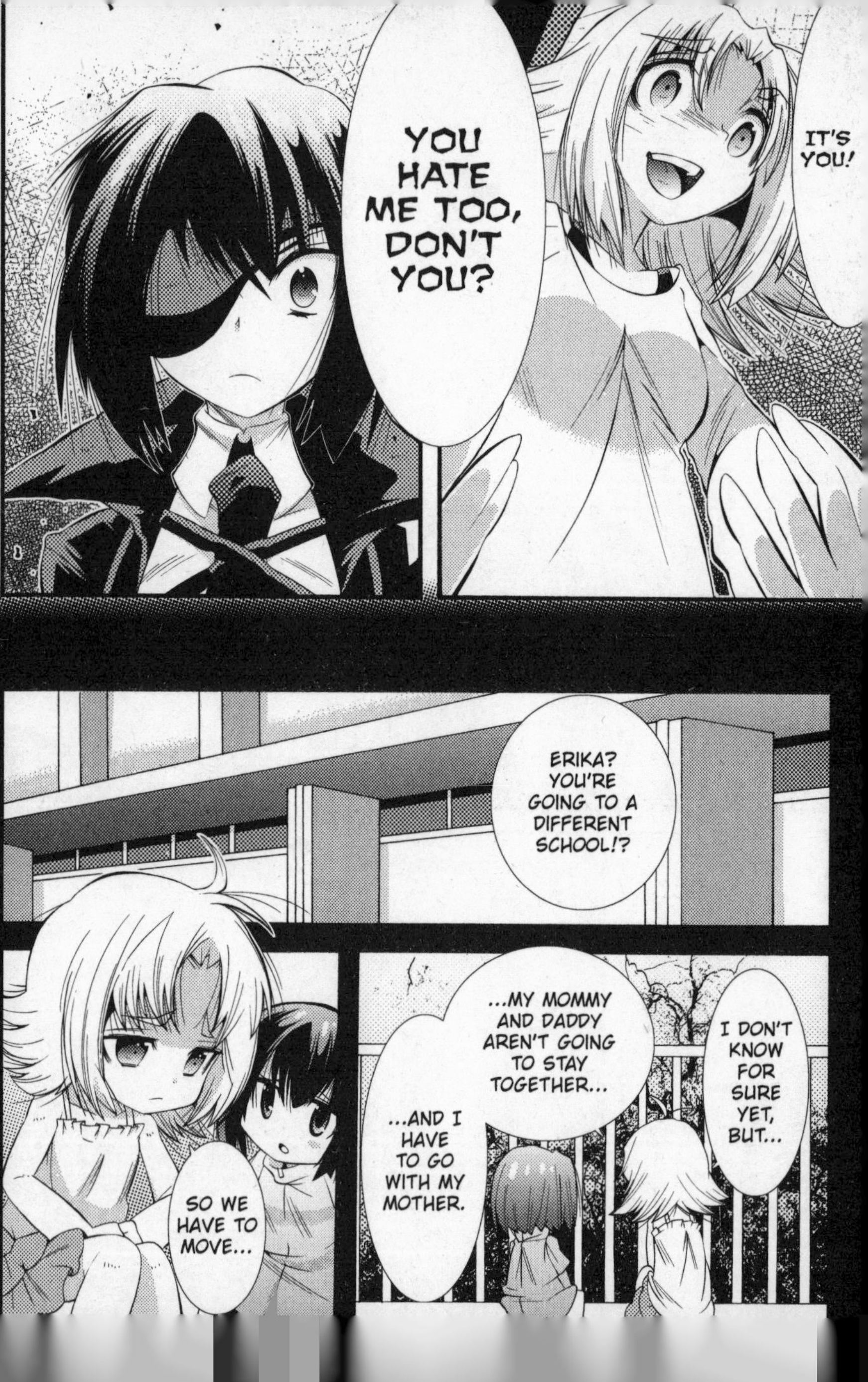
IT'S YOU!
YOU HATE ME TOO, DON'T YOU?
ERIKA? YOU'RE GOING TO A DIFFERENT SCHOOL!?
I DON'T KNOW FOR SURE YET, BUT...
...MY MOMMY AND DADDY AREN'T GOING TO STAY TOGETHER...
...AND I HAVE TO GO WITH MY MOTHER.
SO WE HAVE TO MOVE...

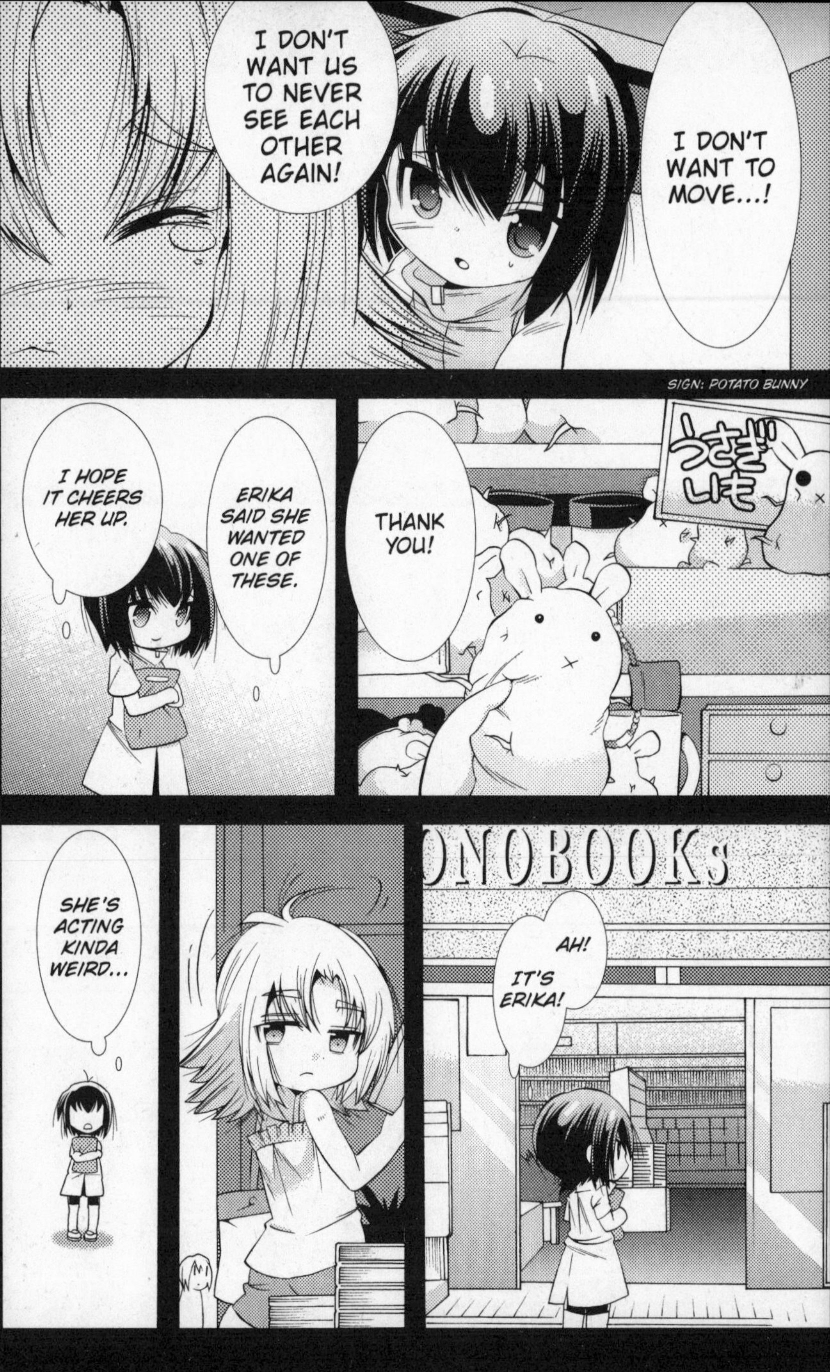
I DON'T WANT TO MOVE...!
I DON'T WANT US TO NEVER SEE EACH OTHER AGAIN!
SIGN: POTATO BUNNY
うさぎいも
THANK YOU!
ERIKA SAID SHE WANTED ONE OF THESE.
I HOPE IT CHEERS HER UP.
ONOBOOKs
AH! IT'S ERIKA!
SHE'S ACTING KINDA WEIRD...

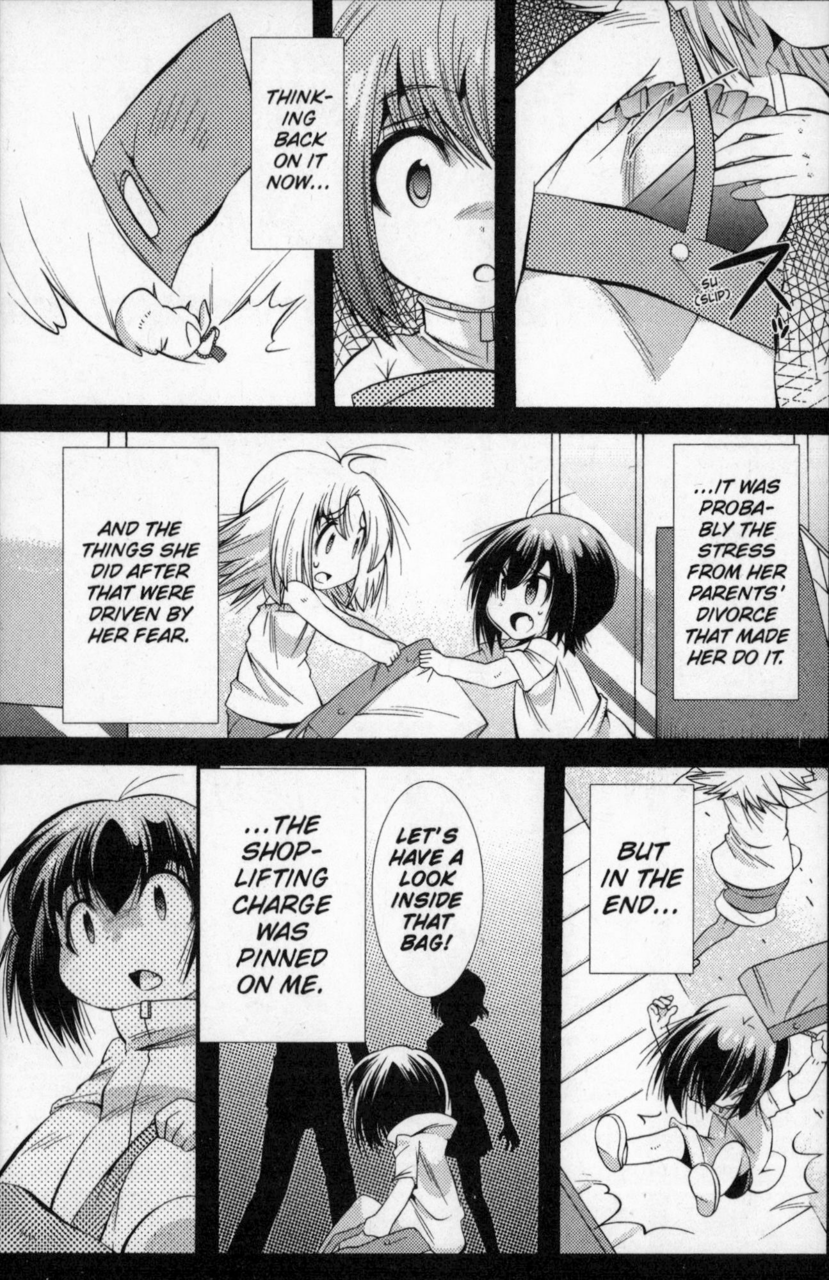
SU (SLIP)
THINKING BACK ON IT NOW...
...IT WAS PROBABLY THE STRESS FROM HER PARENTS' DIVORCE THAT MADE HER DO IT.
AND THE THINGS SHE DID AFTER THAT WERE DRIVEN BY HER FEAR.
BUT IN THE END...
LET'S HAVE A LOOK INSIDE THAT BAG!
...THE SHOPLIFTING CHARGE WAS PINNED ON ME.

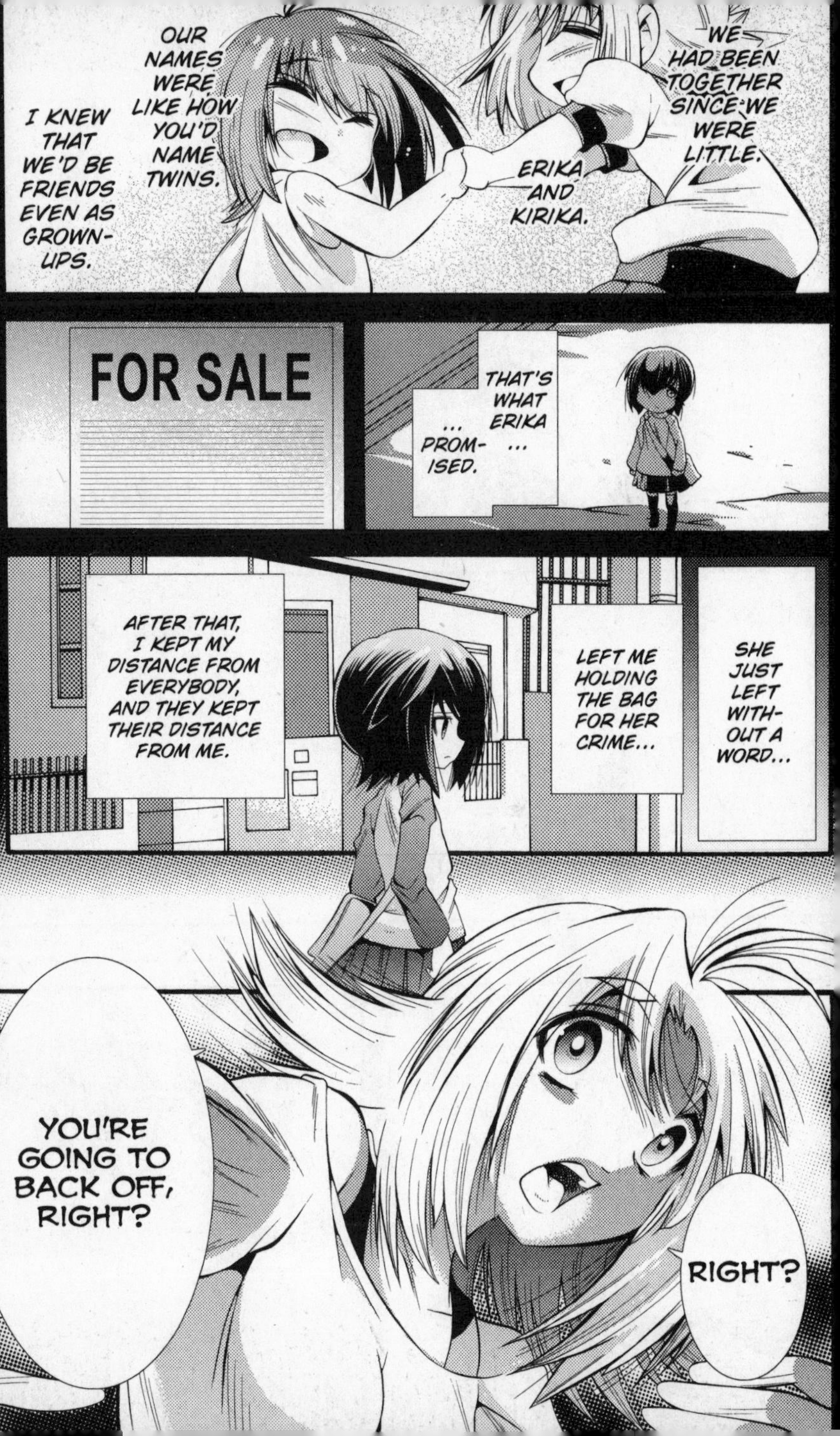
WE HAD BEEN TOGETHER SINCE WE WERE LITTLE.
ERIKA AND KIRIKA.
OUR NAMES WERE LIKE HOW YOU'D NAME TWINS.
I KNEW THAT WE'D BE FRIENDS EVEN AS GROWN-UPS.
THAT'S WHAT ERIKA ...
... PROM-ISED.
FOR SALE
SHE JUST LEFT WITH-OUT A WORD...
LEFT ME HOLDING THE BAG FOR HER CRIME...
AFTER THAT, I KEPT MY DISTANCE FROM EVERYBODY, AND THEY KEPT THEIR DISTANCE FROM ME.
YOU'RE GOING TO BACK OFF, RIGHT?
RIGHT?

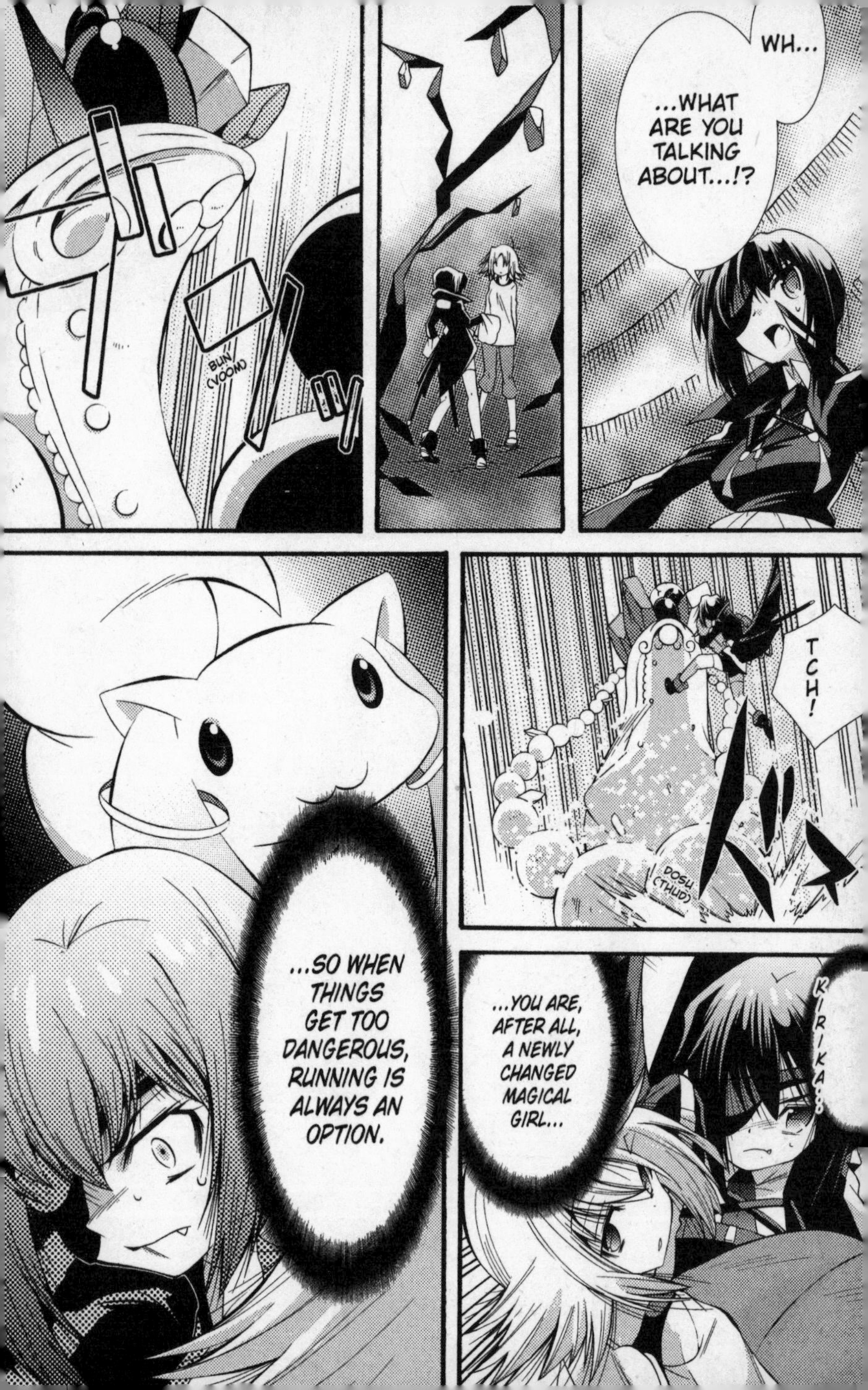
WH...
...WHAT ARE YOU TALKING ABOUT...!?
BUN (VOOM)
TCH!
DOSU (THUD)
KIRIKA...
...YOU ARE, AFTER ALL, A NEWLY CHANGED MAGICAL GIRL...
...SO WHEN THINGS GET TOO DANGEROUS, RUNNING IS ALWAYS AN OPTION.

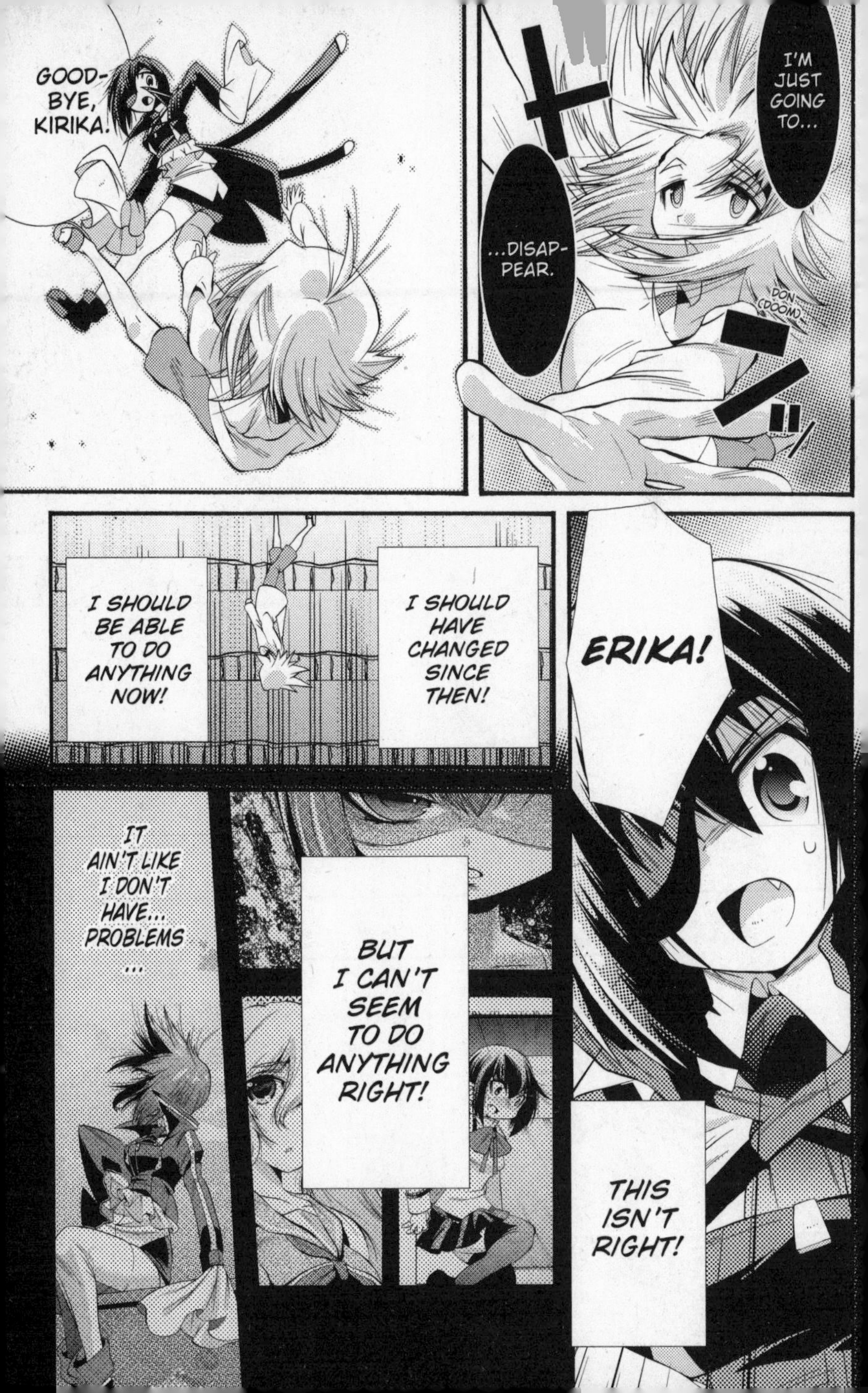
I'M JUST GOING TO...
...DISAP-PEAR.
DON (DOOM)
!!
GOOD-BYE, KIRIKA.
ERIKA!
THIS ISN'T RIGHT!
I SHOULD HAVE CHANGED SINCE THEN!
I SHOULD BE ABLE TO DO ANYTHING NOW!
BUT I CAN'T SEEM TO DO ANYTHING RIGHT!
IT AIN'T LIKE I DON'T HAVE... PROBLEMS...

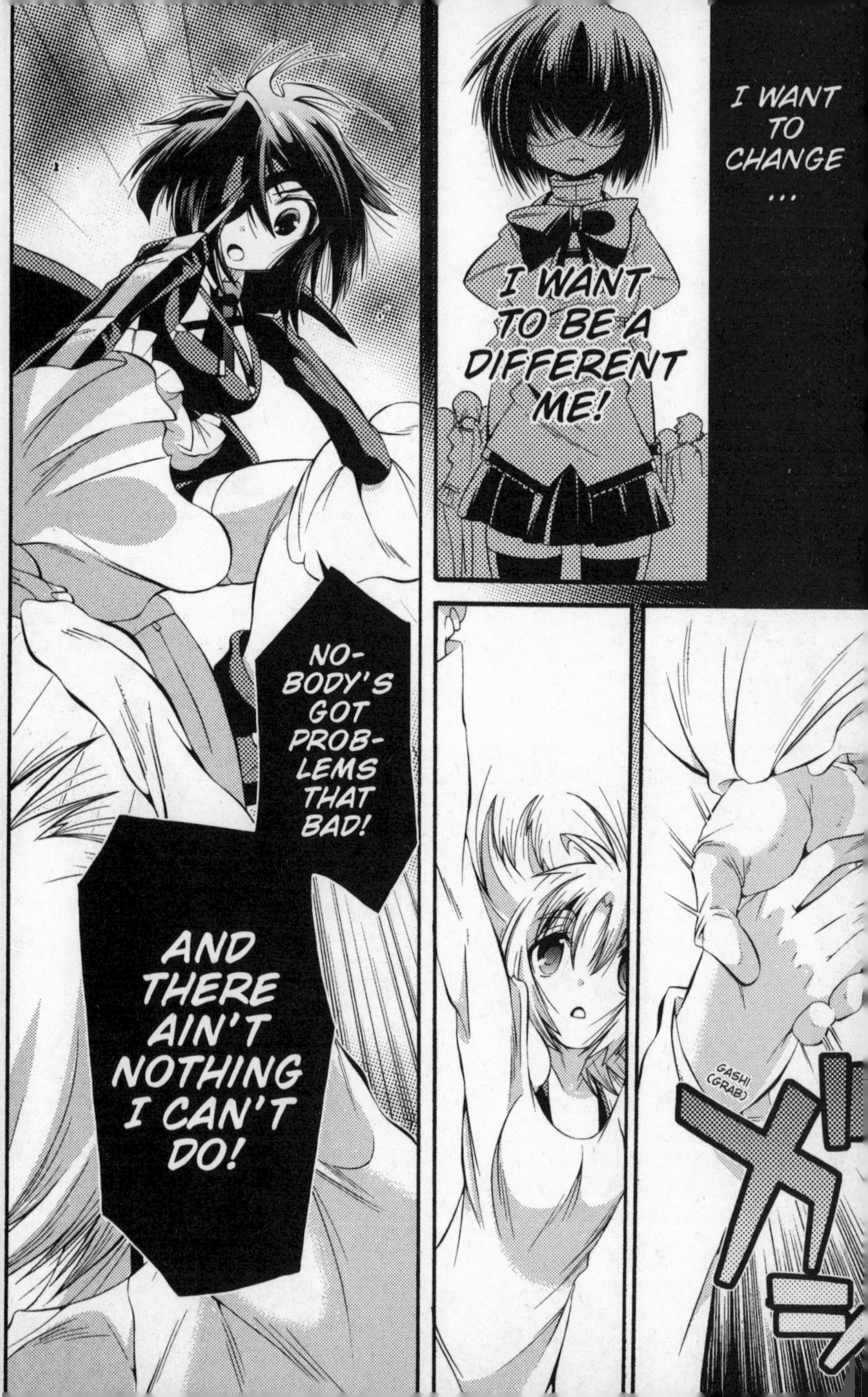
I WANT TO CHANGE ...
I WANT TO BE A DIFFERENT ME!
GASHI (GRAB)
NO-BODY'S GOT PROB-LEMS THAT BAD!
AND THERE AIN'T NOTHING I CAN'T DO!

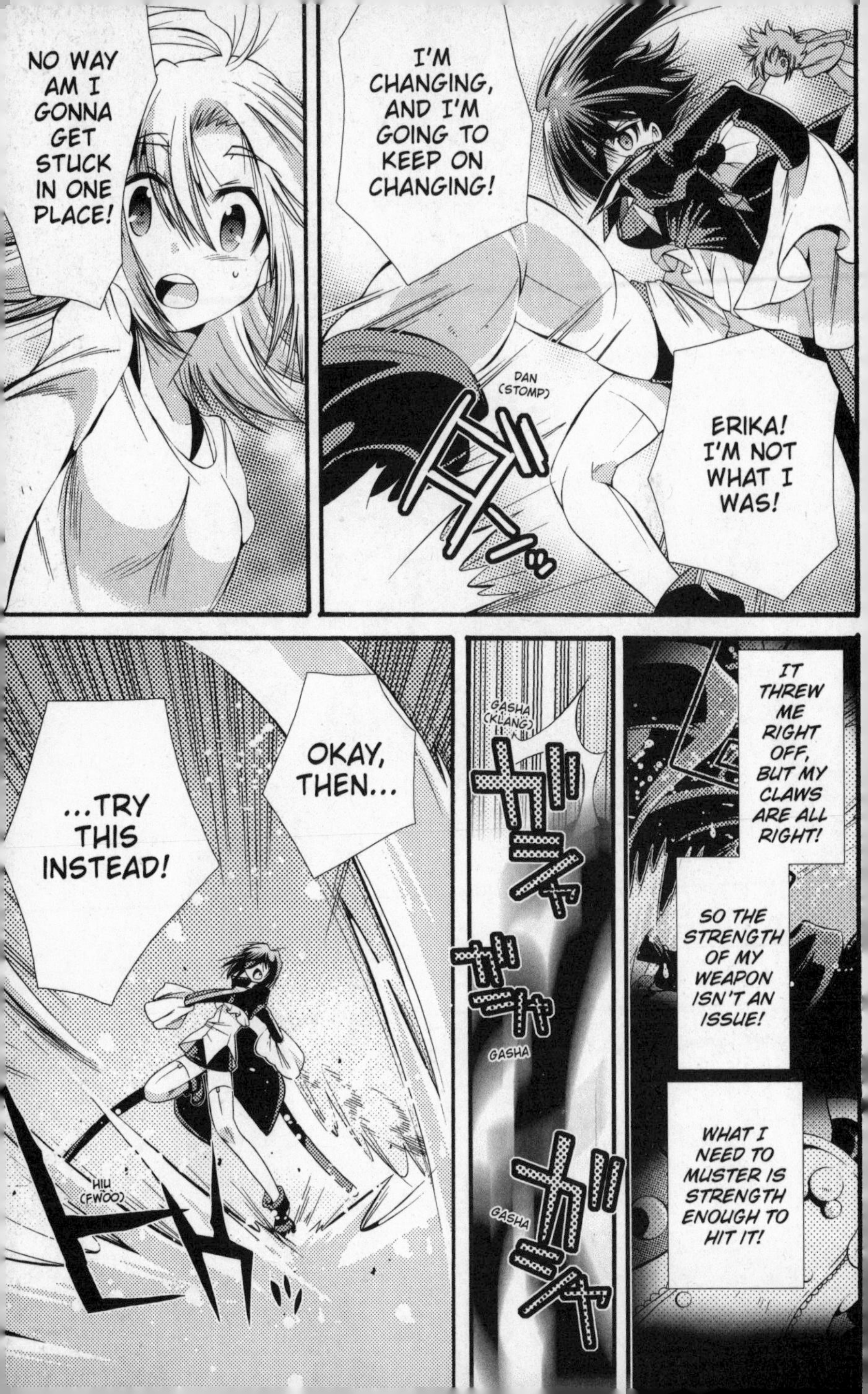
I'M CHANGING, AND I'M GOING TO KEEP ON CHANGING!
DAN (STOMP)
ERIKA! I'M NOT WHAT I WAS!
NO WAY AM I GONNA GET STUCK IN ONE PLACE!
IT THREW ME RIGHT OFF, BUT MY CLAWS ARE ALL RIGHT!
SO THE STRENGTH OF MY WEAPON ISN'T AN ISSUE!
WHAT I NEED TO MUSTER IS STRENGTH ENOUGH TO HIT IT!
GASHA (KLANG)
GASHA
GASHA
OKAY, THEN...
...TRY THIS INSTEAD!
HIU (FWOO)

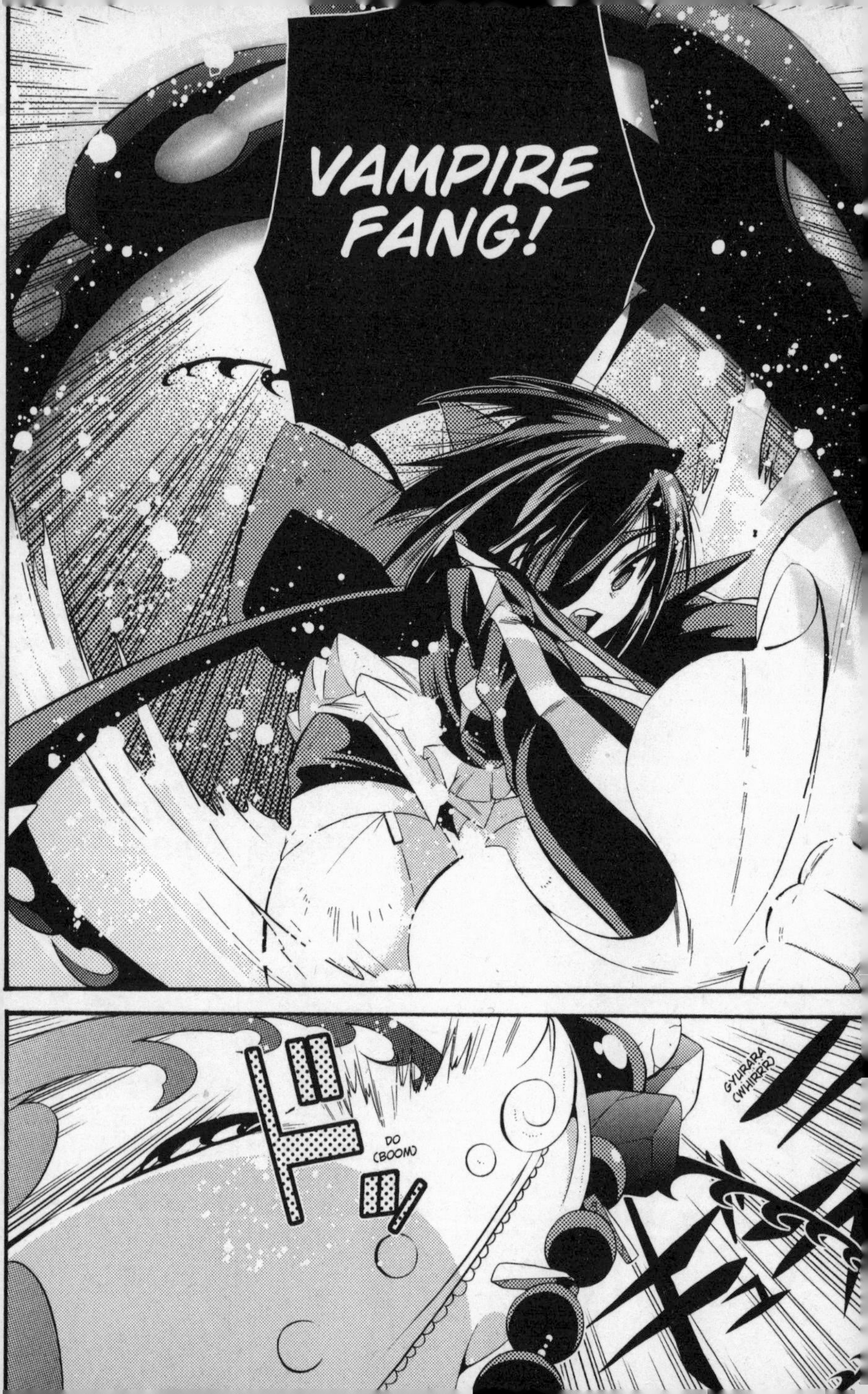
VAMPIRE FANG!
GYURARA (WHIRRR)
DO (BOOM)

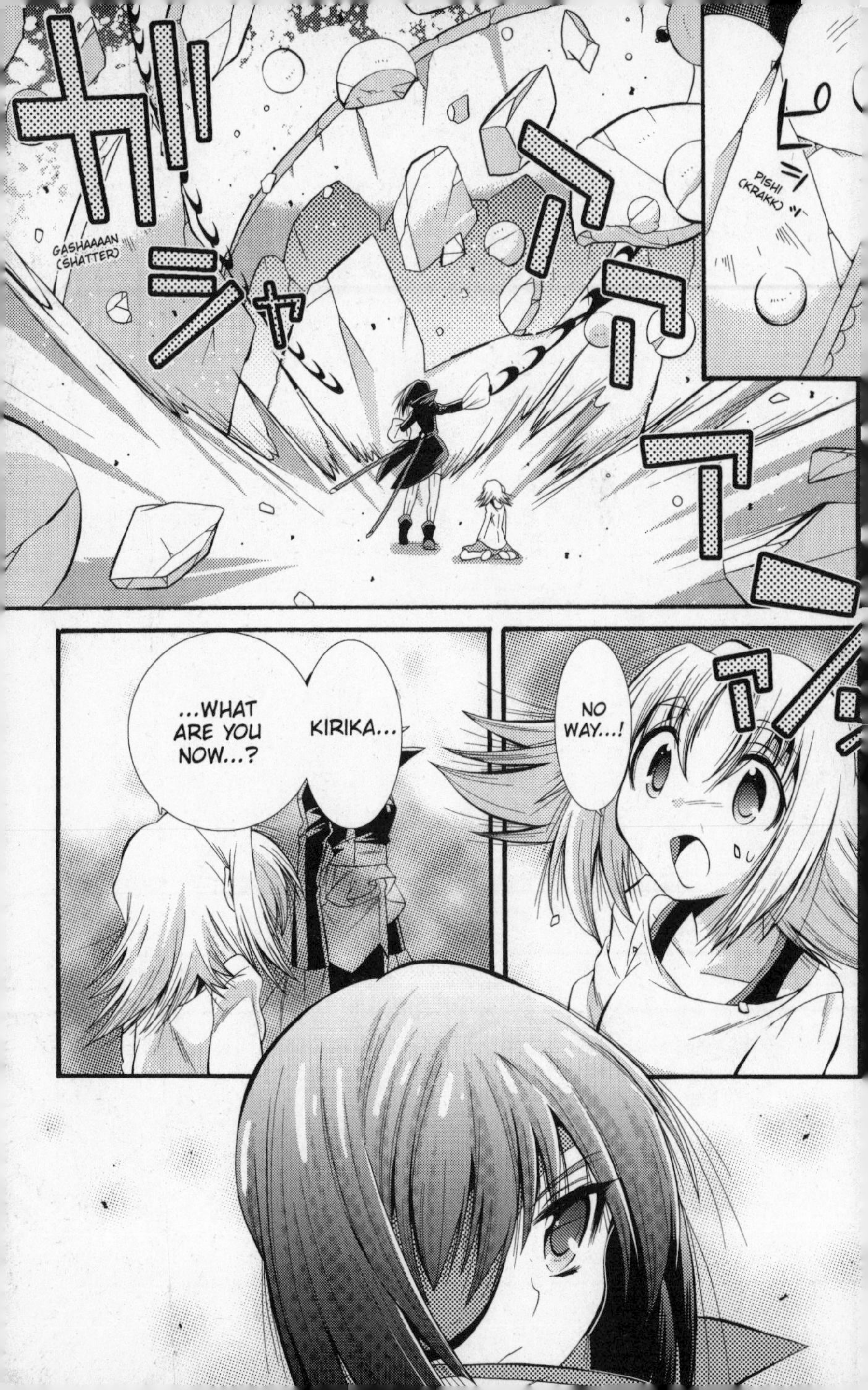
PISHI (KRAKK)
GASHAAAAN (SHATTER)
NO WAY...!
KIRIKA...
...WHAT ARE YOU NOW...?

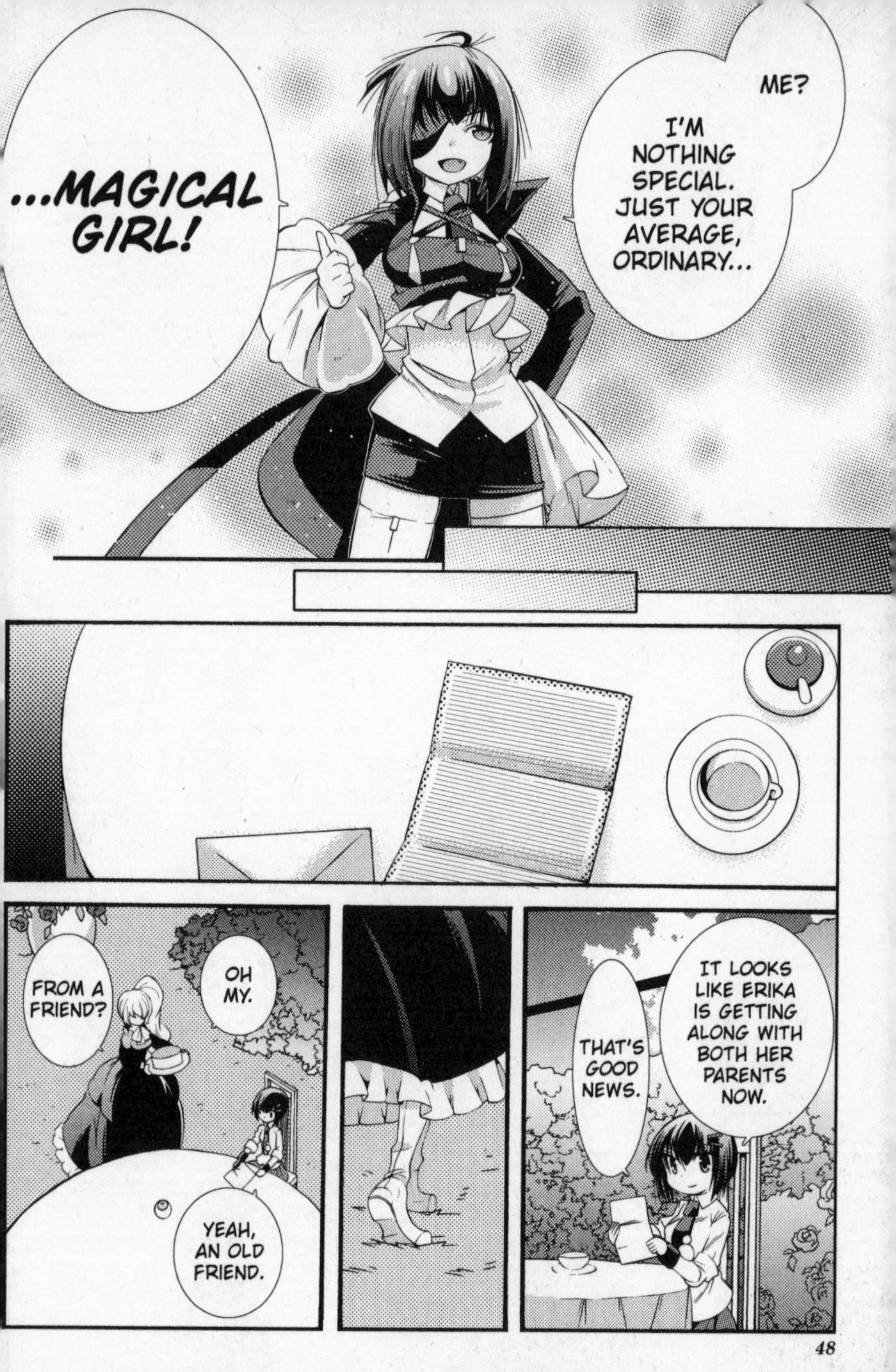
ME?
I'M NOTHING SPECIAL. JUST YOUR AVERAGE, ORDINARY...
...MAGICAL GIRL!
IT LOOKS LIKE ERIKA IS GETTING ALONG WITH BOTH HER PARENTS NOW.
THAT'S GOOD NEWS.
OH MY.
FROM A FRIEND?
YEAH, AN OLD FRIEND.

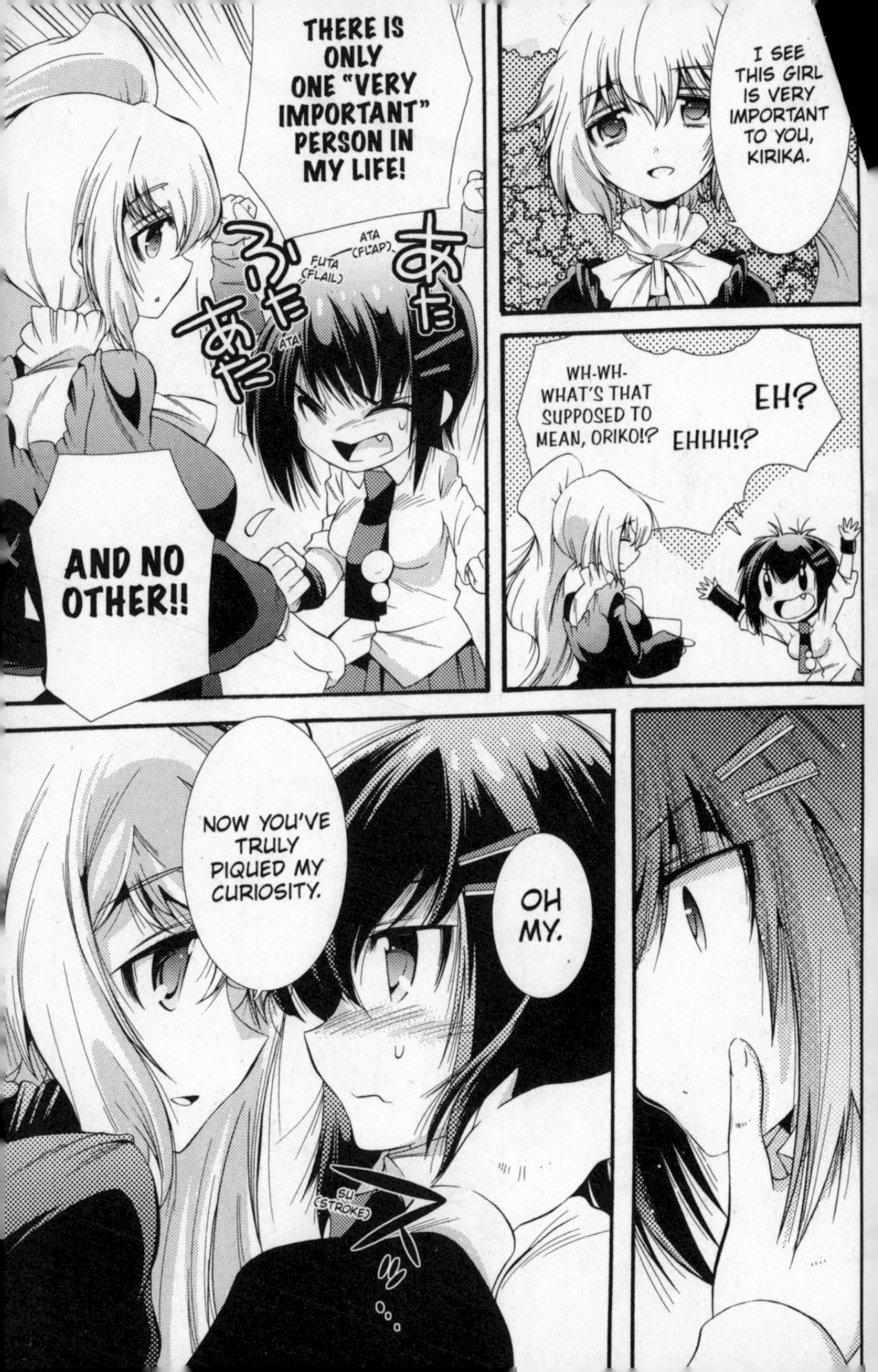
I SEE THIS GIRL IS VERY IMPORTANT TO YOU, KIRIKA.
EH?
EHHH!?
WH-WH-WHAT'S THAT SUPPOSED TO MEAN, ORIKO!?
THERE IS ONLY ONE "VERY IMPORTANT" PERSON IN MY LIFE!
あた
ATA (FLAP)
ふた
FUTA (FLAIL)
あた
ATA
AND NO OTHER!!
NOW YOU'VE TRULY PIQUED MY CURIOSITY.
OH MY.
SU (STROKE)

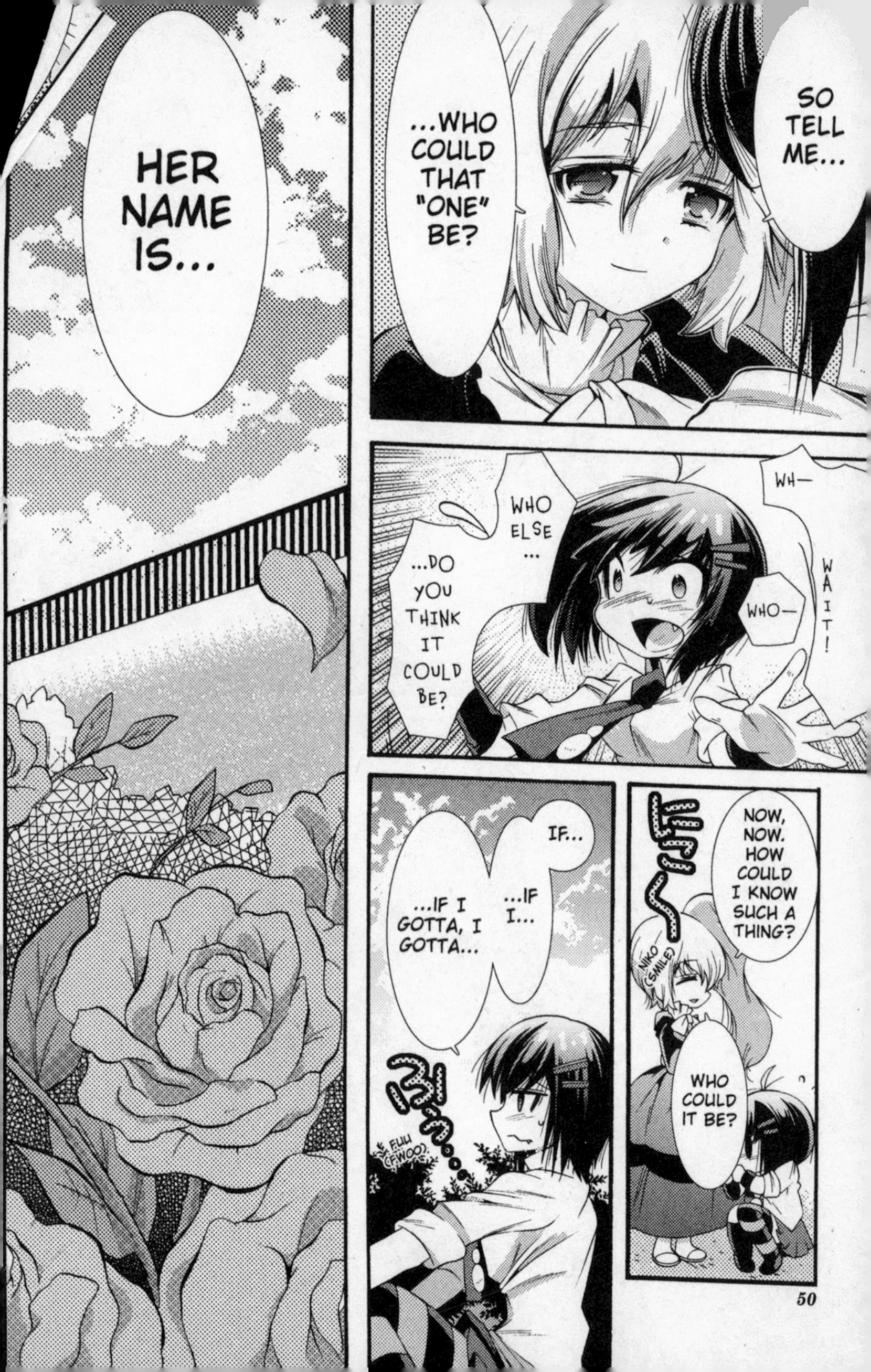
SO TELL ME...
...WHO COULD THAT "ONE" BE?
WH—
WHO ELSE ...
WAIT!
WHO—
...DO YOU THINK IT COULD BE?
NOW, NOW. HOW COULD I KNOW SUCH A THING?
NIKO (SMILE)
WHO COULD IT BE?
IF...
...IF I...
...IF I GOTTA, I GOTTA...
FUU (F-WOO)
HER NAME IS...

PUELLA MAGI
ORIKO ★ MAGICA
[extra story]

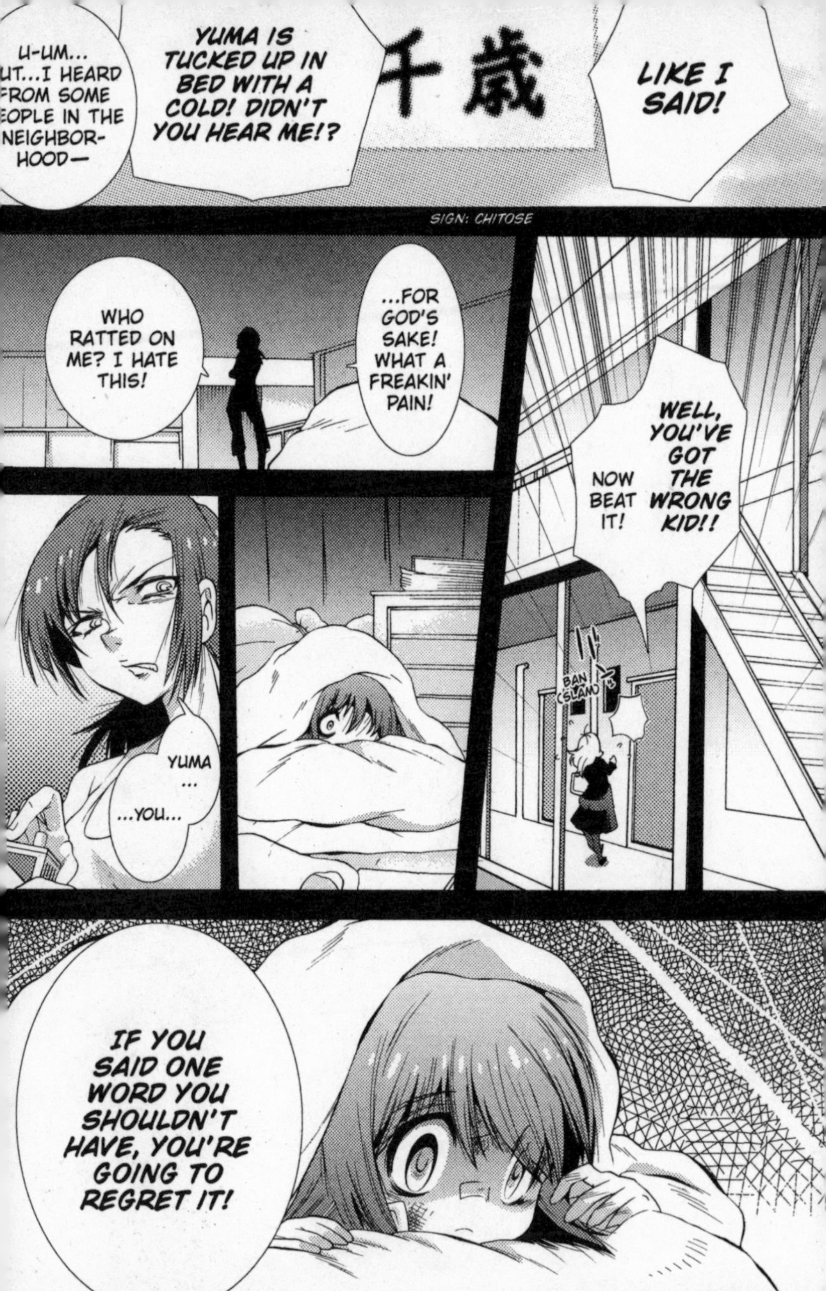

LIKE I SAID!
千歳
YUMA IS TUCKED UP IN BED WITH A COLD! DIDN'T YOU HEAR ME!?
U-UM... UT...I HEARD FROM SOME EOPLE IN THE NEIGHBOR-HOOD—
SIGN: CHITOSE
WELL, YOU'VE GOT THE WRONG KID!!
NOW BEAT IT!
BAN (SLAM)
...FOR GOD'S SAKE! WHAT A FREAKIN' PAIN!
WHO RATTED ON ME? I HATE THIS!
YUMA ...
...YOU...
IF YOU SAID ONE WORD YOU SHOULDN'T HAVE, YOU'RE GOING TO REGRET IT!

~symmetry diamond~ [part 1]

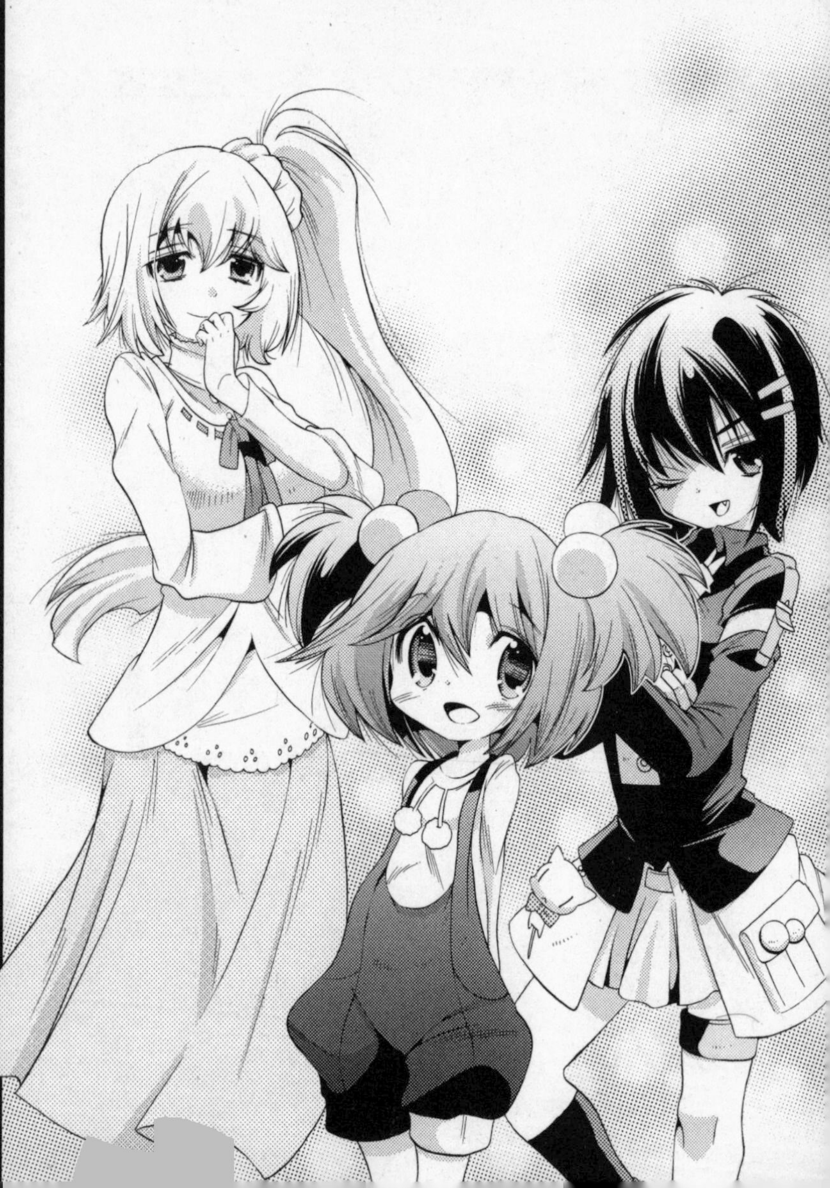

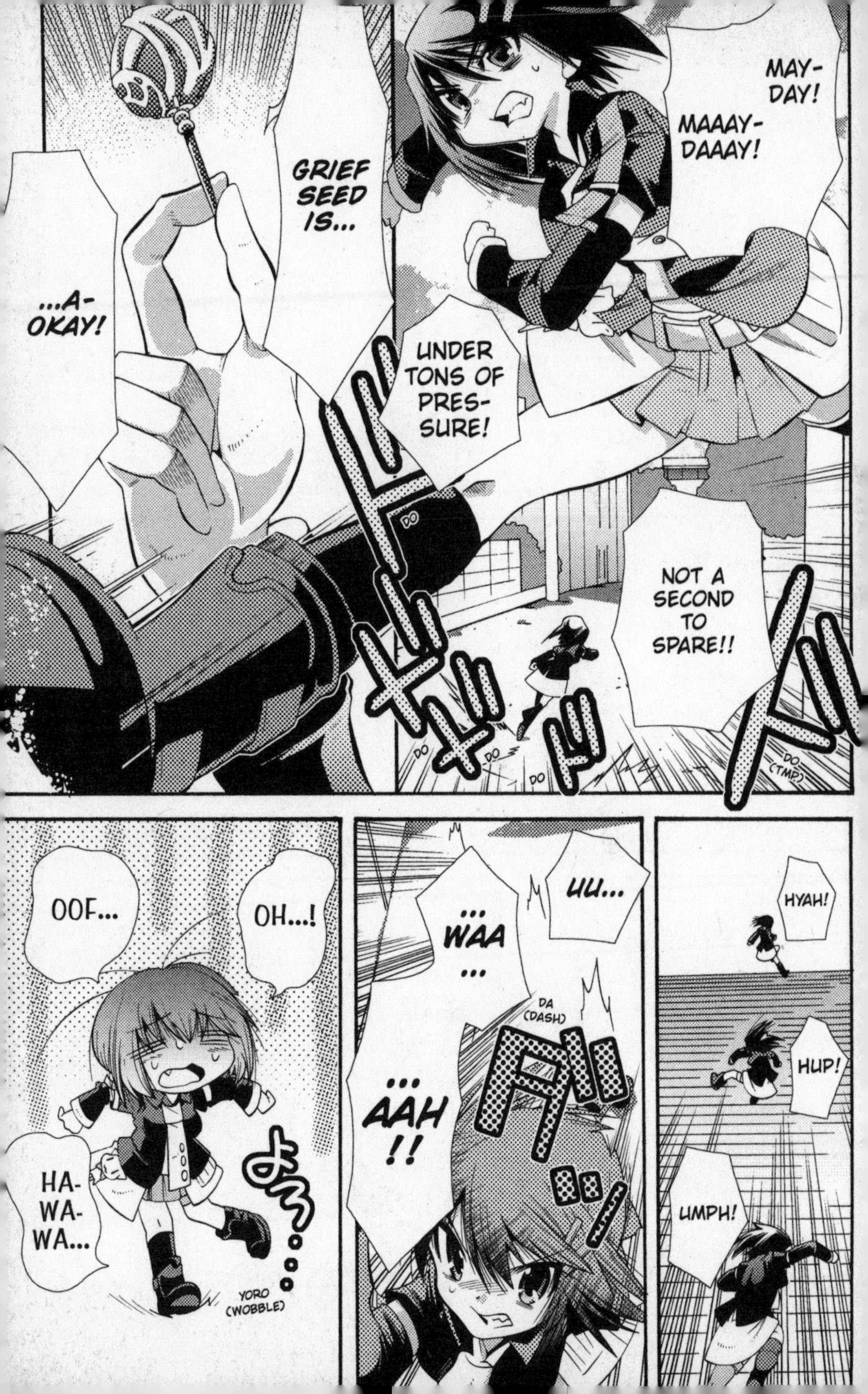
MAY-DAY!
MAAAY-DAAAY!
UNDER TONS OF PRES-SURE!
NOT A SECOND TO SPARE!!
DO
DO (TMP)
DO
DO
DO
GRIEF SEED IS...
...A-OKAY!
HYAH!
HUP!
UMPH!
UU...
...WÄA...
DA (DASH)
...ÄAH!!
OH...!
OOF...
HA-WA-WA...
YORO (WOBBLE)

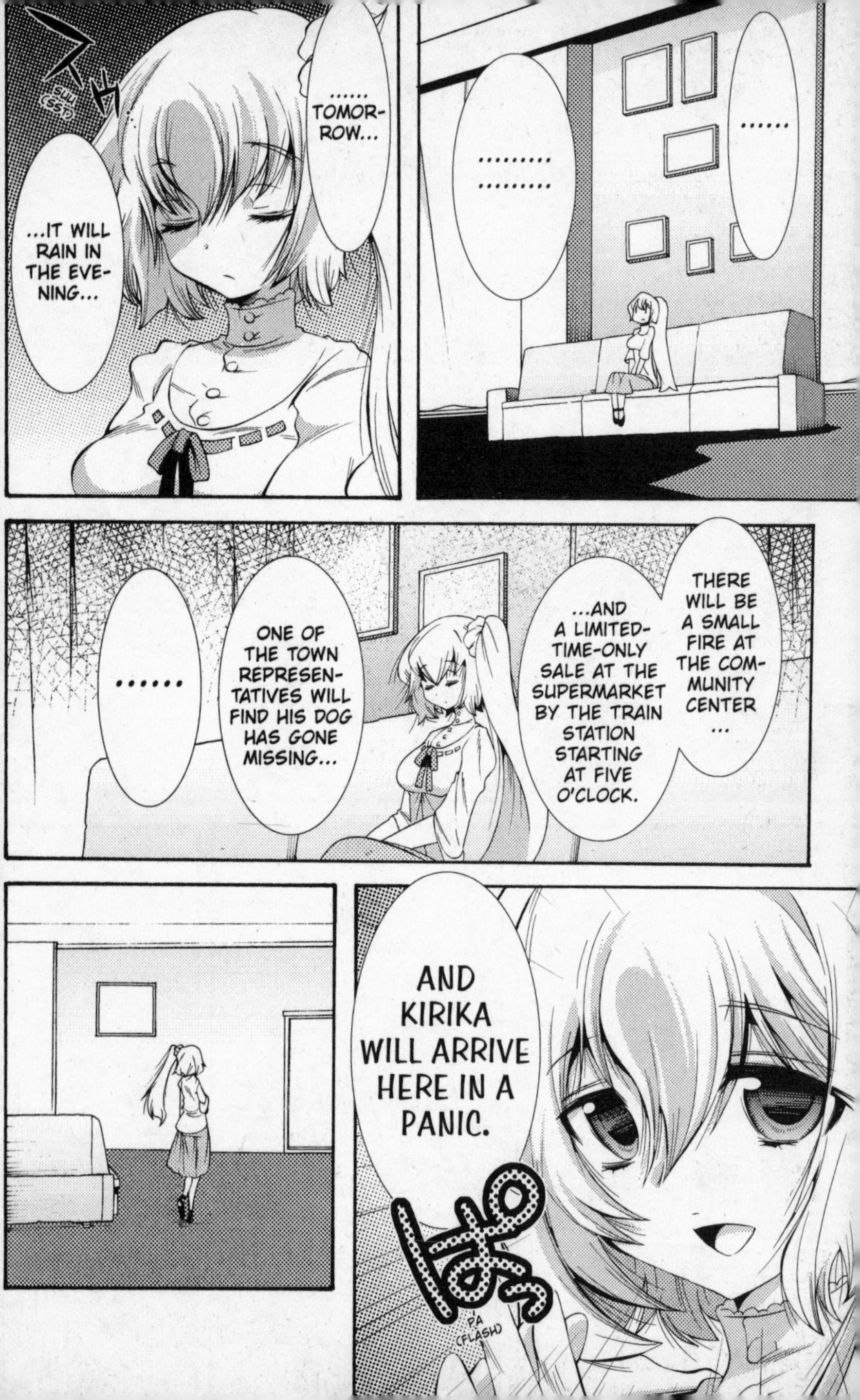
......
....
....
......
TOMOR-
ROW...
SUU (SST)
...IT WILL RAIN IN THE EVE-NING...
THERE WILL BE A SMALL FIRE AT THE COM-MUNITY CENTER ...
...AND A LIMITED-TIME-ONLY SALE AT THE SUPERMARKET BY THE TRAIN STATION STARTING AT FIVE O'CLOCK.
ONE OF THE TOWN REPRESEN-TATIVES WILL FIND HIS DOG HAS GONE MISSING...
......
AND KIRIKA WILL ARRIVE HERE IN A PANIC.
PA (FLASH)

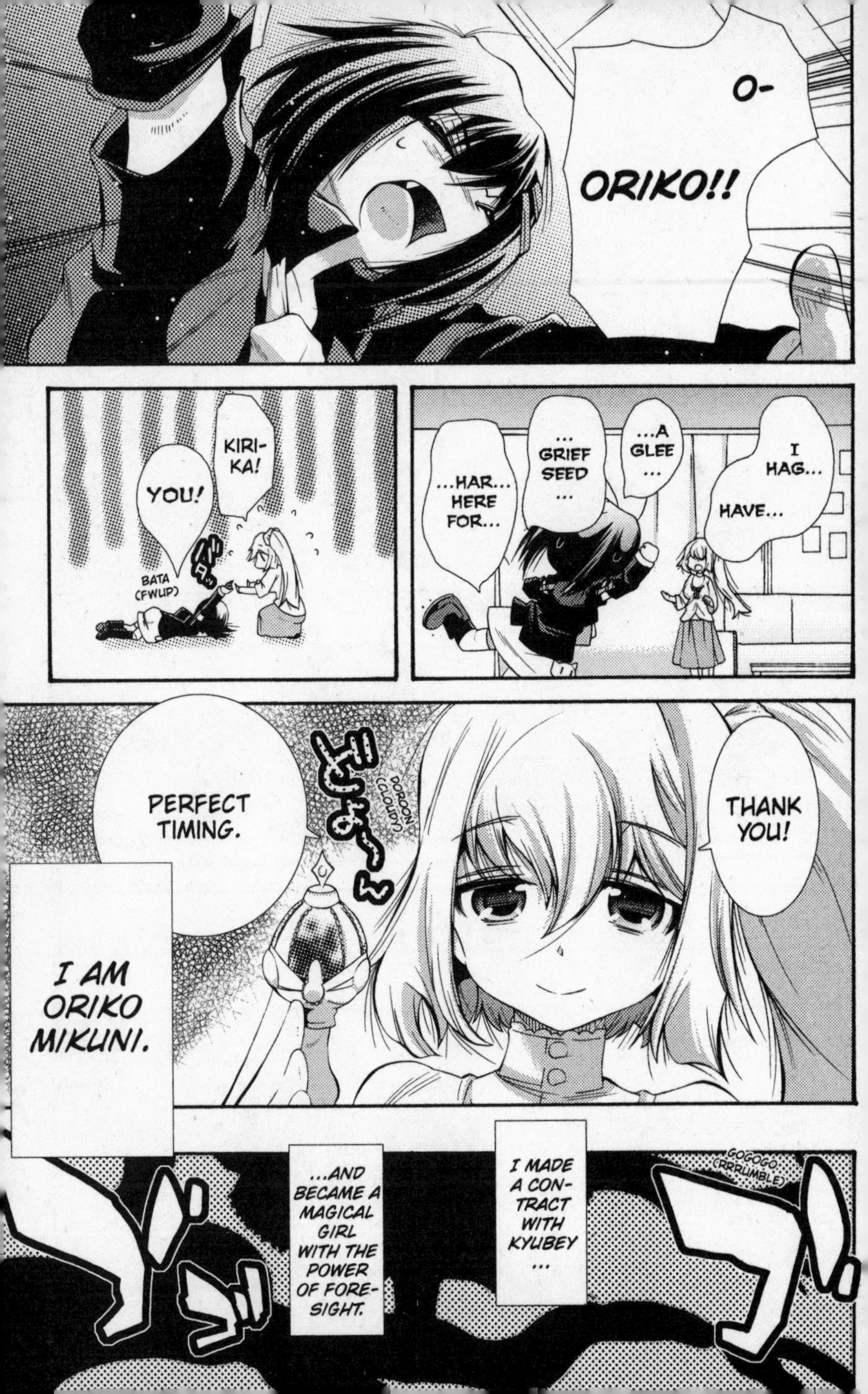
O-
ORIKO!!
I HAG... HAVE...
...A GLEE ...
... GRIEF SEED ...
...HAR... HERE FOR...
KIRI-KA!
YOU!
BATA (FWUP)
THANK YOU!
DOROON (CLOUDY)
PERFECT TIMING.
I AM ORIKO MIKUNI.
GOGOGO (RRRUMBLE)
I MADE A CONTRACT WITH KYUBEY ...
...AND BECAME A MAGICAL GIRL WITH THE POWER OF FORESIGHT.

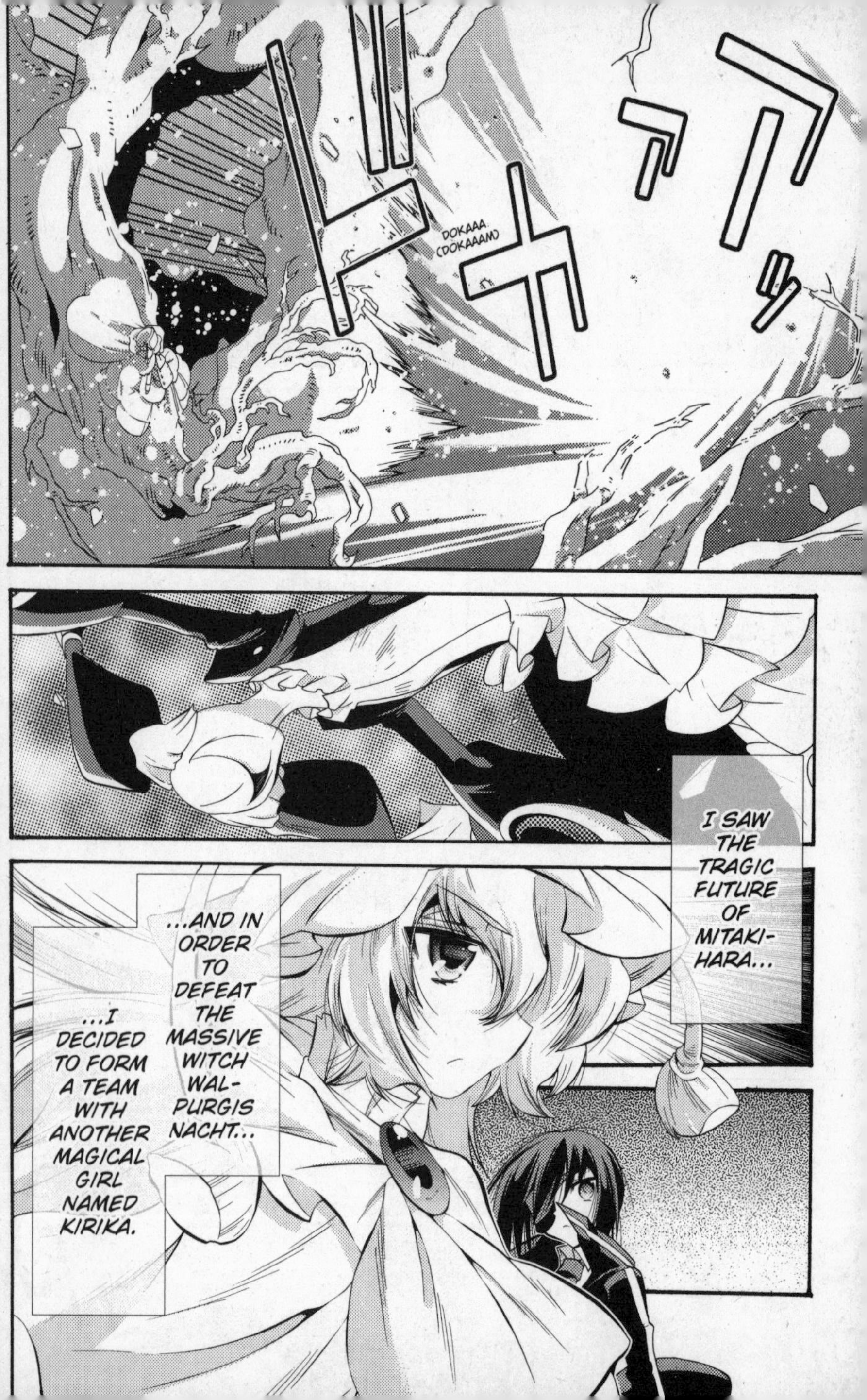
DOKAAA (DOKAAAM)
I SAW THE TRAGIC FUTURE OF MITAKI-HARA...
...AND IN ORDER TO DEFEAT THE MASSIVE WITCH WAL-PURGIS NACHT...
...I DECIDED TO FORM A TEAM WITH ANOTHER MAGICAL GIRL NAMED KIRIKA.

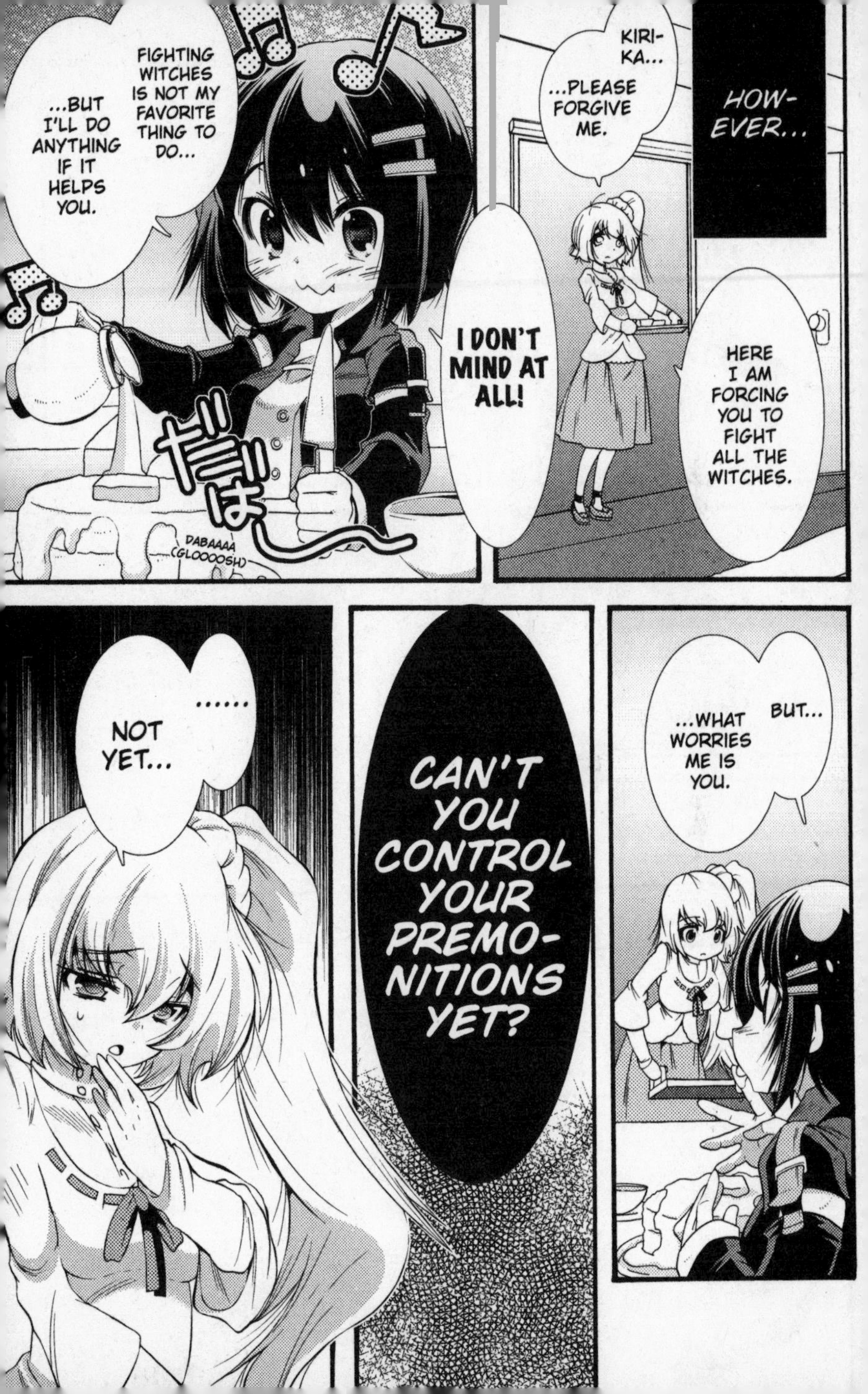
HOW-EVER...
KIRI-KA... ...PLEASE FORGIVE ME.
HERE I AM FORCING YOU TO FIGHT ALL THE WITCHES.
I DON'T MIND AT ALL!
FIGHTING WITCHES IS NOT MY FAVORITE THING TO DO...
...BUT I'LL DO ANYTHING IF IT HELPS YOU.
だばぁ
DABAAAA (GLOOOOSH)
BUT...
...WHAT WORRIES ME IS YOU.
CAN'T YOU CONTROL YOUR PREMO-NITIONS YET?
......
NOT YET...

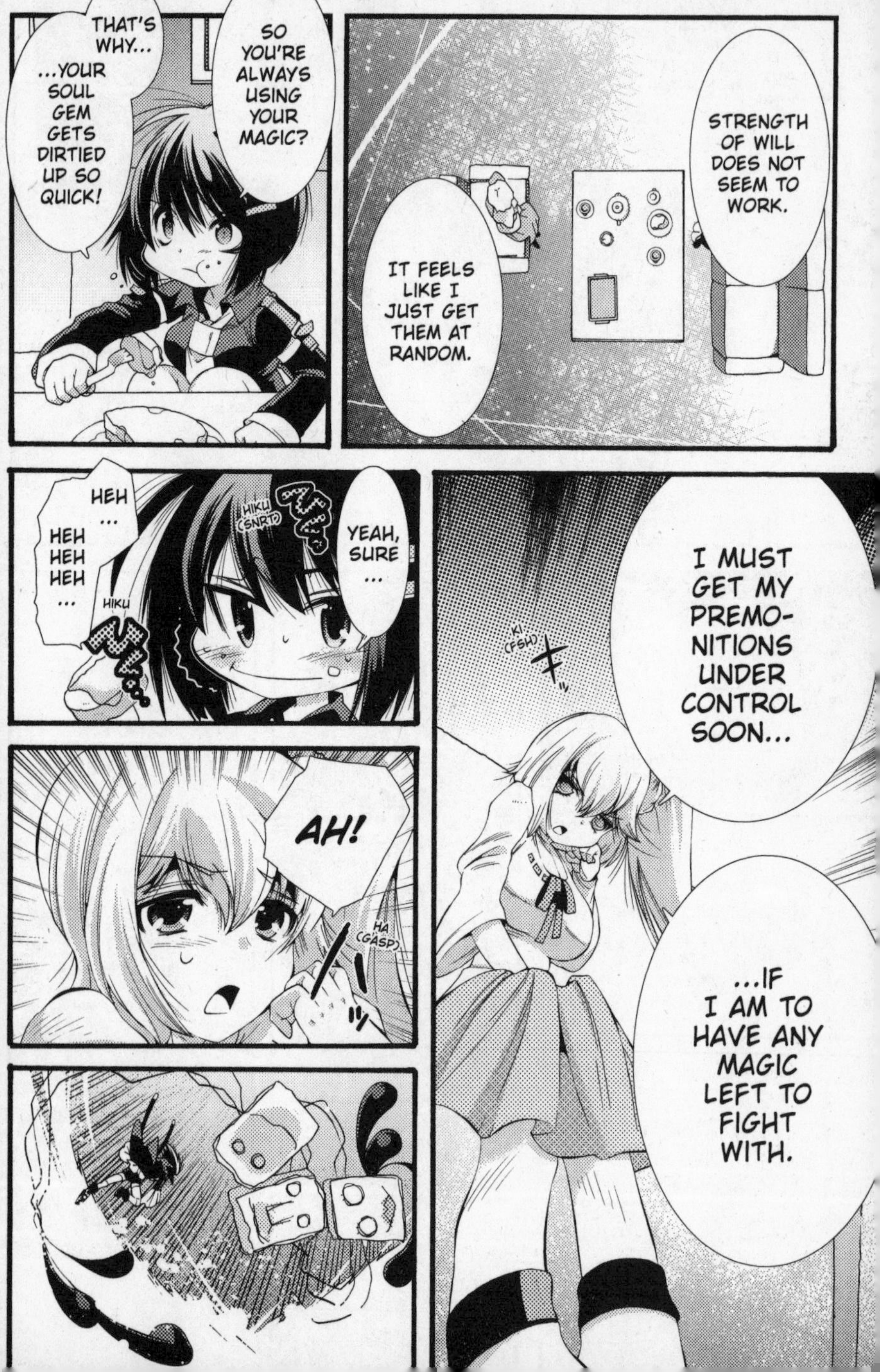

STRENGTH OF WILL DOES NOT SEEM TO WORK.
IT FEELS LIKE I JUST GET THEM AT RANDOM.
SO YOU'RE ALWAYS USING YOUR MAGIC?
THAT'S WHY... ...YOUR SOUL GEM GETS DIRTIED UP SO QUICK!
I MUST GET MY PREMO-NITIONS UNDER CONTROL SOON...
KI (FSH)
...IF I AM TO HAVE ANY MAGIC LEFT TO FIGHT WITH.
YEAH, SURE ...
HIKU (SNRT)
HEH ... HEH HEH HEH ...
HIKU
AH!
HA (GASP)

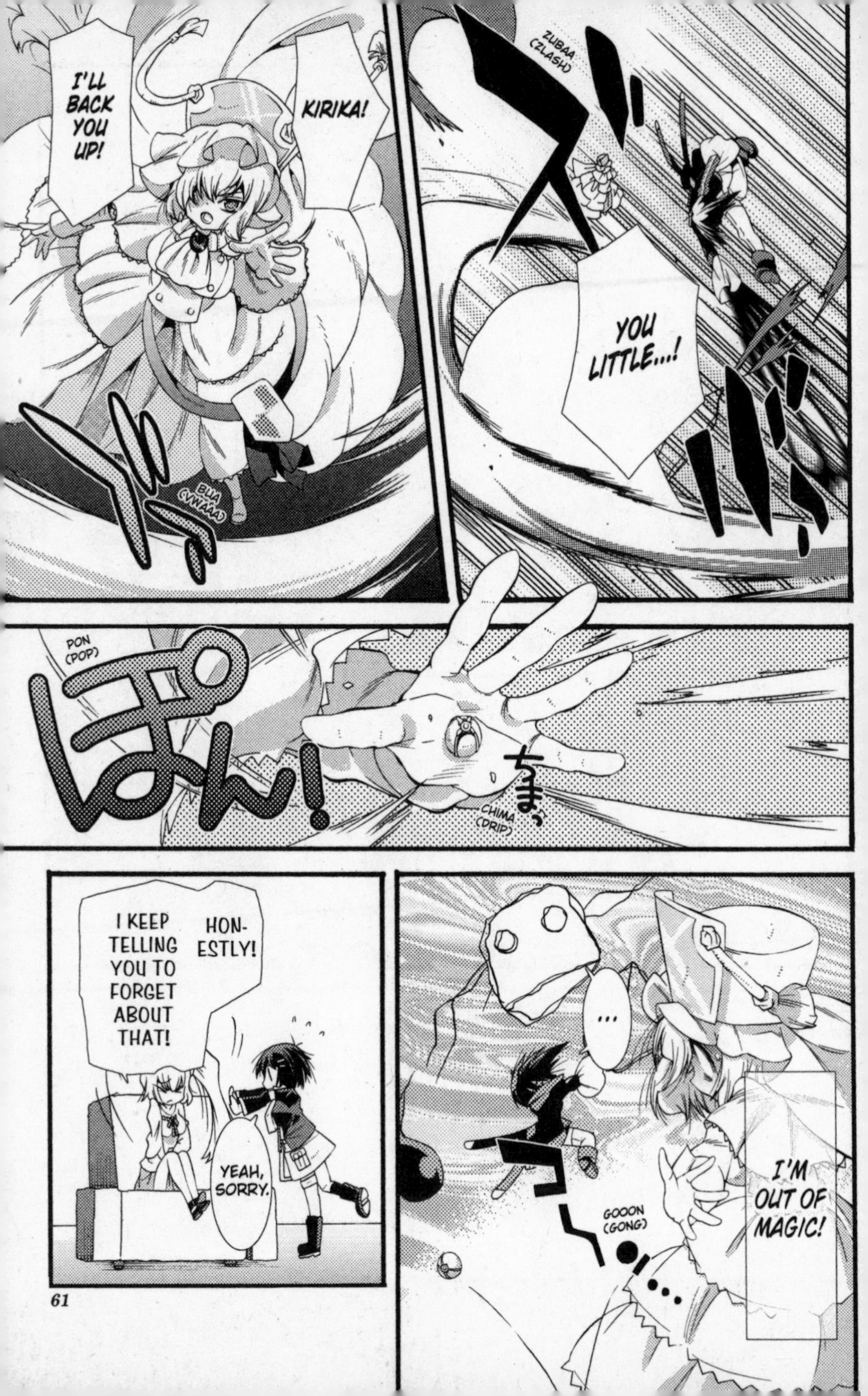
ZUBAA (ZLASH)
YOU LITTLE...!
KIRIKA!
I'LL BACK YOU UP!
BUA (VWAAA)
PON (POP)
CHIMA (DRIP)
...
I'M OUT OF MAGIC!
GOOON (GONG)
HON-ESTLY!
I KEEP TELLING YOU TO FORGET ABOUT THAT!
YEAH, SORRY.

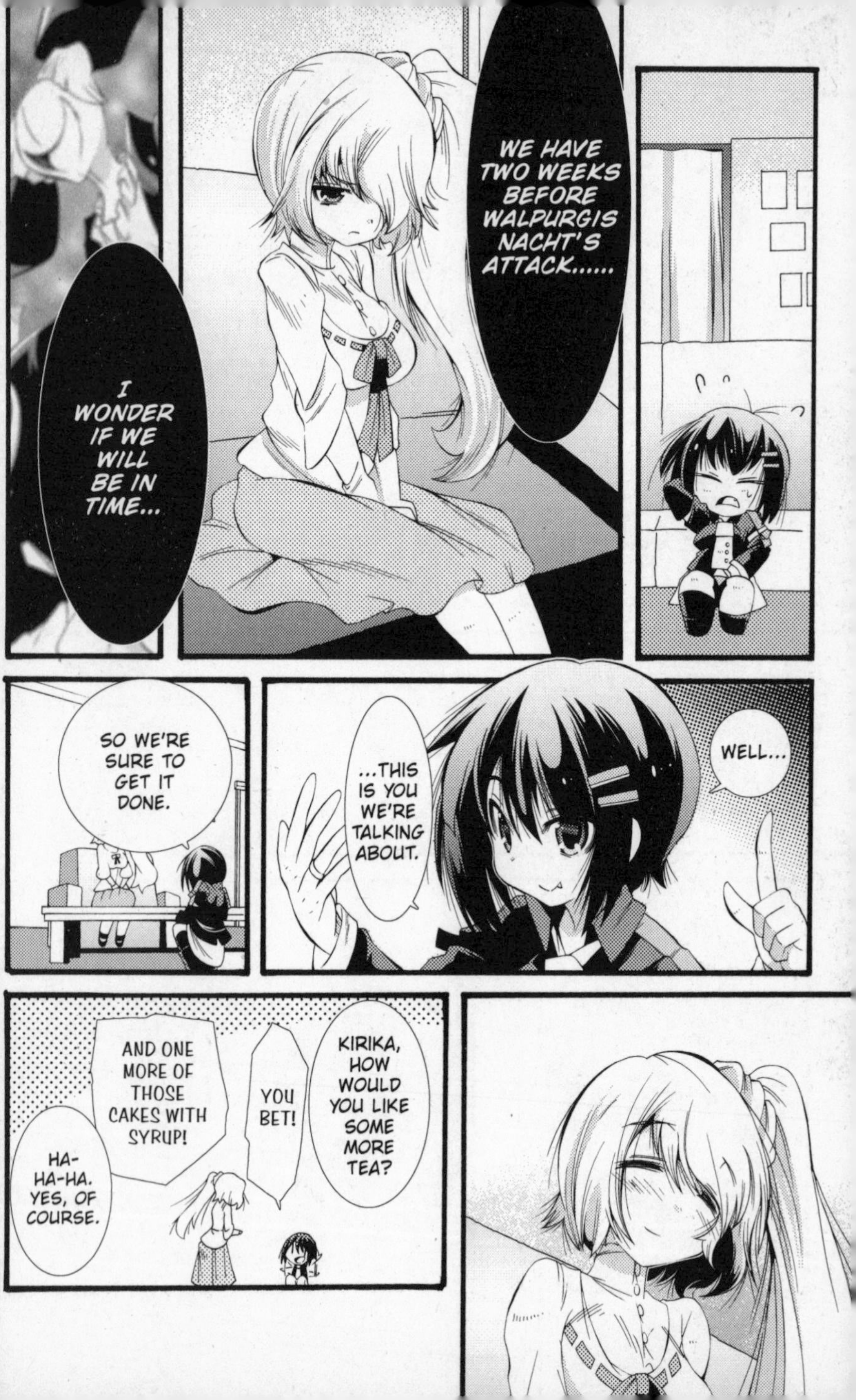

WE HAVE TWO WEEKS BEFORE WALPURGIS NACHT'S ATTACK......
I WONDER IF WE WILL BE IN TIME...
WELL...
...THIS IS YOU WE'RE TALKING ABOUT.
SO WE'RE SURE TO GET IT DONE.
KIRIKA, HOW WOULD YOU LIKE SOME MORE TEA?
YOU BET!
AND ONE MORE OF THOSE CAKES WITH SYRUP!
HA-HA-HA. YES, OF COURSE.

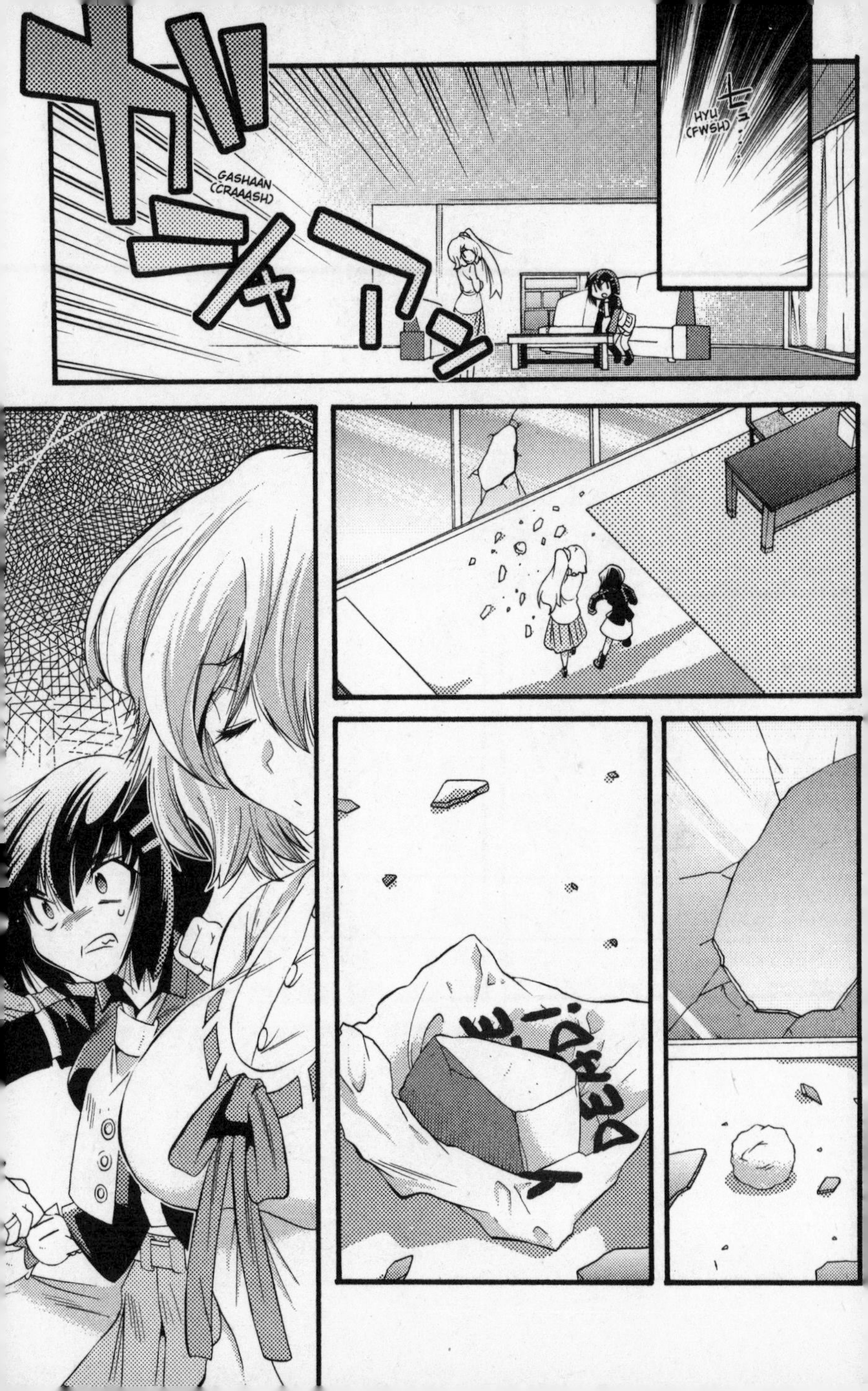
ヒュ…
HYU (FWSH)
ガシャアーン
GASHAAN (CRAAASH)

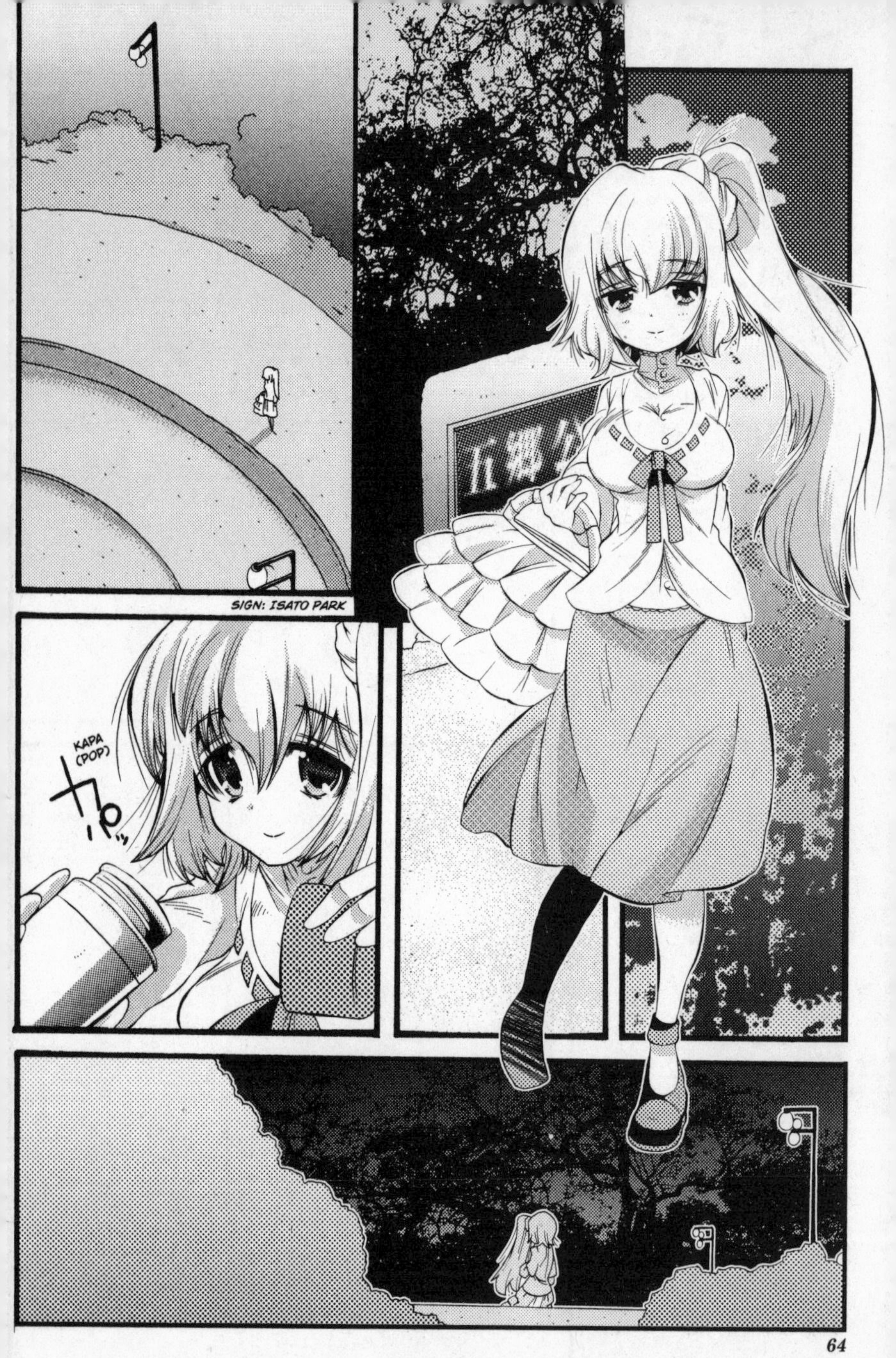
SIGN: ISATO PARK
KAPA
(POP)

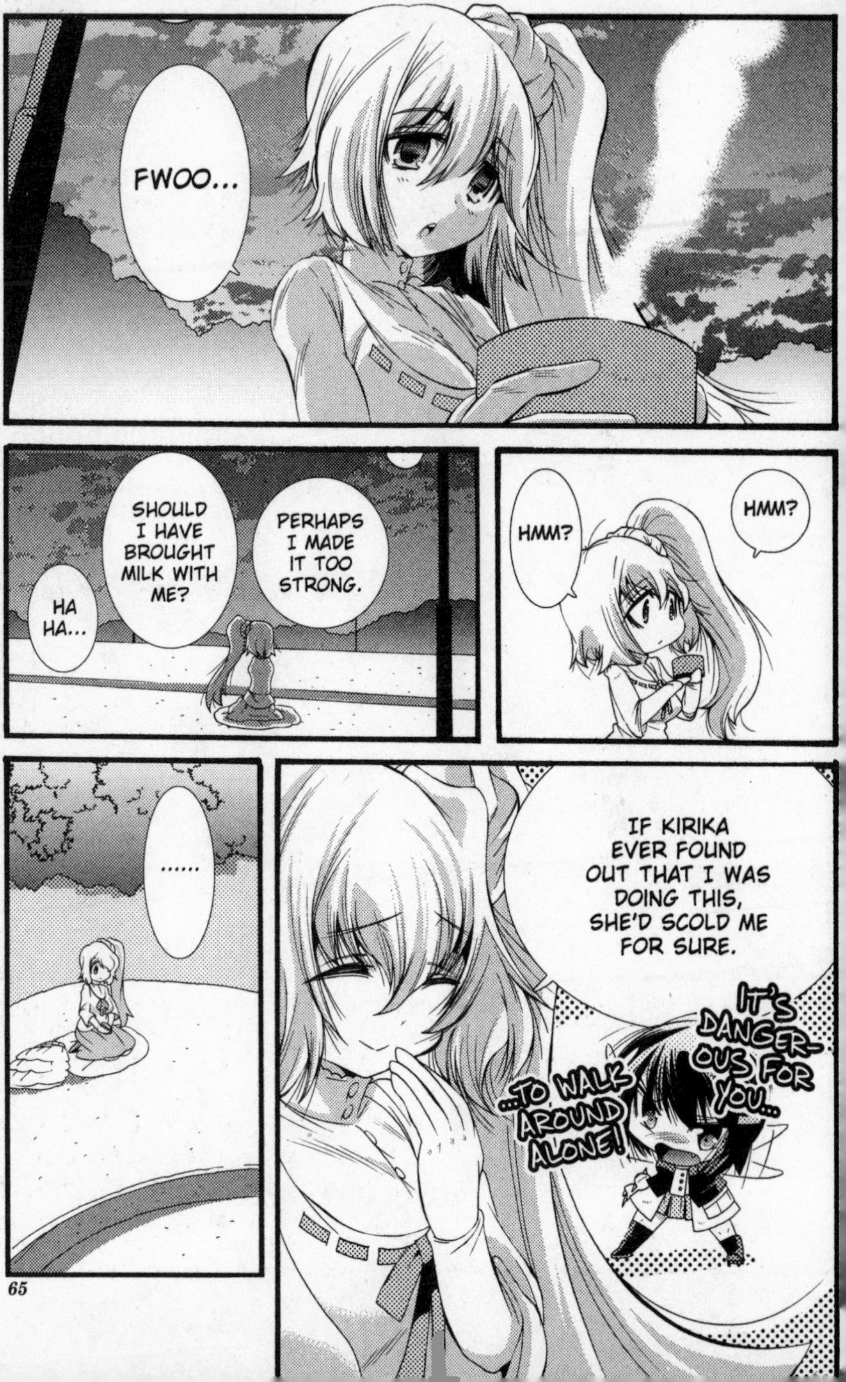
FWOO...
HMM?
HMM?
PERHAPS I MADE IT TOO STRONG.
SHOULD I HAVE BROUGHT MILK WITH ME?
HA HA...
IF KIRIKA EVER FOUND OUT THAT I WAS DOING THIS, SHE'D SCOLD ME FOR SURE.
IT'S DANGER-OUS FOR YOU...
...TO WALK AROUND ALONE!
......

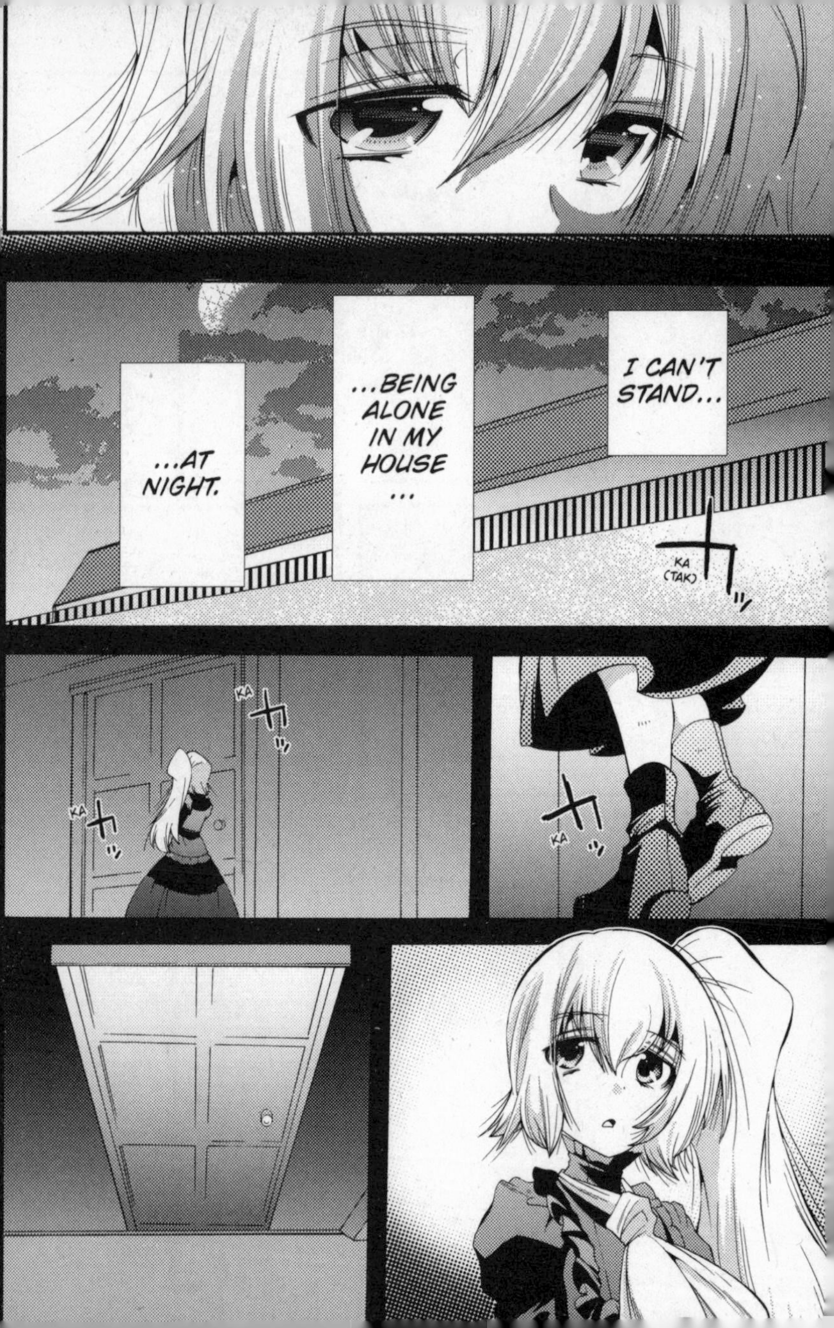
I CAN'T STAND...
...BEING ALONE IN MY HOUSE ...
...AT NIGHT.
KA (TAK)
...
KA
KA
KA

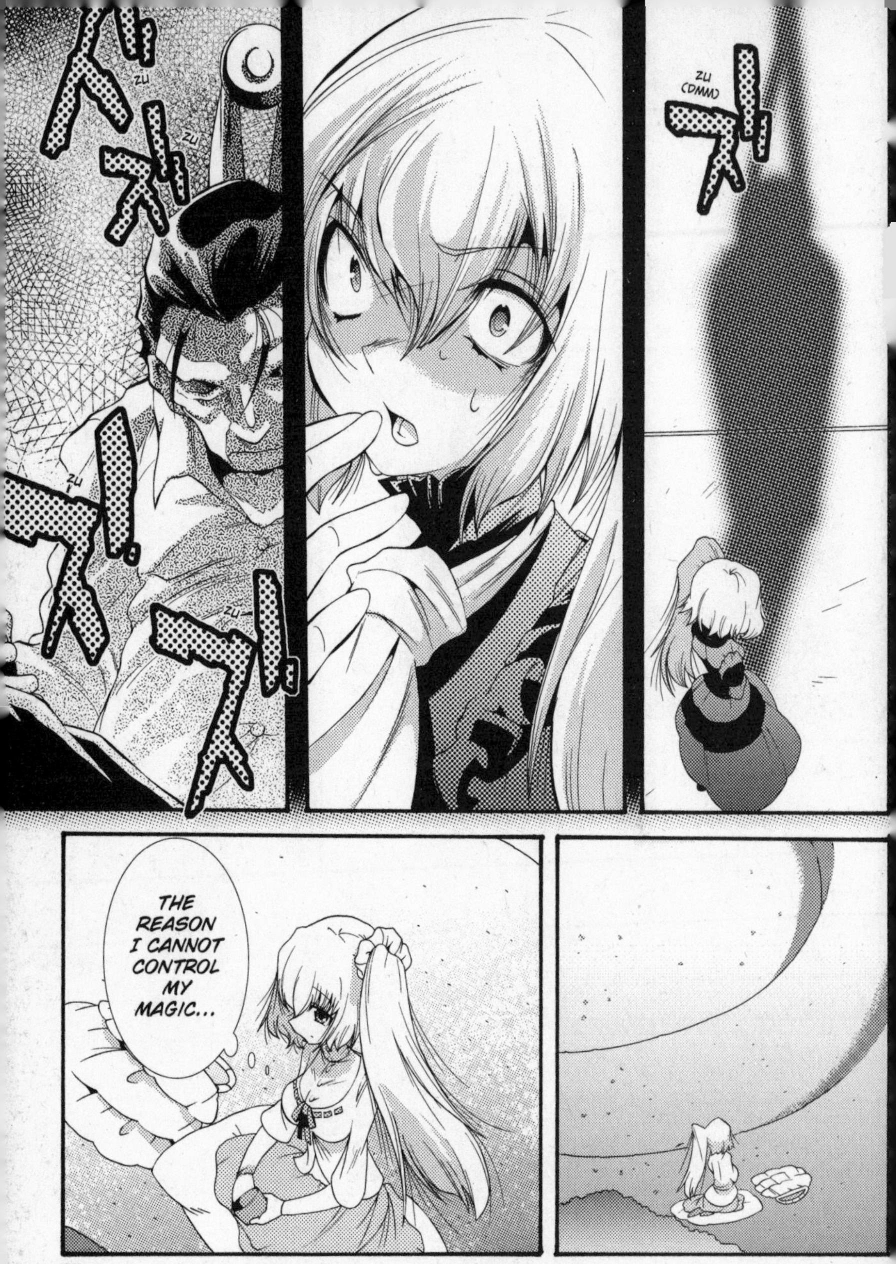
ZU
(DMM)
ZU
ZU
ZU
ZU
THE REASON I CANNOT CONTROL MY MAGIC...

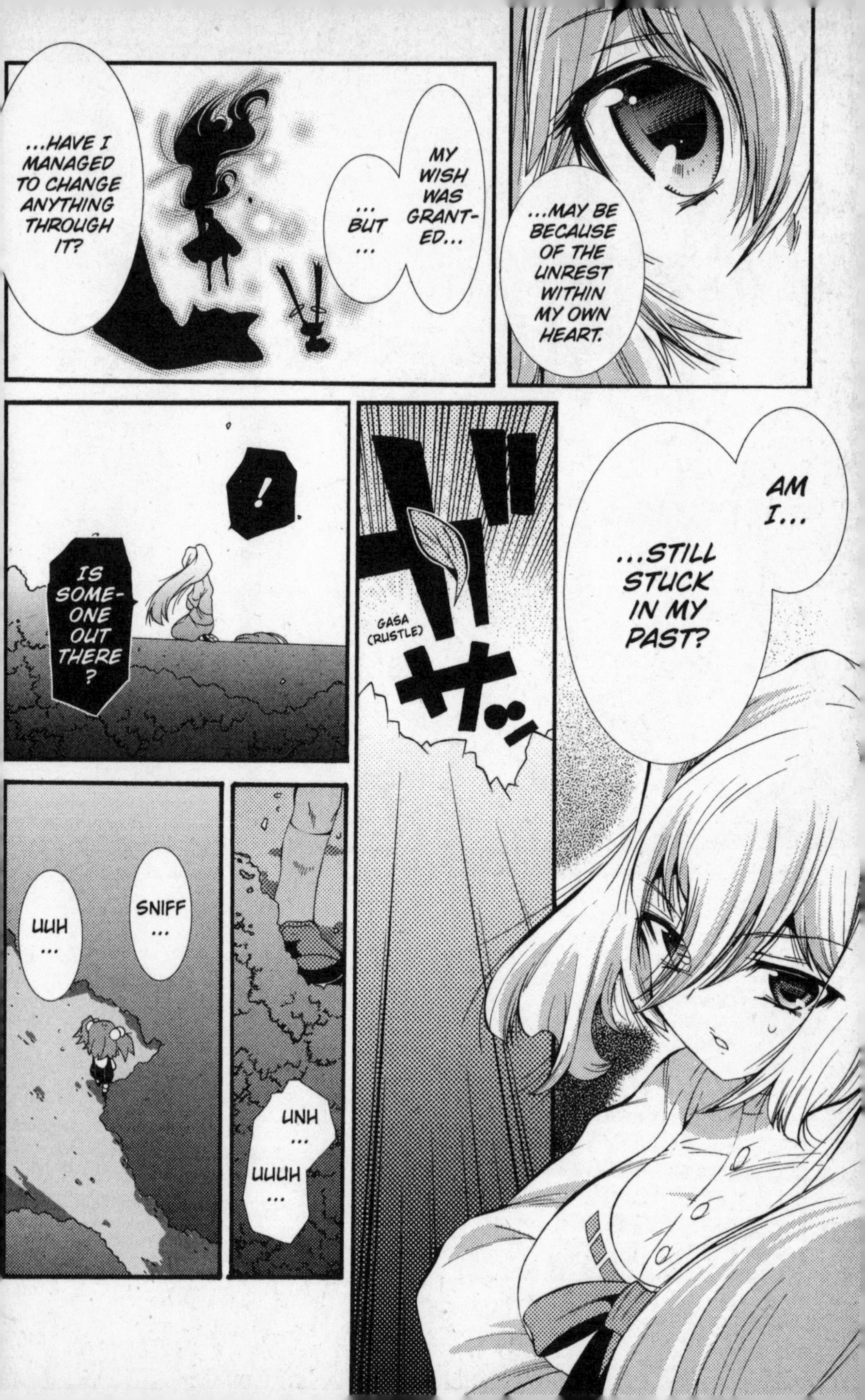
...MAY BE BECAUSE OF THE UNREST WITHIN MY OWN HEART.
MY WISH WAS GRANTED...
...BUT...
...HAVE I MANAGED TO CHANGE ANYTHING THROUGH IT?
AM I...
...STILL STUCK IN MY PAST?
GASA (RUSTLE)
!
IS SOMEONE OUT THERE?
UNH...
UUUH...
SNIFF...
UUH...

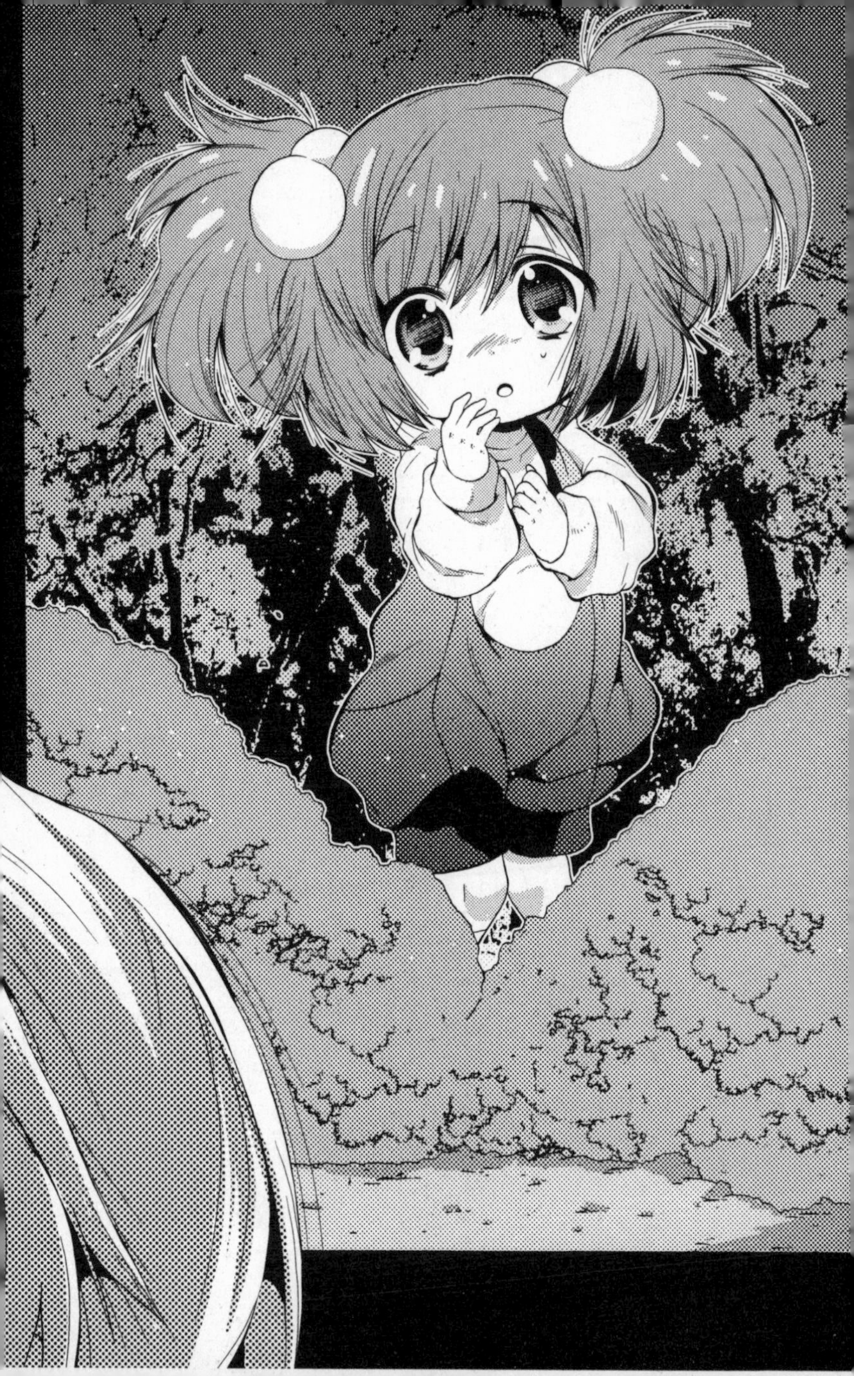

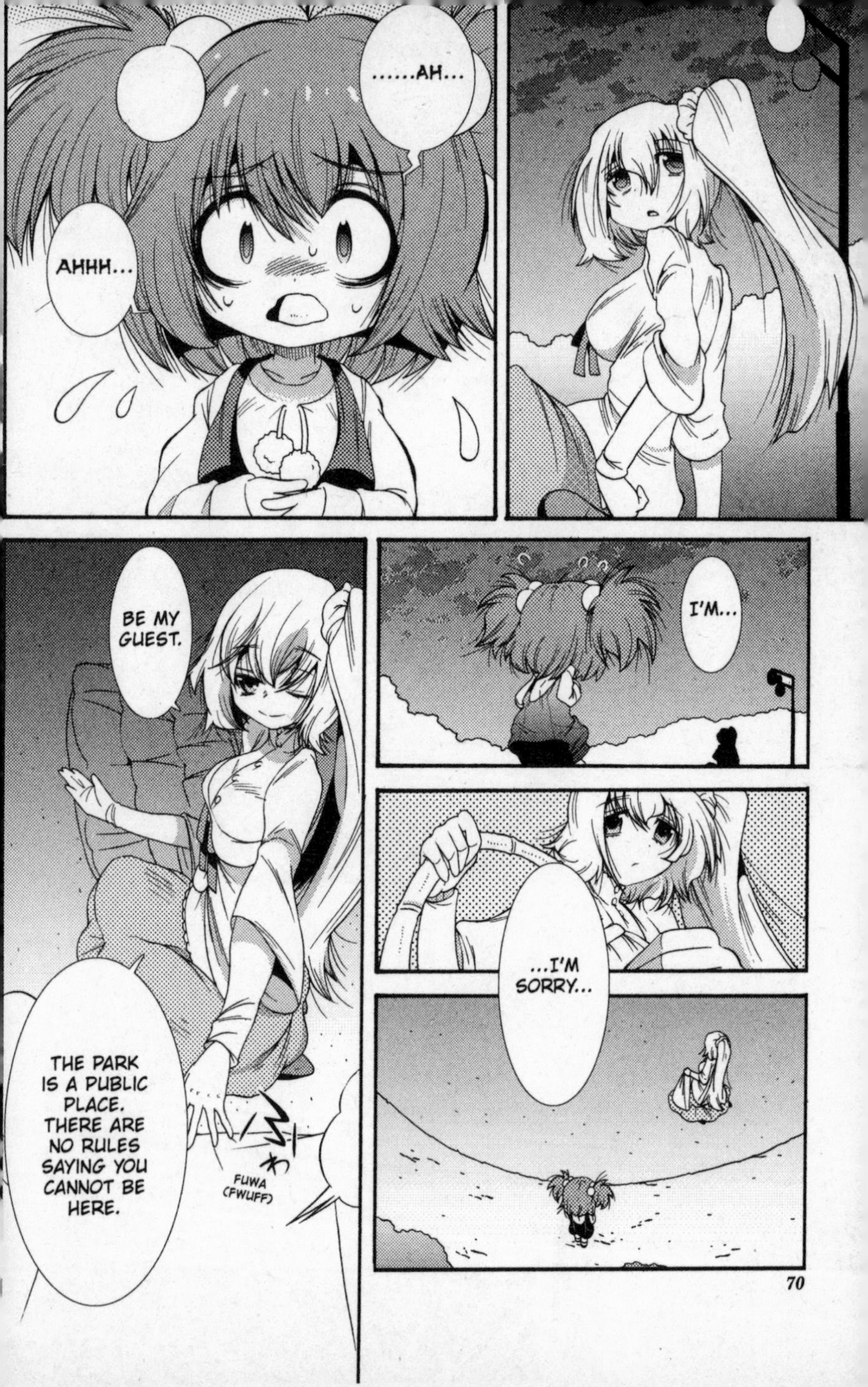
......AH...
AHHH...
I'M...
...I'M SORRY...
BE MY GUEST.
THE PARK IS A PUBLIC PLACE. THERE ARE NO RULES SAYING YOU CANNOT BE HERE.
ふわ
FUWA (FWUFF)

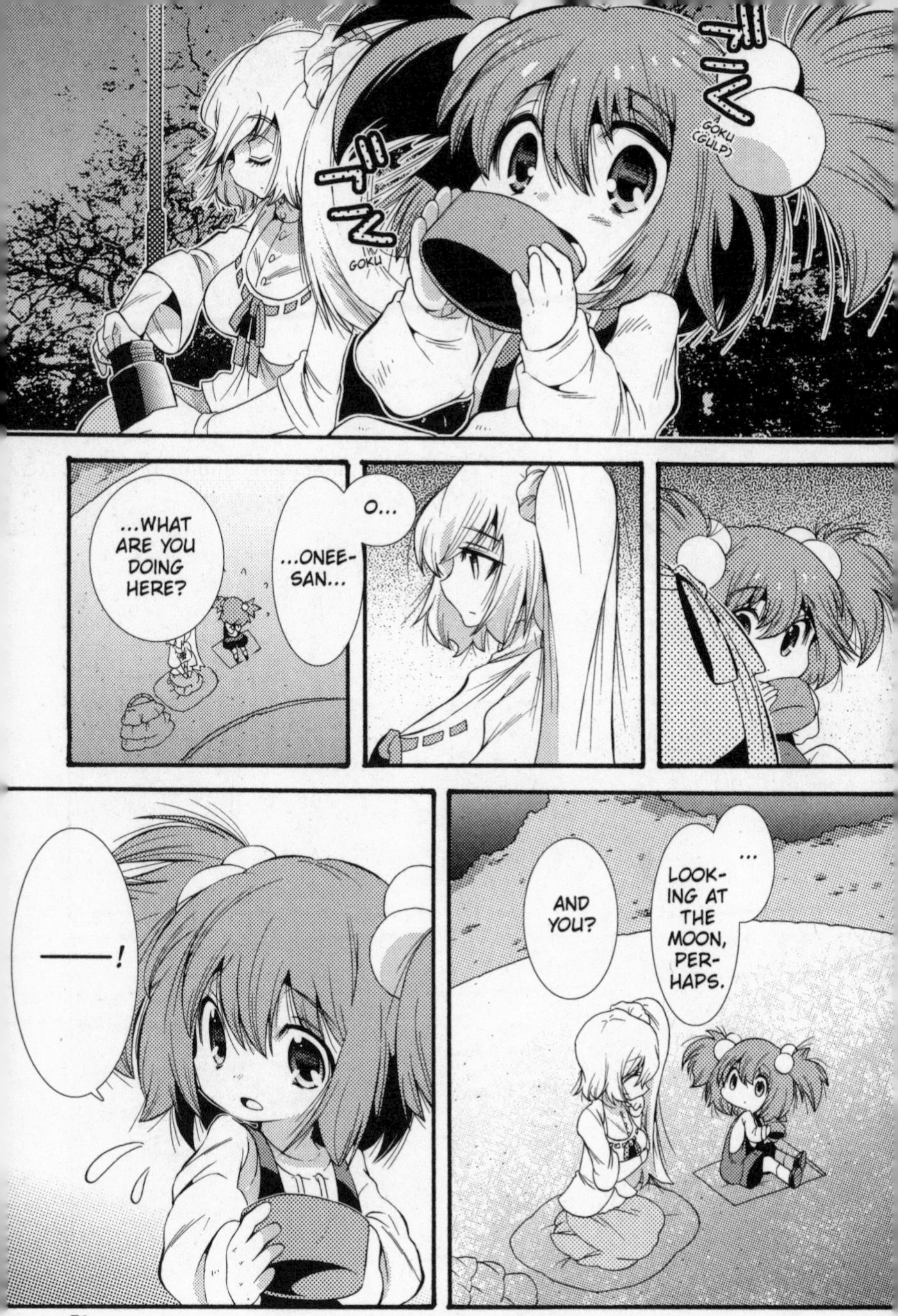
GOKU (GULP)
GOKU
O...
...ONEE-SAN...
...WHAT ARE YOU DOING HERE?
...LOOKING AT THE MOON, PERHAPS.
AND YOU?
——!

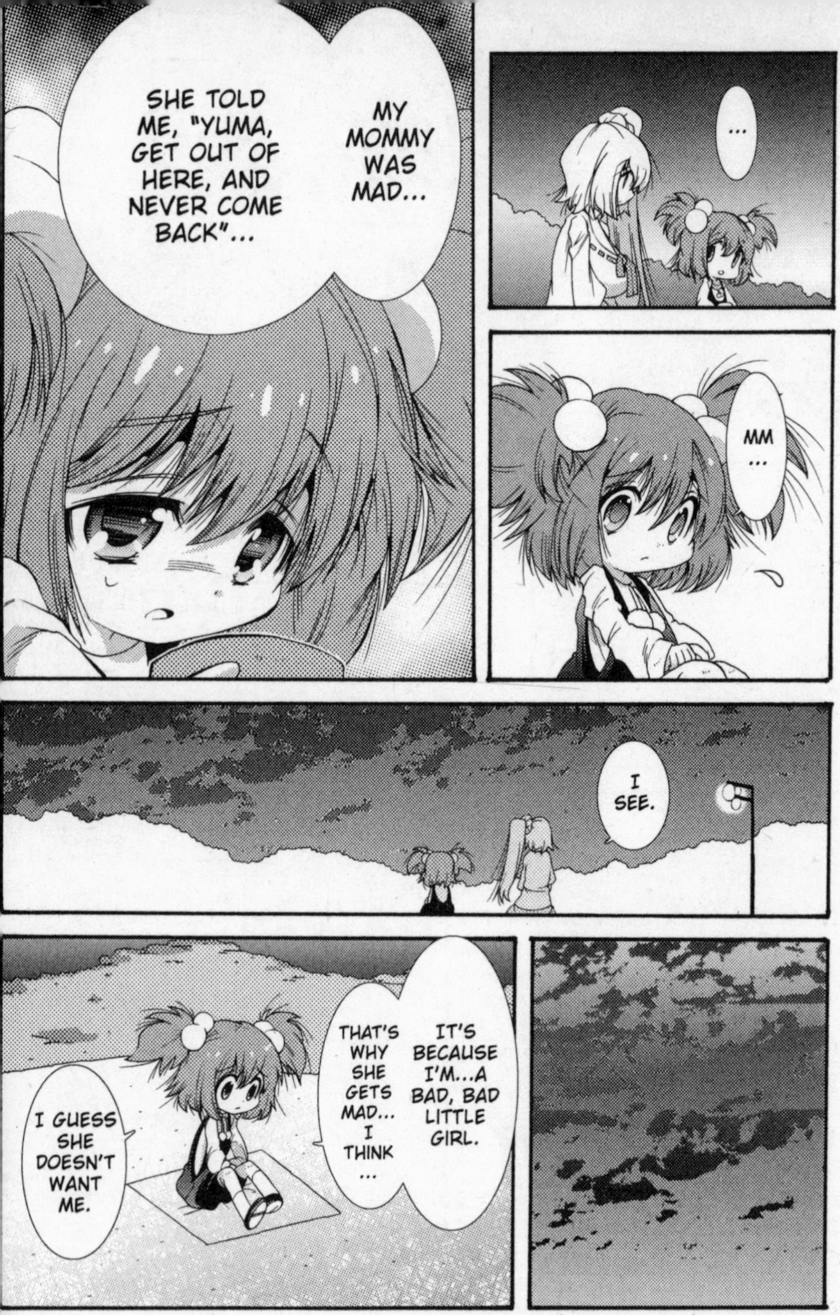
...
MM ...
MY MOMMY WAS MAD...
SHE TOLD ME, "YUMA, GET OUT OF HERE, AND NEVER COME BACK"...
I SEE.
IT'S BECAUSE I'M...A BAD, BAD LITTLE GIRL.
THAT'S WHY SHE GETS MAD... I THINK ...
I GUESS SHE DOESN'T WANT ME.

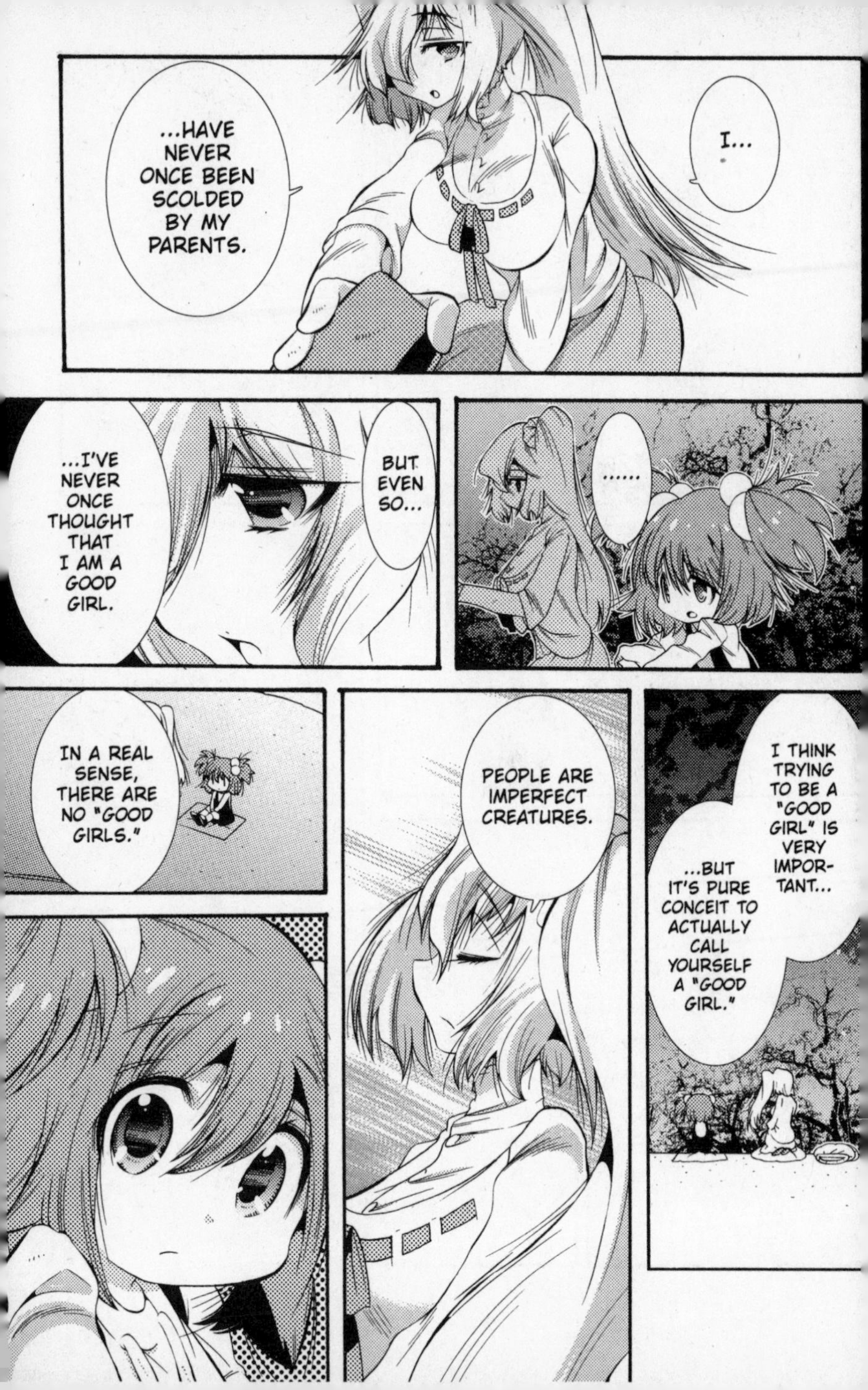
I...
...HAVE NEVER ONCE BEEN SCOLDED BY MY PARENTS.
......
BUT EVEN SO...
...I'VE NEVER ONCE THOUGHT THAT I AM A GOOD GIRL.
I THINK TRYING TO BE A "GOOD GIRL" IS VERY IMPOR-TANT...
...BUT IT'S PURE CONCEIT TO ACTUALLY CALL YOURSELF A "GOOD GIRL."
PEOPLE ARE IMPERFECT CREATURES.
IN A REAL SENSE, THERE ARE NO "GOOD GIRLS."

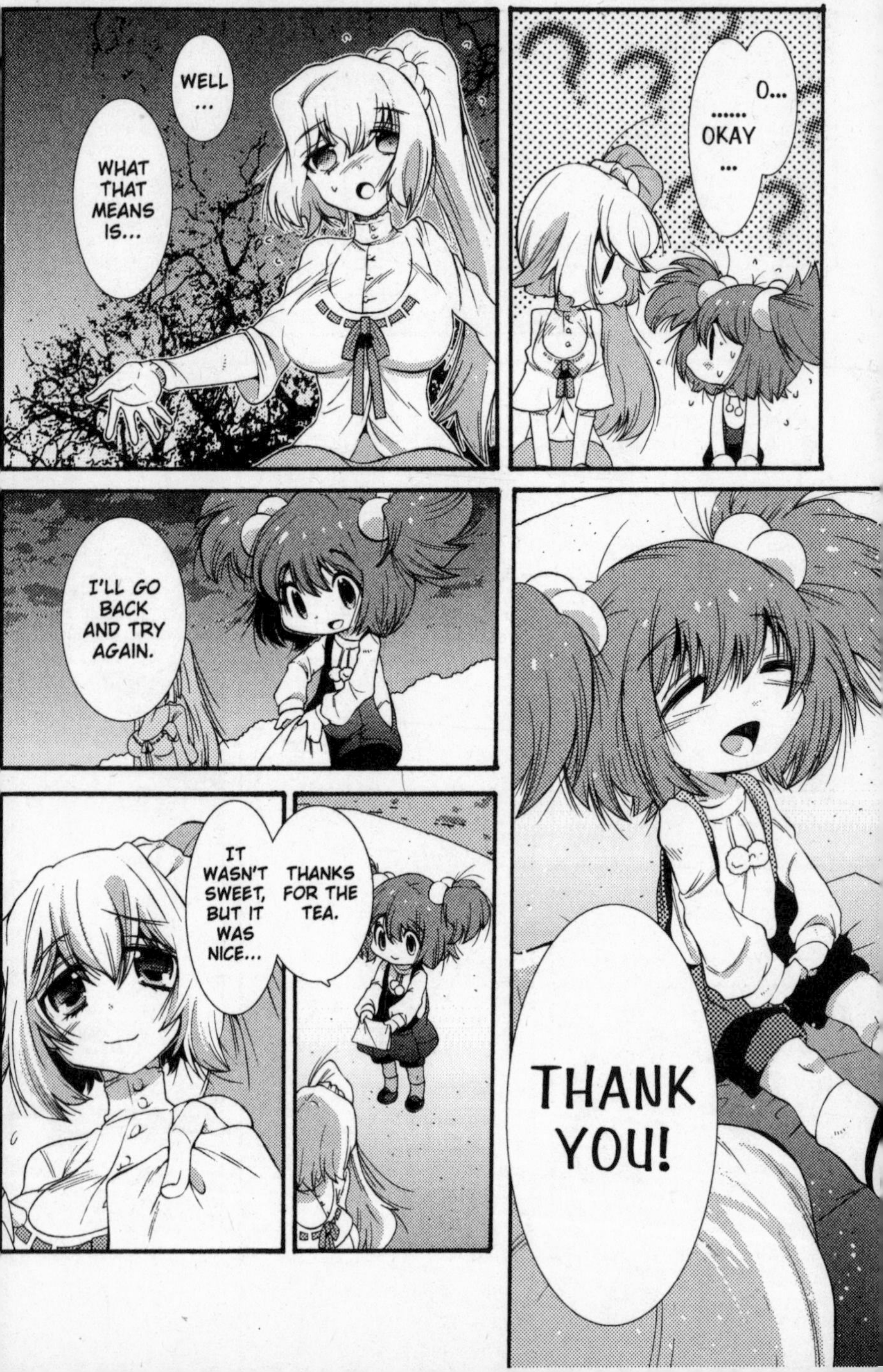
O... ...... OKAY ...
WELL ...
WHAT THAT MEANS IS...
THANK YOU!
I'LL GO BACK AND TRY AGAIN.
THANKS FOR THE TEA.
IT WASN'T SWEET, BUT IT WAS NICE...

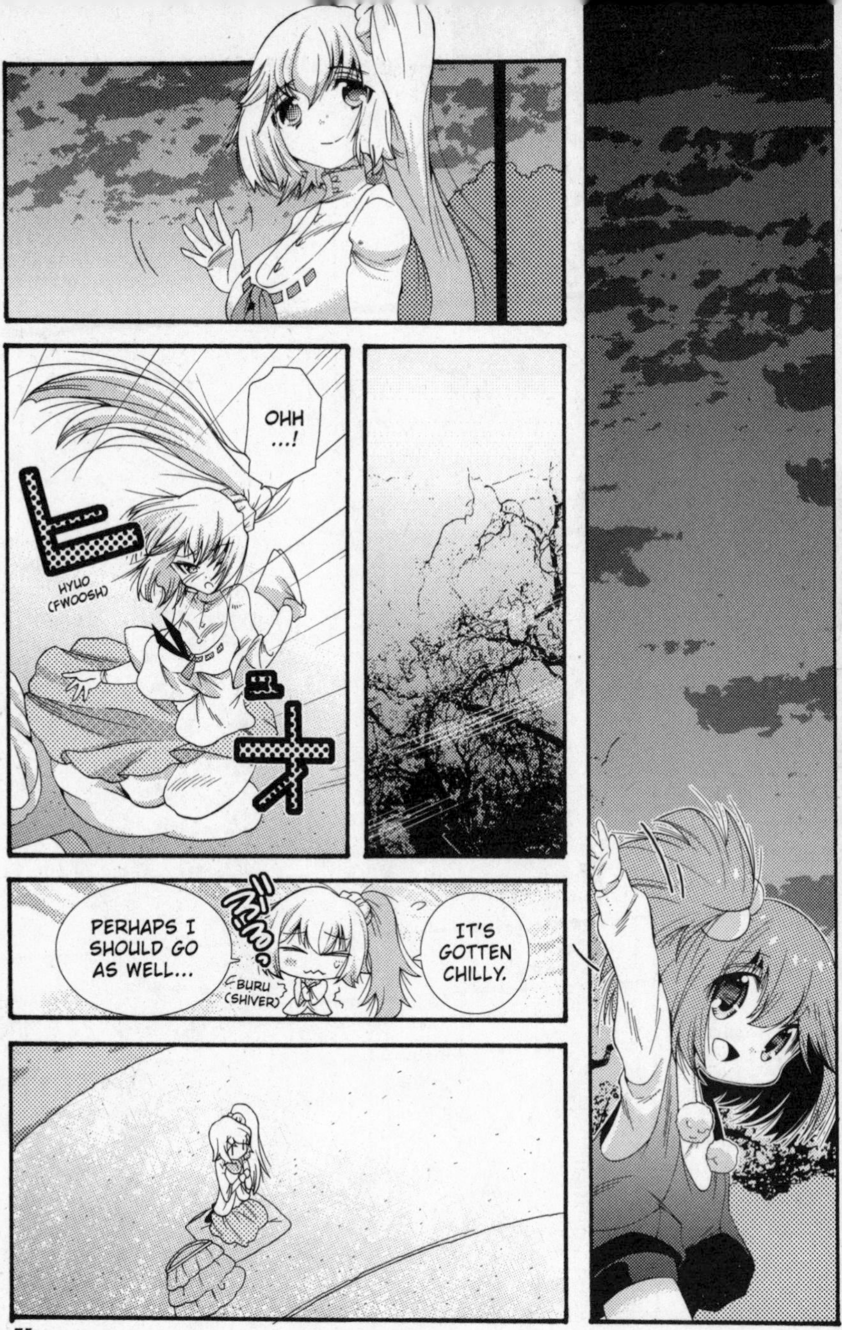
OHH ...!
HYUO (FWOOSH)
IT'S GOTTEN CHILLY.
BURU (SHIVER)
PERHAPS I SHOULD GO AS WELL...

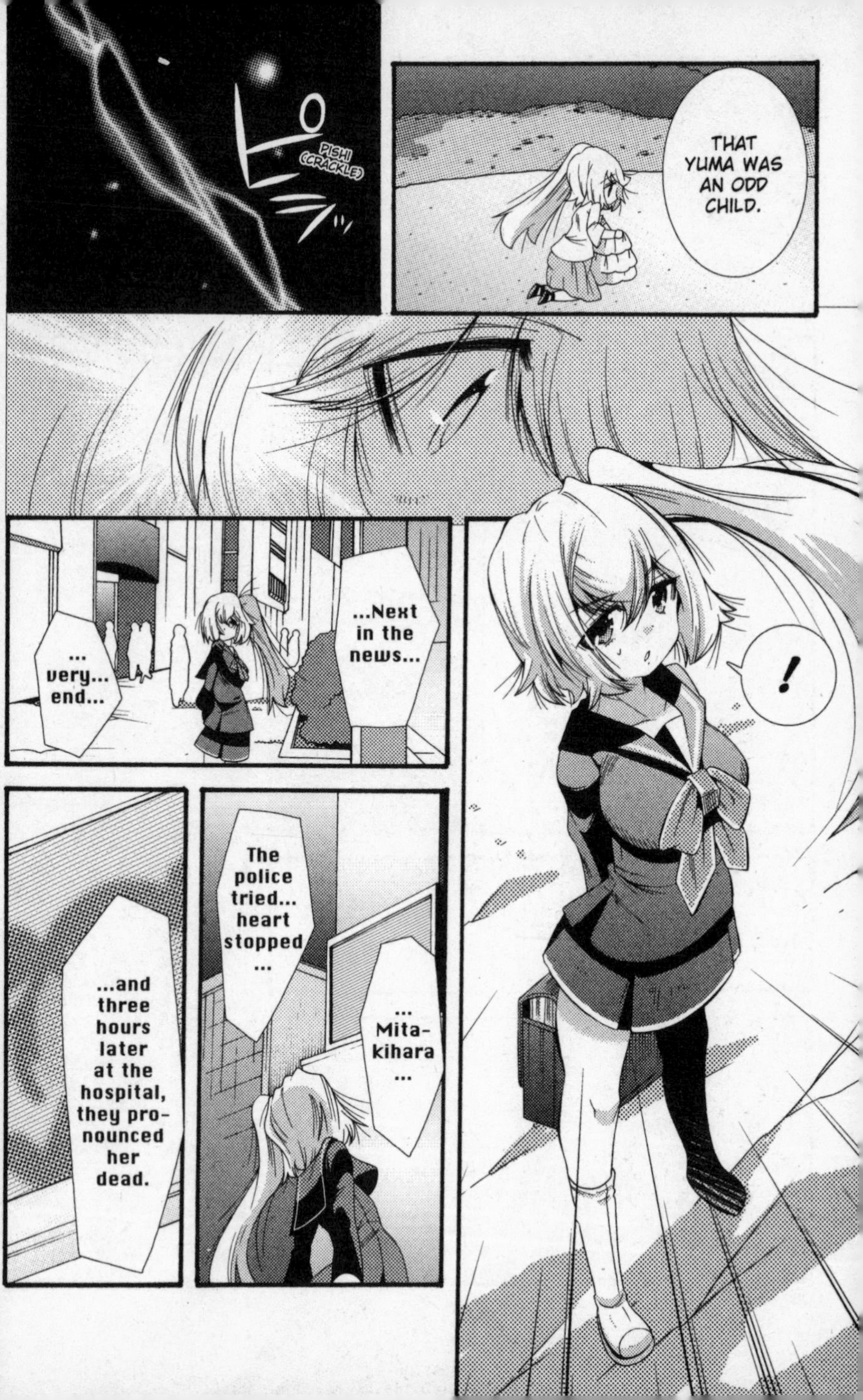
THAT YUMA WAS AN ODD CHILD.
PISHI (CRACKLE)
!
...Next in the news...
... very... end...
The police tried... heart stopped ...
... Mita-kihara ...
...and three hours later at the hospital, they pronounced her dead.

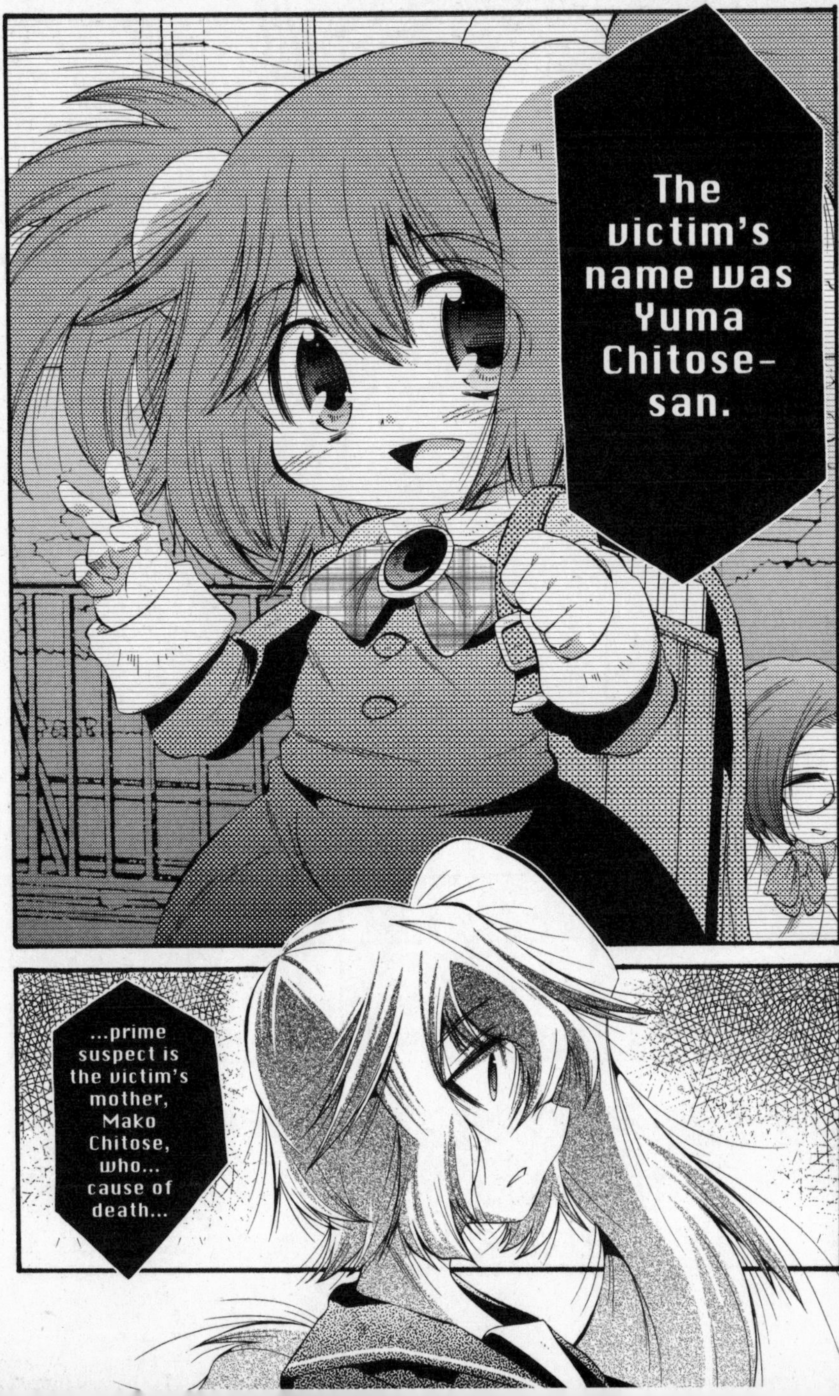
The victim's name was Yuma Chitose-san.
...prime suspect is the victim's mother, Mako Chitose, who... cause of death...

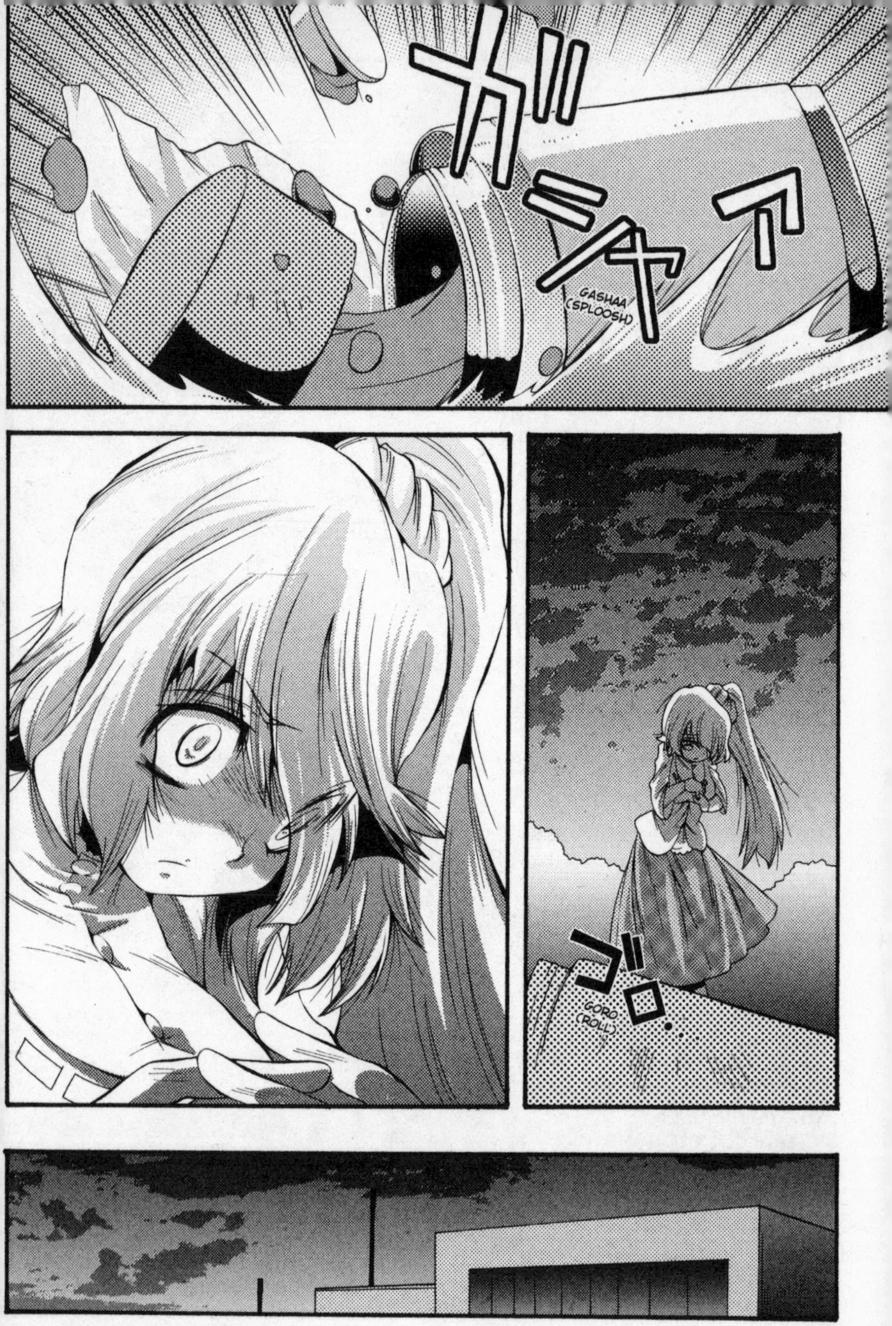
ガシャア
GASHAA (SPLOOSH)
ゴロ
GORO (ROLL)

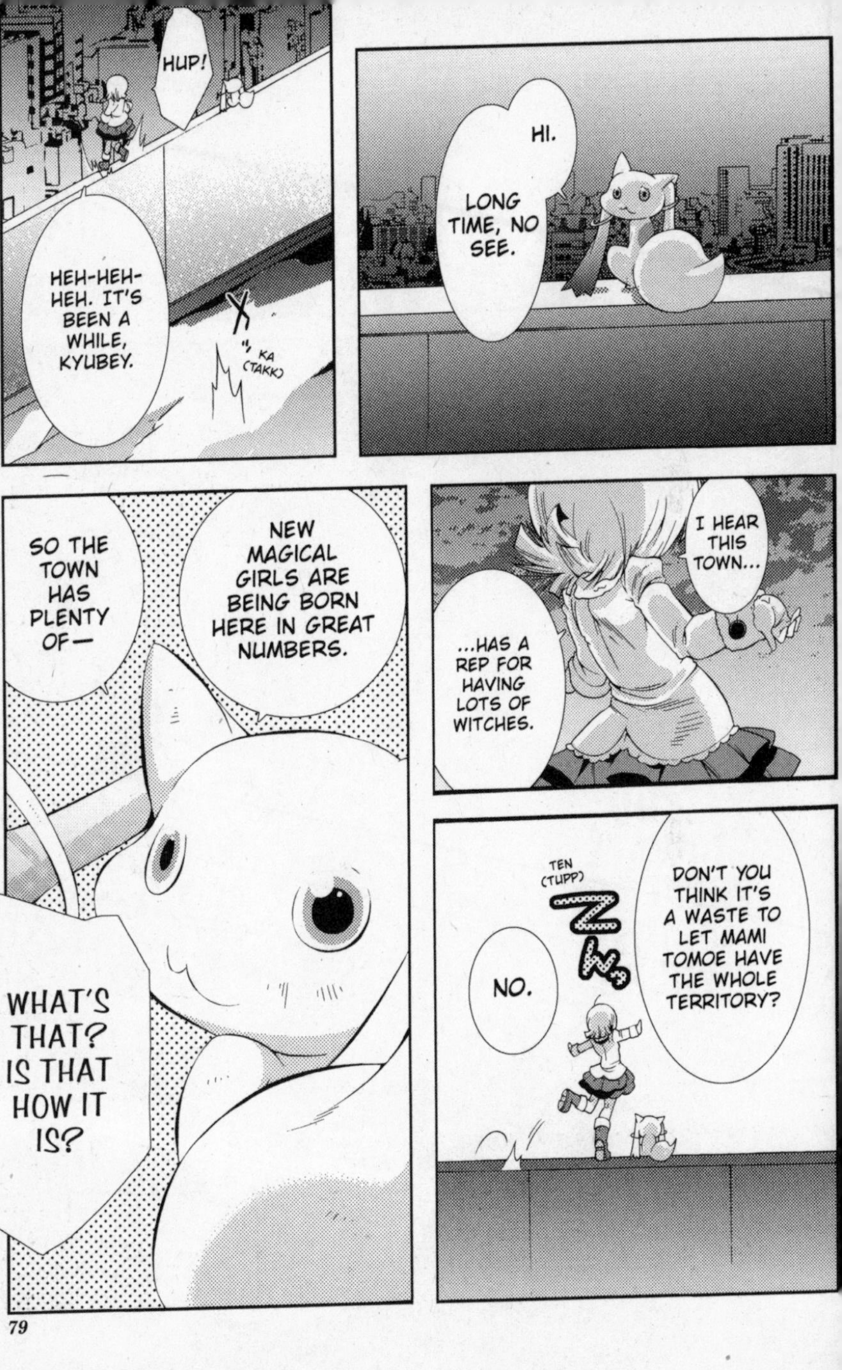
HI.
LONG TIME, NO SEE.
HUP!
HEH-HEH-HEH. IT'S BEEN A WHILE, KYUBEY.
KA (TAKK)
I HEAR THIS TOWN...
...HAS A REP FOR HAVING LOTS OF WITCHES.
DON'T YOU THINK IT'S A WASTE TO LET MAMI TOMOE HAVE THE WHOLE TERRITORY?
TEN (TUPP)
NO.
NEW MAGICAL GIRLS ARE BEING BORN HERE IN GREAT NUMBERS.
SO THE TOWN HAS PLENTY OF—
WHAT'S THAT? IS THAT HOW IT IS?

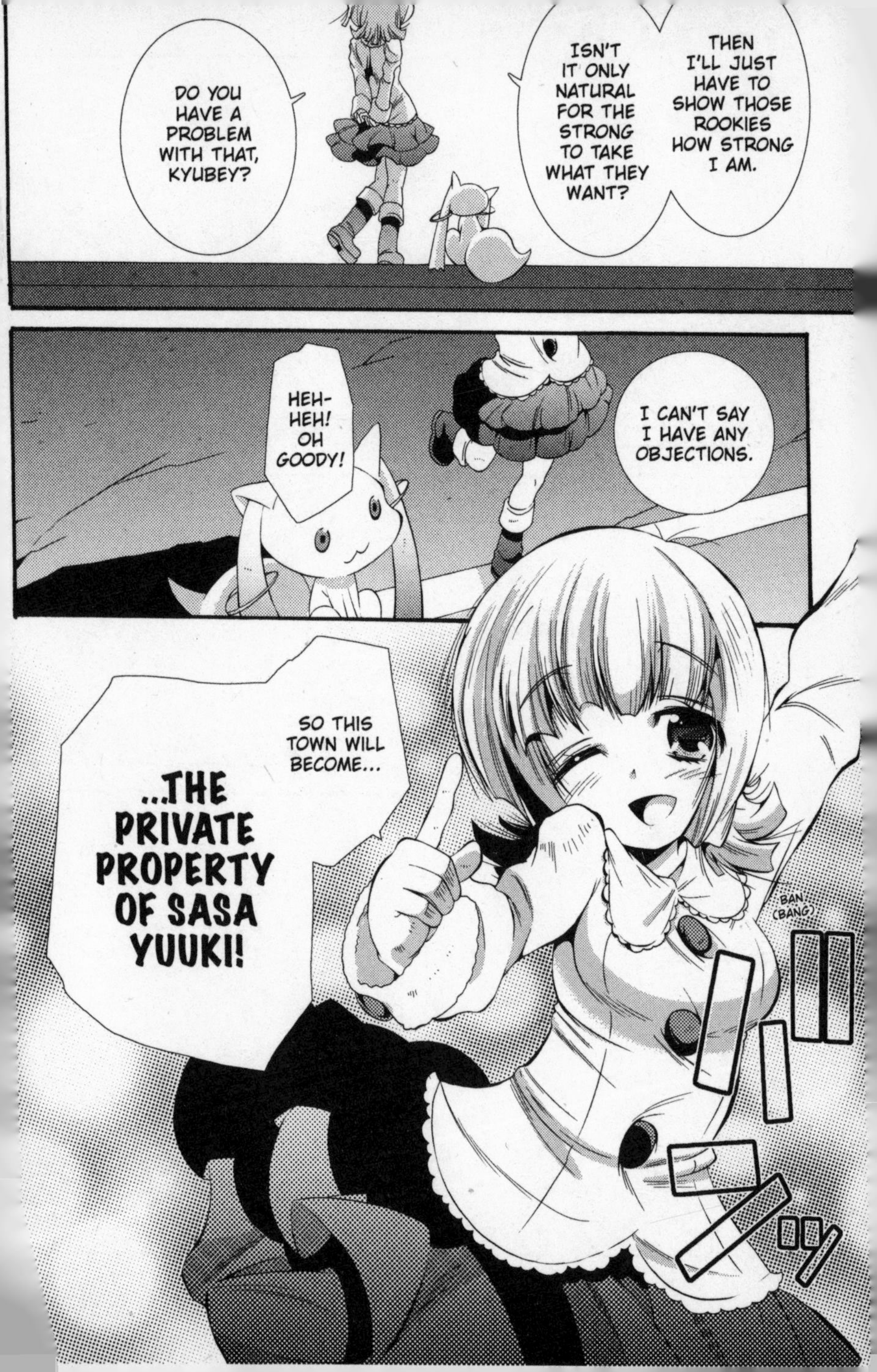
THEN I'LL JUST HAVE TO SHOW THOSE ROOKIES HOW STRONG I AM.
ISN'T IT ONLY NATURAL FOR THE STRONG TO TAKE WHAT THEY WANT?
DO YOU HAVE A PROBLEM WITH THAT, KYUBEY?
I CAN'T SAY I HAVE ANY OBJECTIONS.
HEH-HEH! OH GOODY!
SO THIS TOWN WILL BECOME...
...THE PRIVATE PROPERTY OF SASA YUUKI!
BAN (BANG)

PUELLA MAGI
ORIKO ★ MAGICA
[extra story]

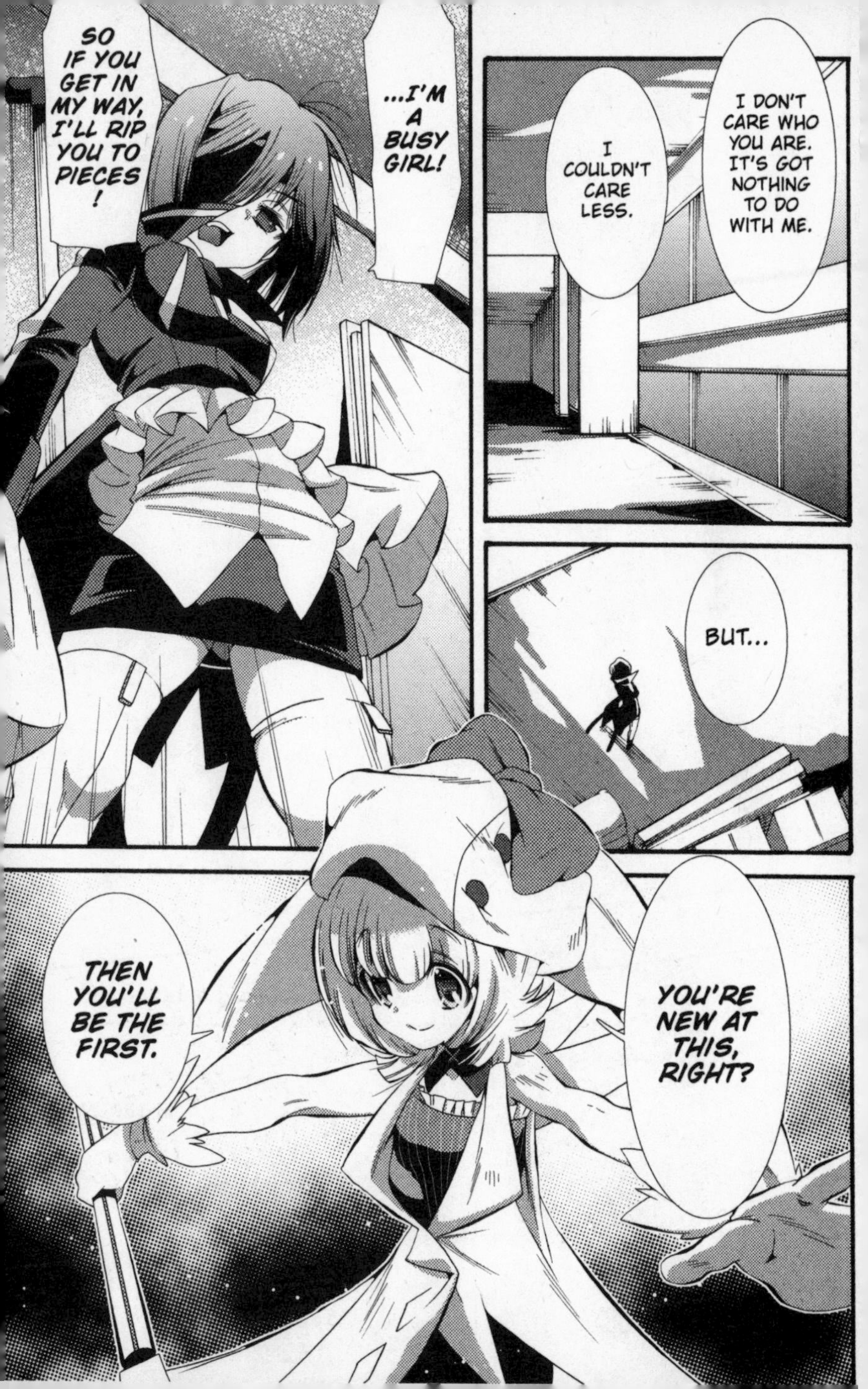
I DON'T CARE WHO YOU ARE. IT'S GOT NOTHING TO DO WITH ME.
I COULDN'T CARE LESS.
BUT...
...I'M A BUSY GIRL!
SO IF YOU GET IN MY WAY, I'LL RIP YOU TO PIECES!
YOU'RE NEW AT THIS, RIGHT?
THEN YOU'LL BE THE FIRST.

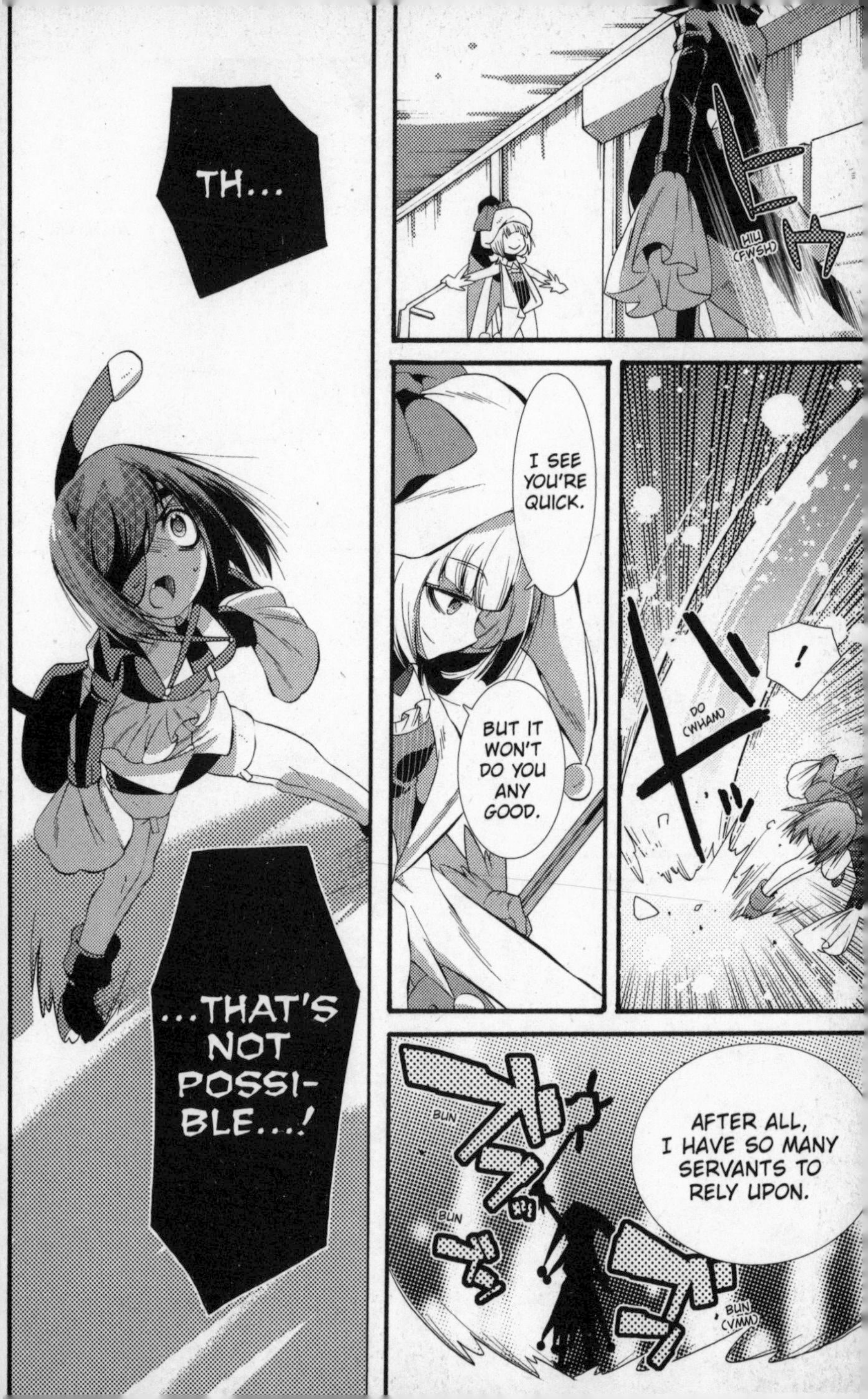
HIU (FWSH)
!
DO (WHAM)
I SEE YOU'RE QUICK.
BUT IT WON'T DO YOU ANY GOOD.
BUN
BUN
BUN (VMM)
AFTER ALL, I HAVE SO MANY SERVANTS TO RELY UPON.
TH...
...THAT'S NOT POSSI-BLE...!

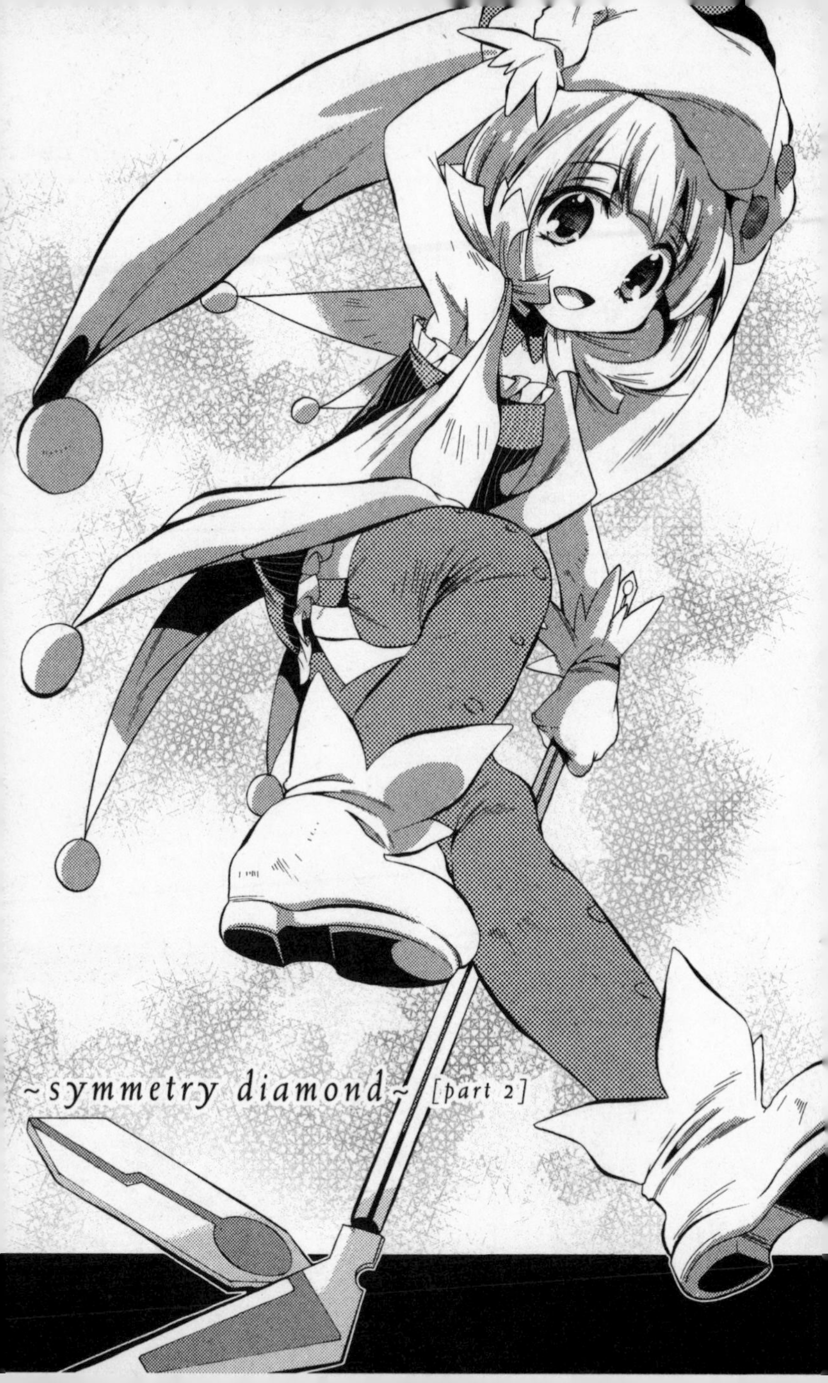
~symmetry diamond~ [part 2]

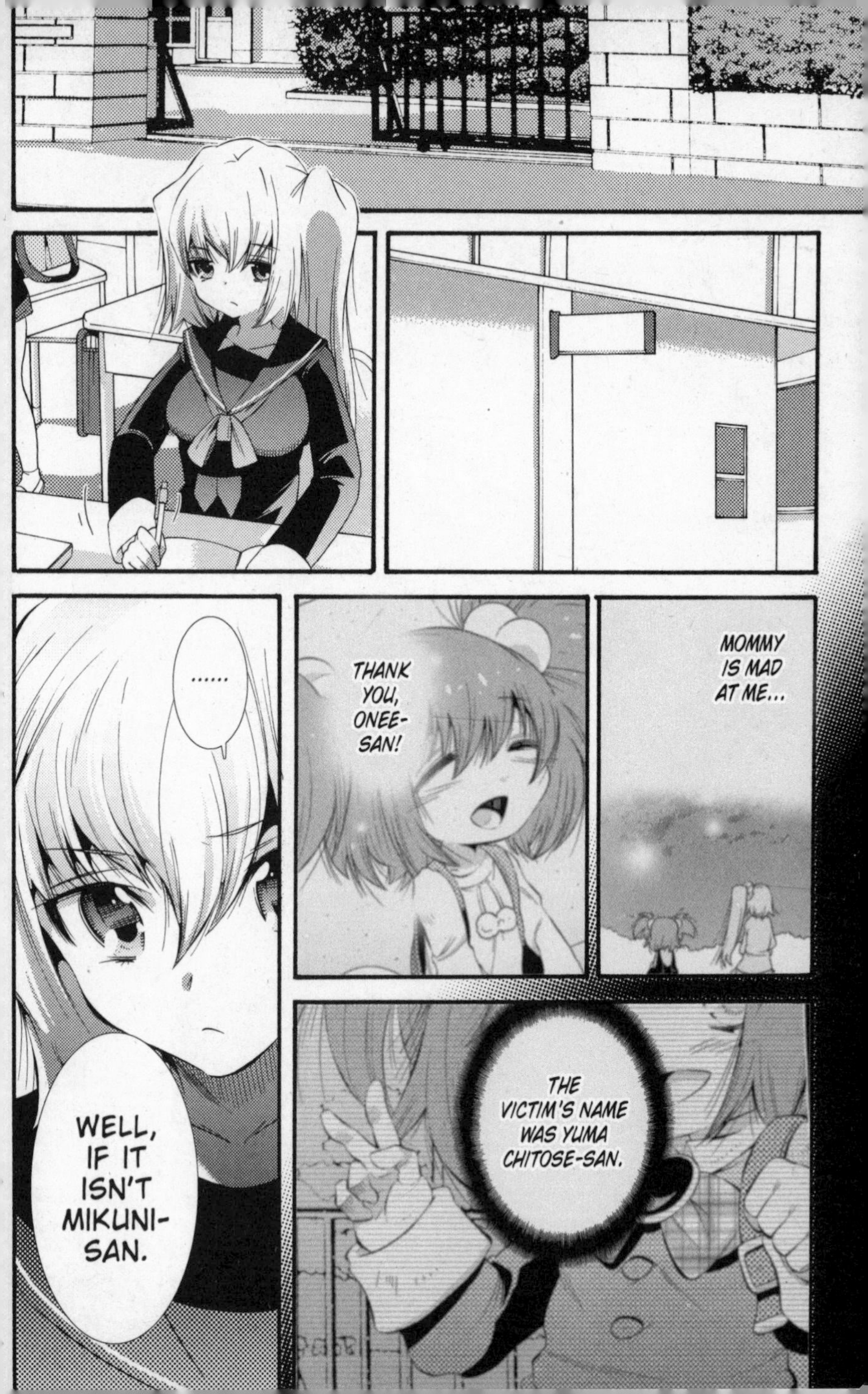
MOMMY IS MAD AT ME...
THANK YOU, ONEE-SAN!
THE VICTIM'S NAME WAS YUMA CHITOSE-SAN.
......
WELL, IF IT ISN'T MIKUNI-SAN.

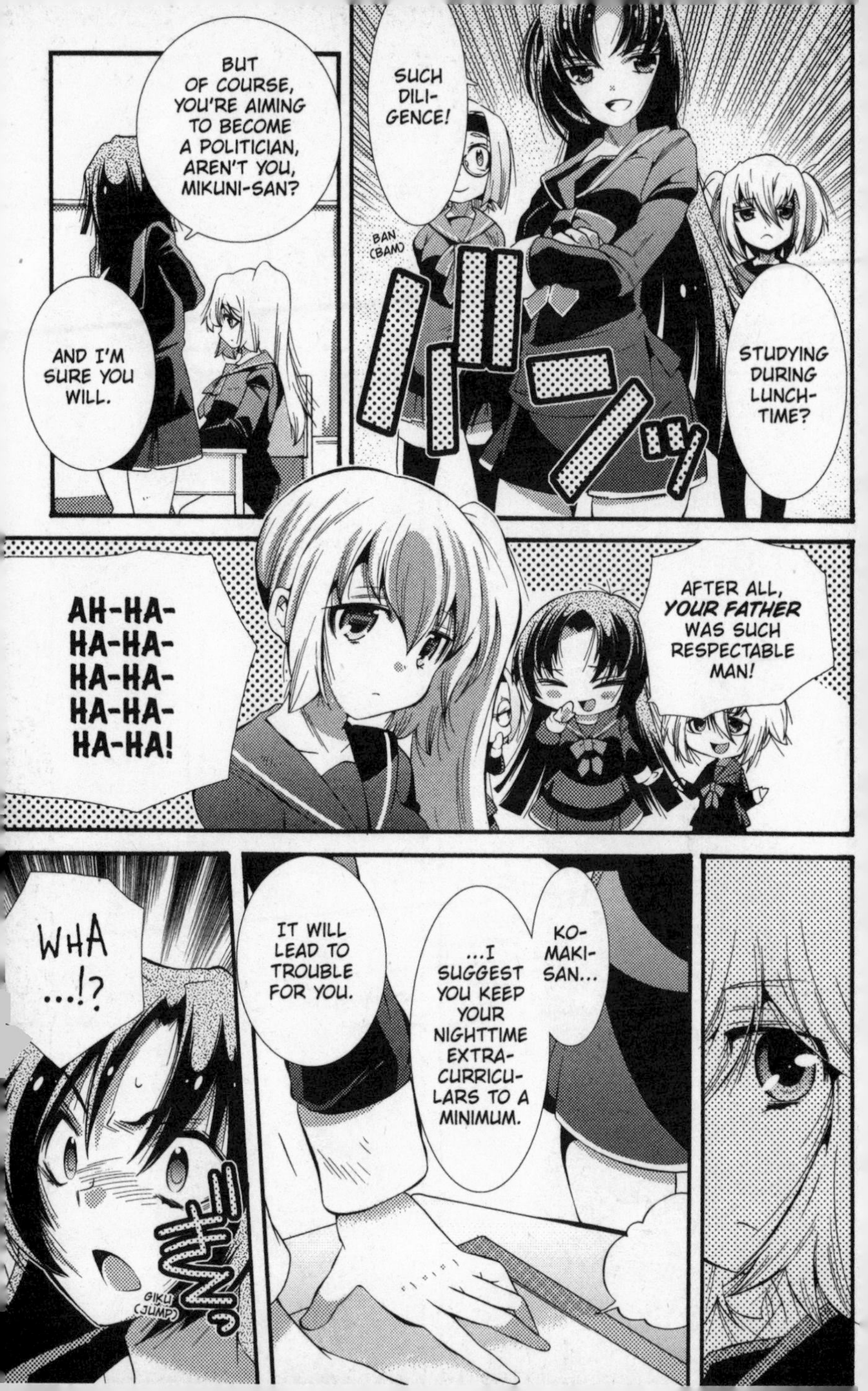
STUDYING DURING LUNCH-TIME?
SUCH DILI-GENCE!
BAN (BAM)
BUT OF COURSE, YOU'RE AIMING TO BECOME A POLITICIAN, AREN'T YOU, MIKUNI-SAN?
AND I'M SURE YOU WILL.
AFTER ALL, ***YOUR FATHER*** WAS SUCH RESPECTABLE MAN!
AH-HA-HA-HA-HA-HA-HA-HA-HA-HA!
KO-MAKI-SAN...
...I SUGGEST YOU KEEP YOUR NIGHTTIME EXTRA-CURRICU-LARS TO A MINIMUM.
IT WILL LEAD TO TROUBLE FOR YOU.
WHA ...!?
GIKU (JUMP)

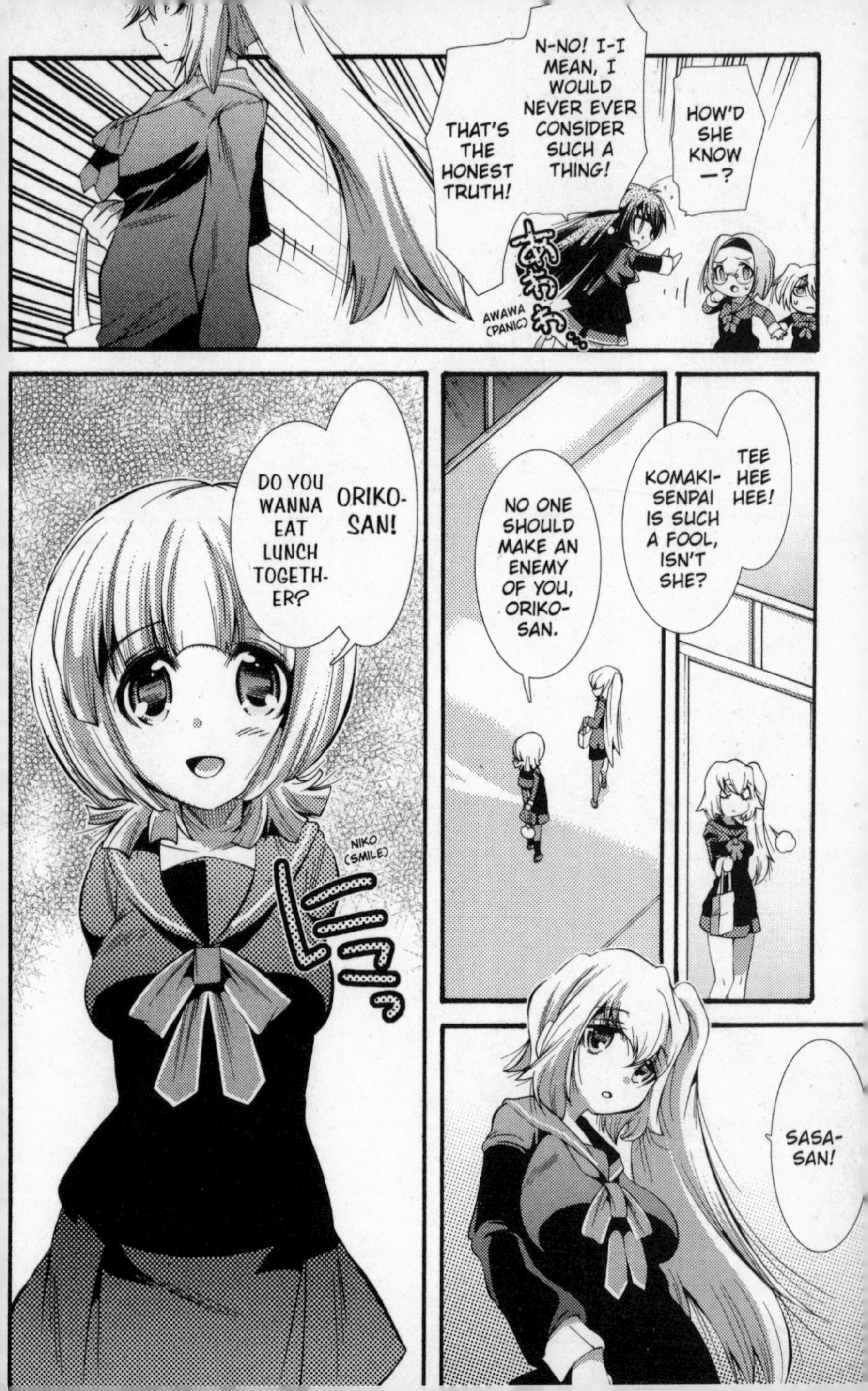
HOW'D SHE KNOW—?
N-NO! I-I MEAN, I WOULD NEVER EVER CONSIDER SUCH A THING!
THAT'S THE HONEST TRUTH!
AWAWA (PANIC)
TEE HEE HEE!
KOMAKI-SENPAI IS SUCH A FOOL, ISN'T SHE?
NO ONE SHOULD MAKE AN ENEMY OF YOU, ORIKO-SAN.
SASA-SAN!
ORIKO-SAN!
DO YOU WANNA EAT LUNCH TOGETH-ER?
NIKO (SMILE)

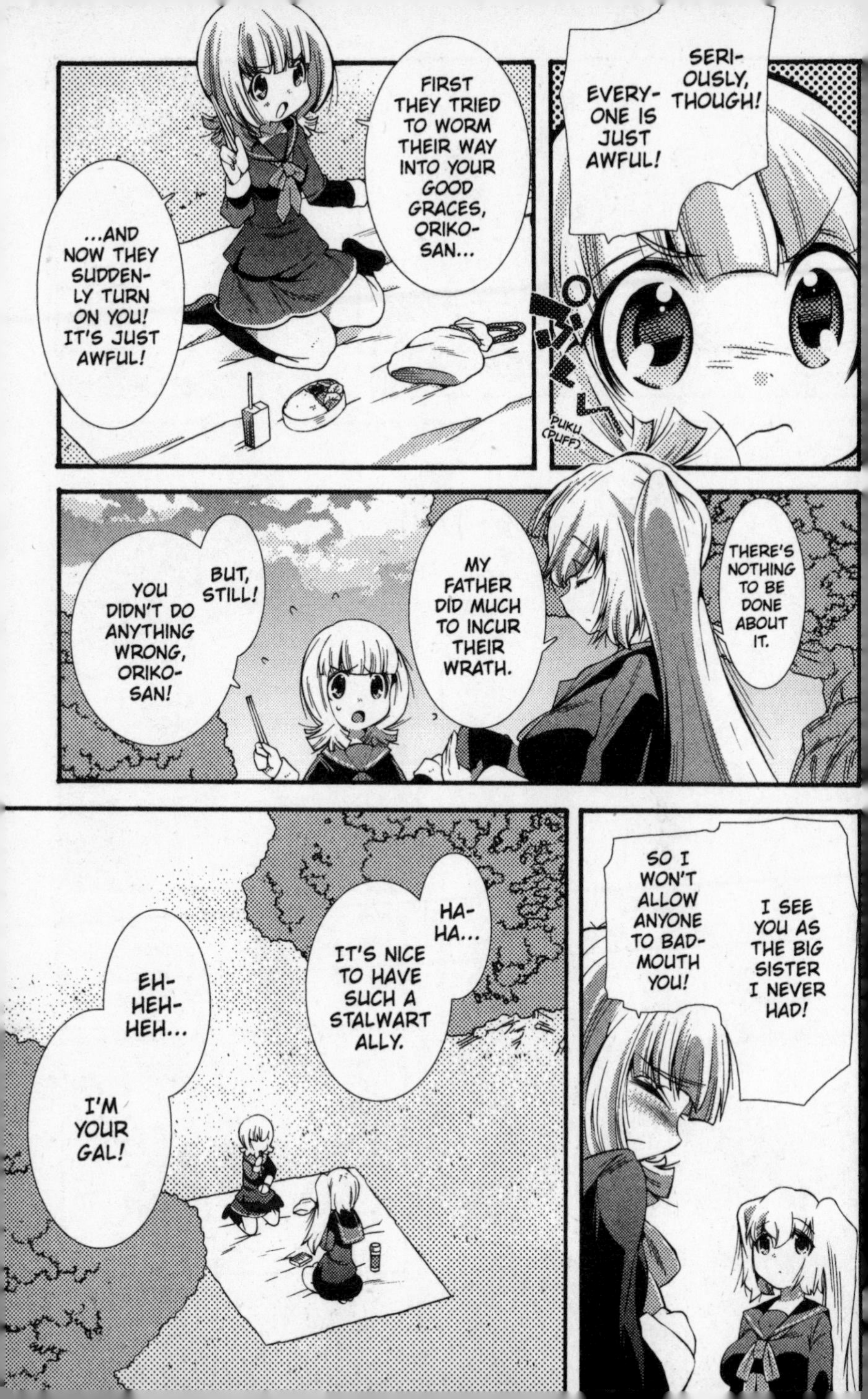
SERIOUSLY, THOUGH!
EVERYONE IS JUST AWFUL!
PUKU (PUFF)
FIRST THEY TRIED TO WORM THEIR WAY INTO YOUR GOOD GRACES, ORIKO-SAN...
...AND NOW THEY SUDDENLY TURN ON YOU! IT'S JUST AWFUL!
THERE'S NOTHING TO BE DONE ABOUT IT.
MY FATHER DID MUCH TO INCUR THEIR WRATH.
BUT, STILL!
YOU DIDN'T DO ANYTHING WRONG, ORIKO-SAN!
I SEE YOU AS THE BIG SISTER I NEVER HAD!
SO I WON'T ALLOW ANYONE TO BAD-MOUTH YOU!
HA-HA...
IT'S NICE TO HAVE SUCH A STALWART ALLY.
EH-HEH-HEH...
I'M YOUR GAL!

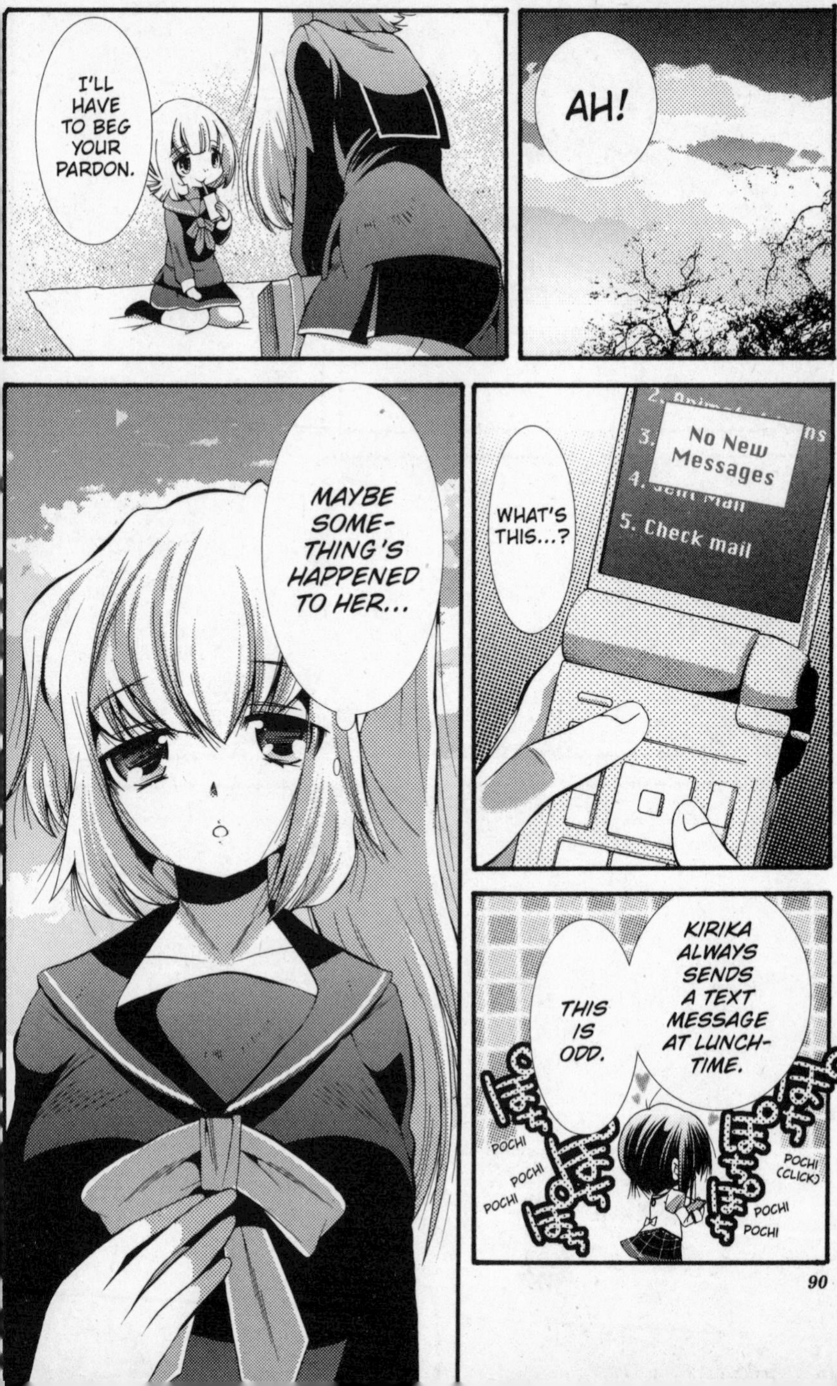
AH!
I'LL HAVE TO BEG YOUR PARDON.
WHAT'S THIS...?
No New Messages
5. Check mail
KIRIKA ALWAYS SENDS A TEXT MESSAGE AT LUNCH-TIME.
THIS IS ODD.
POCHI (CLICK)
POCHI
POCHI
POCHI
POCHI
POCHI
MAYBE SOME-THING'S HAPPENED TO HER...

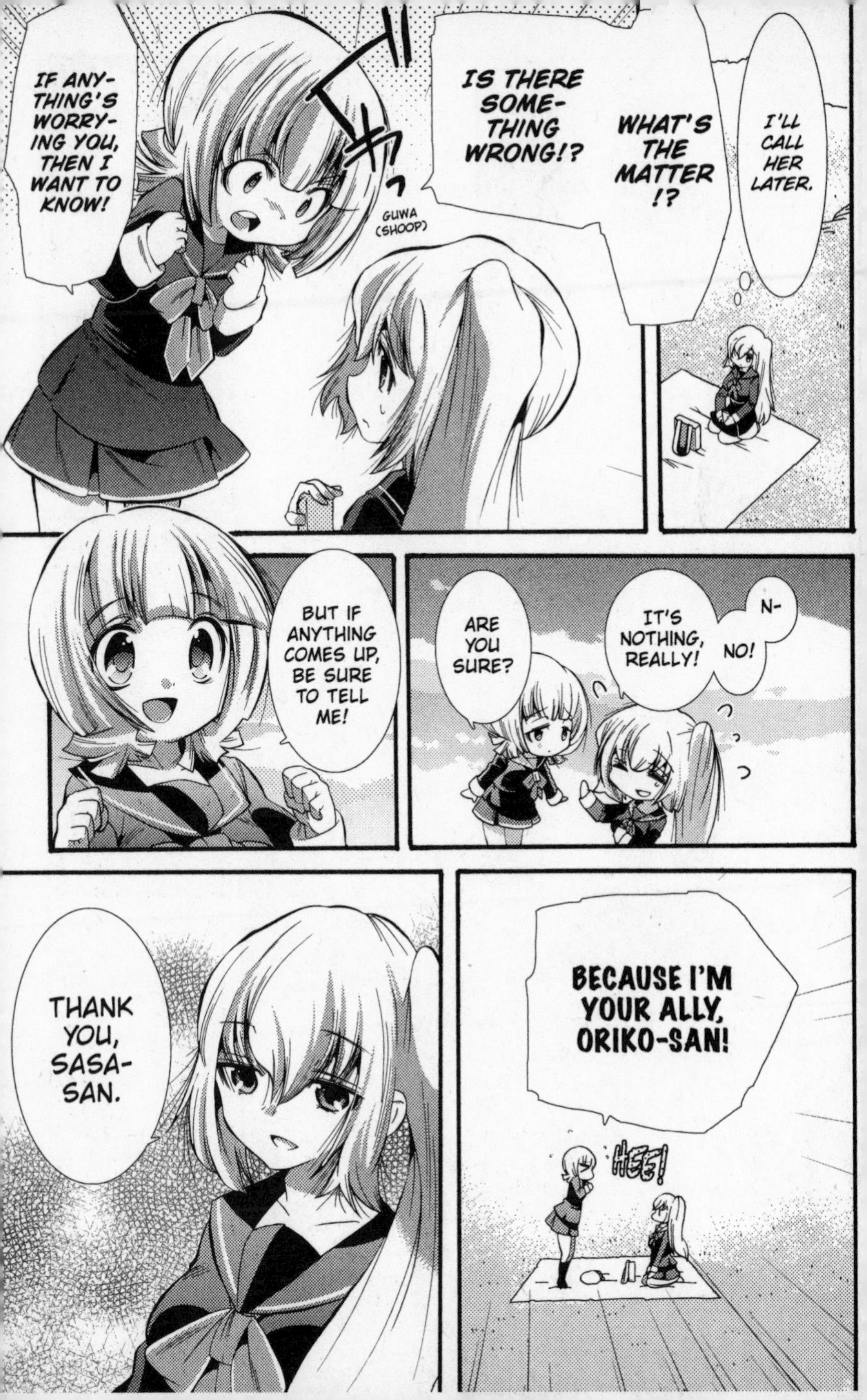
I'LL CALL HER LATER.
WHAT'S THE MATTER !?
IS THERE SOME-THING WRONG!?
GUWA (SHOOP)
IF ANY-THING'S WORRY-ING YOU, THEN I WANT TO KNOW!
N- NO!
IT'S NOTHING, REALLY!
ARE YOU SURE?
BUT IF ANYTHING COMES UP, BE SURE TO TELL ME!
BECAUSE I'M YOUR ALLY, ORIKO-SAN!
HEE!
THANK YOU, SASA-SAN.

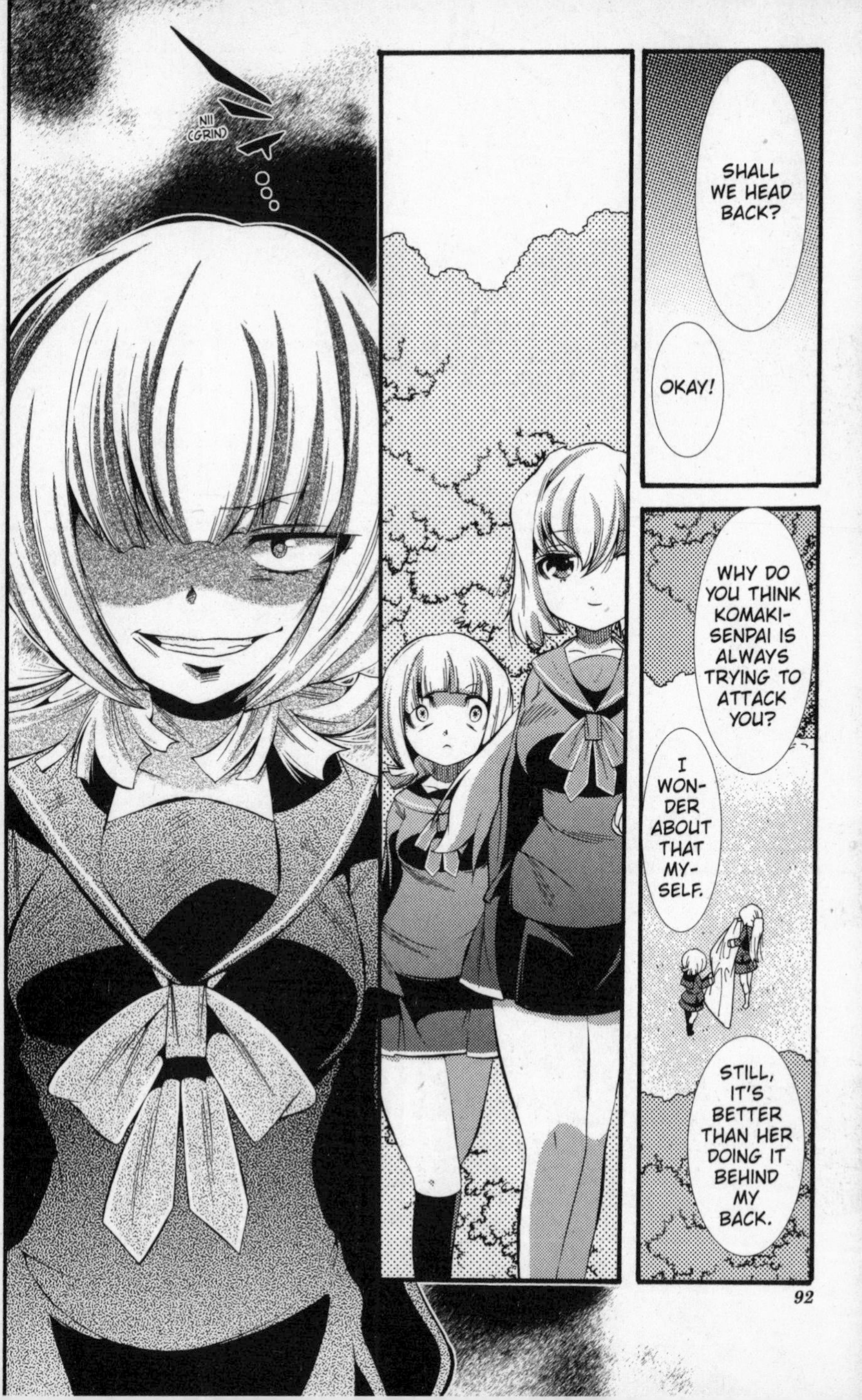
SHALL WE HEAD BACK?
OKAY!
WHY DO YOU THINK KOMAKI-SENPAI IS ALWAYS TRYING TO ATTACK YOU?
I WON-DER ABOUT THAT MY-SELF.
STILL, IT'S BETTER THAN HER DOING IT BEHIND MY BACK.
NII (GRIN)

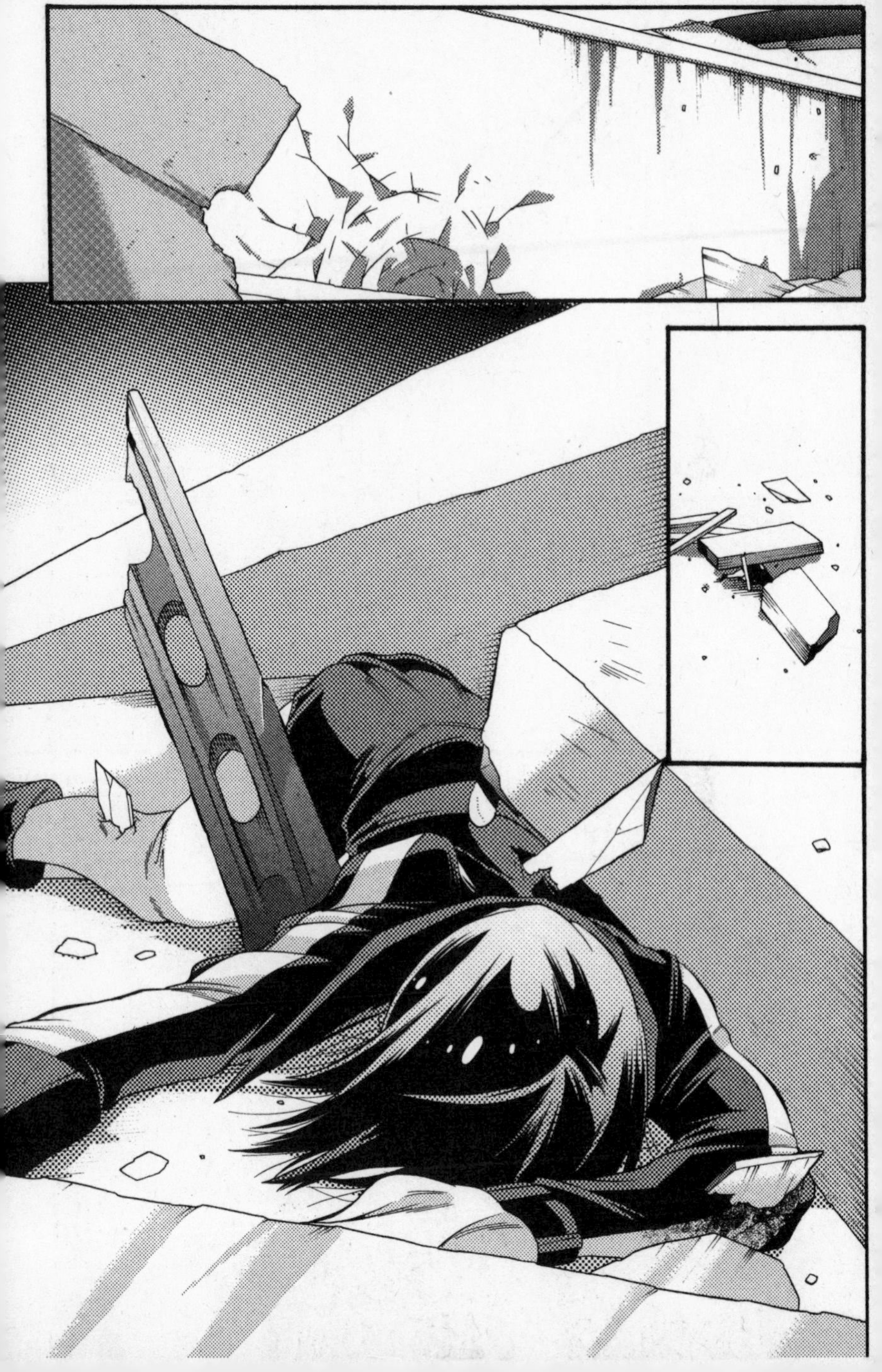

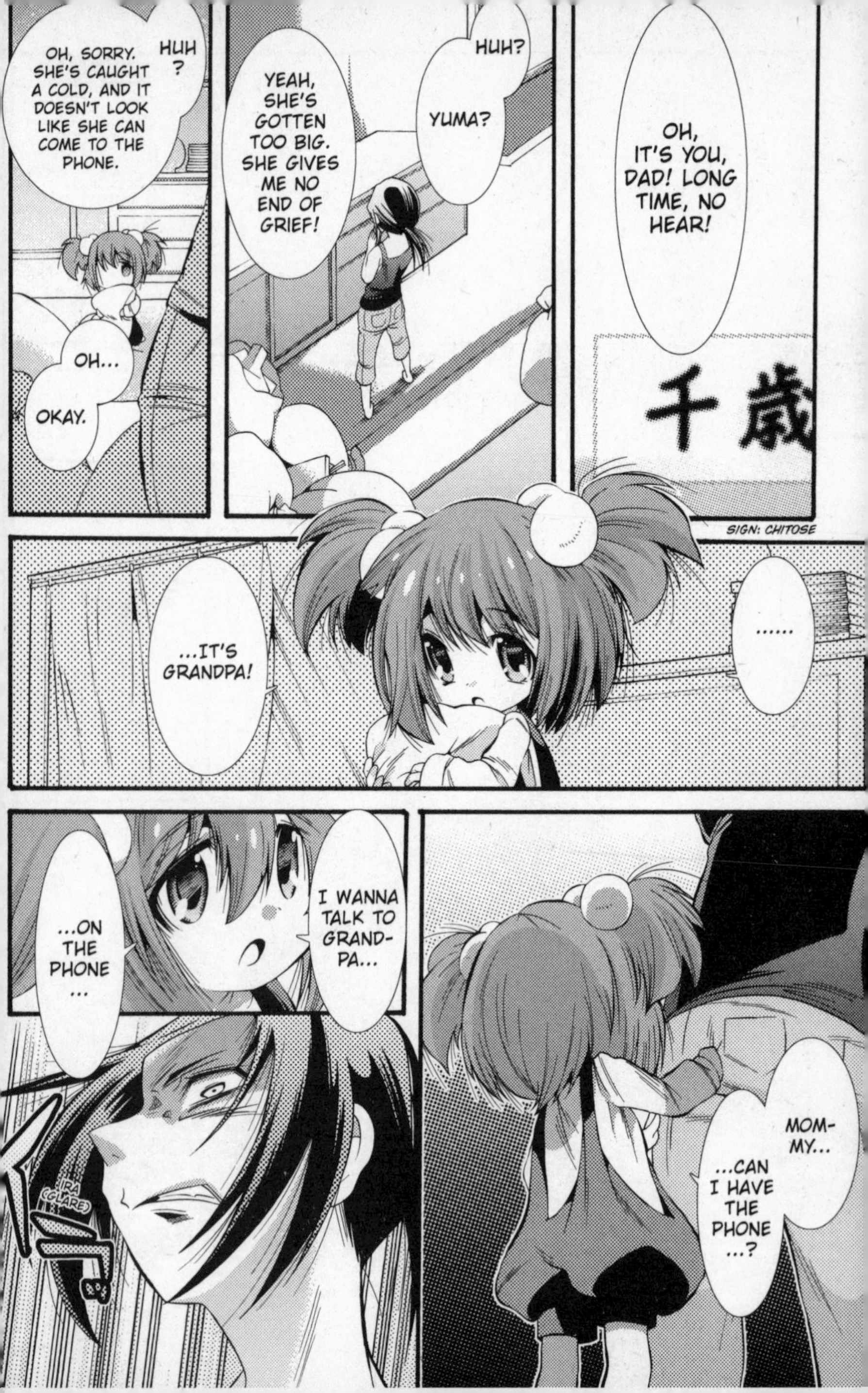
OH, IT'S YOU, DAD! LONG TIME, NO HEAR!
千歳
SIGN: CHITOSE
HUH?
YUMA?
YEAH, SHE'S GOTTEN TOO BIG. SHE GIVES ME NO END OF GRIEF!
HUH ?
OH, SORRY. SHE'S CAUGHT A COLD, AND IT DOESN'T LOOK LIKE SHE CAN COME TO THE PHONE.
OH...
OKAY.
......
...IT'S GRANDPA!
MOM-MY...
...CAN I HAVE THE PHONE ...?
I WANNA TALK TO GRAND-PA...
...ON THE PHONE ...
IRA (GLARE)

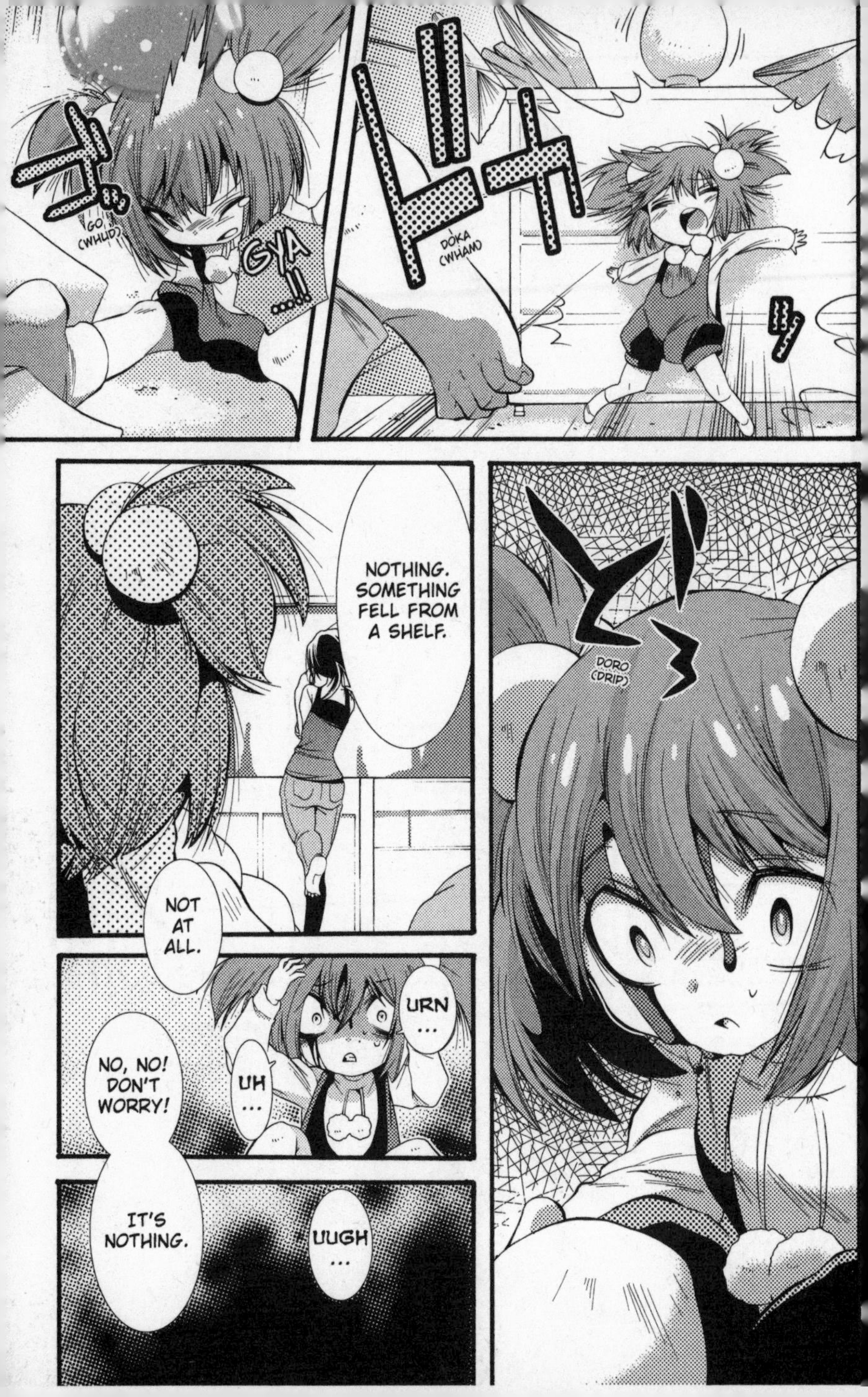

DOKA (WHAM)
GO (WHUD)
GYA!!
DORO (DRIP)
NOTHING. SOMETHING FELL FROM A SHELF.
URN...
NOT AT ALL.
UH...
NO, NO! DON'T WORRY!
UUGH...
IT'S NOTHING.

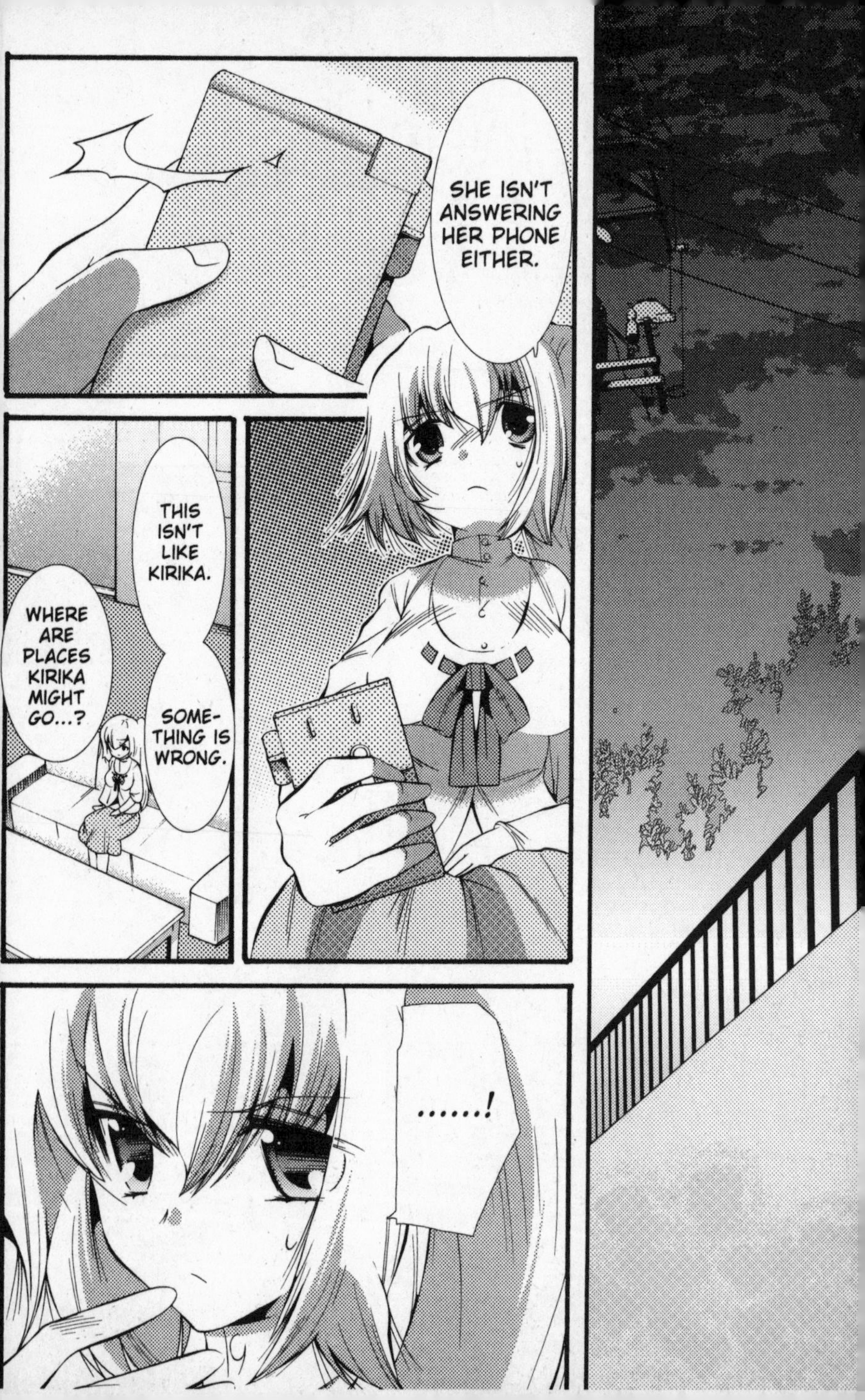
SHE ISN'T ANSWERING HER PHONE EITHER.
THIS ISN'T LIKE KIRIKA.
SOMETHING IS WRONG.
WHERE ARE PLACES KIRIKA MIGHT GO...?
......!

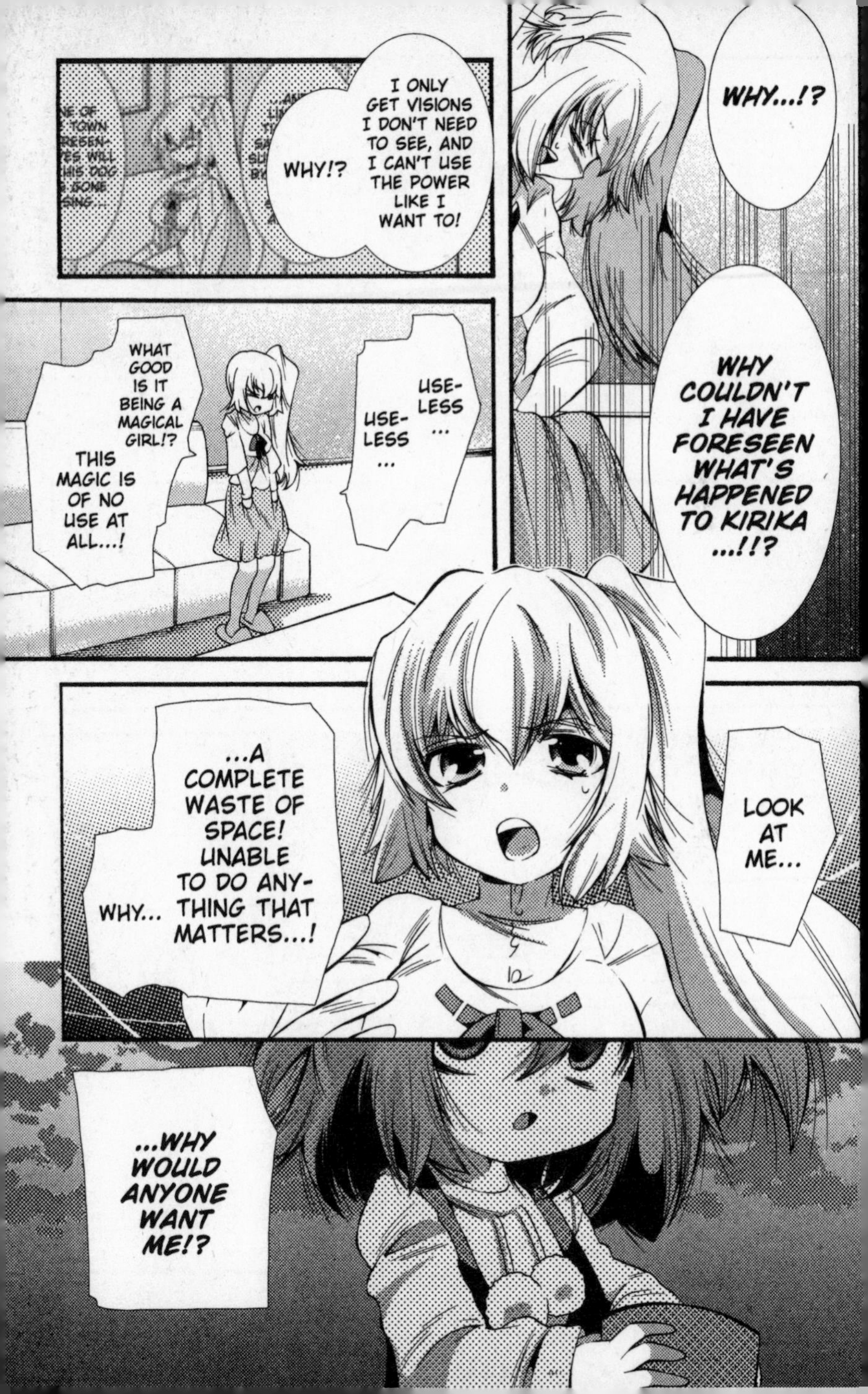
WHY...!?
WHY COULDN'T I HAVE FORESEEN WHAT'S HAPPENED TO KIRIKA...!!?
I ONLY GET VISIONS I DON'T NEED TO SEE, AND I CAN'T USE THE POWER LIKE I WANT TO!
WHY!?
USE-LESS...
USE-LESS...
WHAT GOOD IS IT BEING A MAGICAL GIRL!?
THIS MAGIC IS OF NO USE AT ALL...!
LOOK AT ME...
...A COMPLETE WASTE OF SPACE! UNABLE TO DO ANY-THING THAT MATTERS...!
WHY...
...WHY WOULD ANYONE WANT ME!?

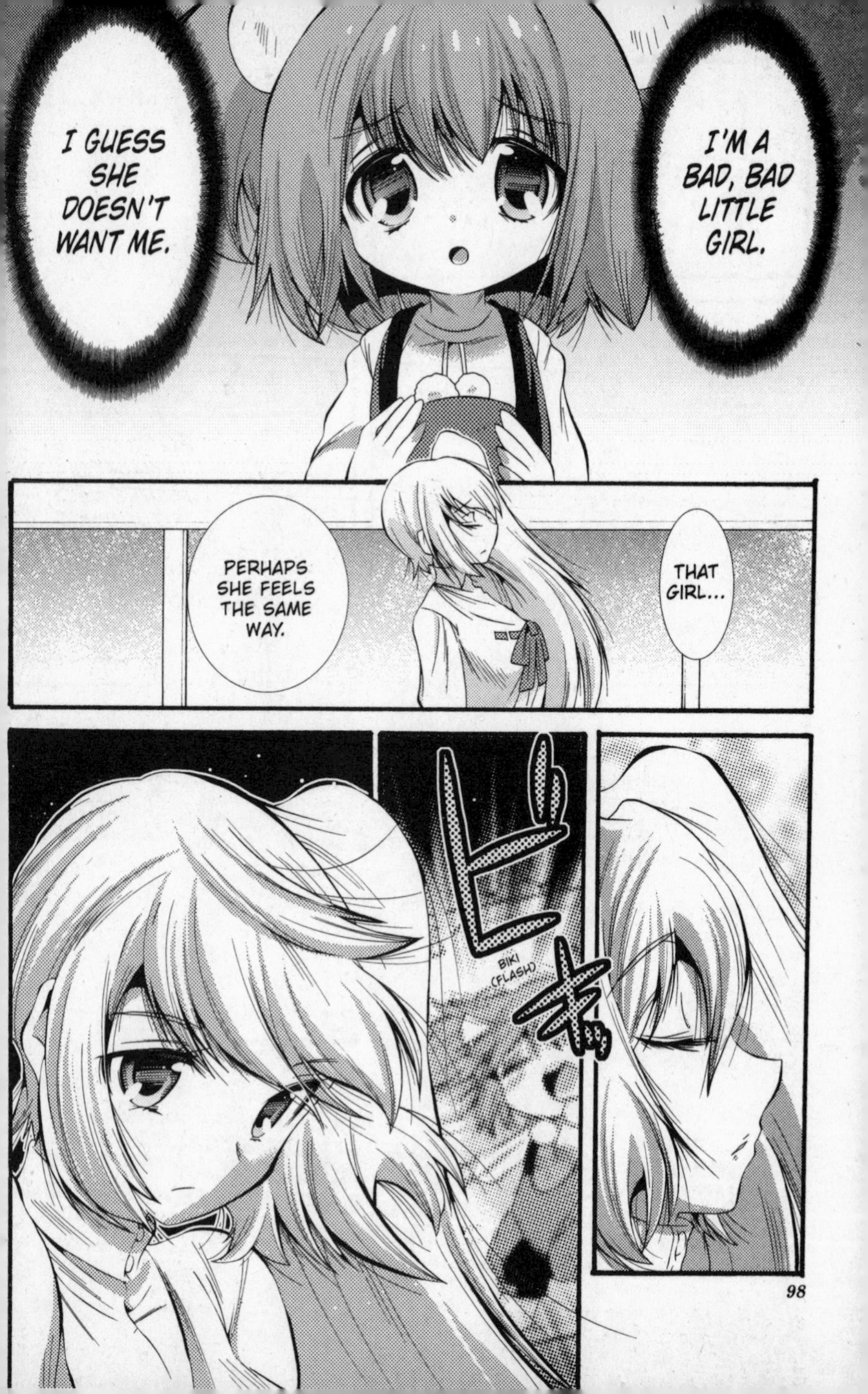
I'M A BAD, BAD LITTLE GIRL.
I GUESS SHE DOESN'T WANT ME.
THAT GIRL...
PERHAPS SHE FEELS THE SAME WAY.
BIKI (FLASH)

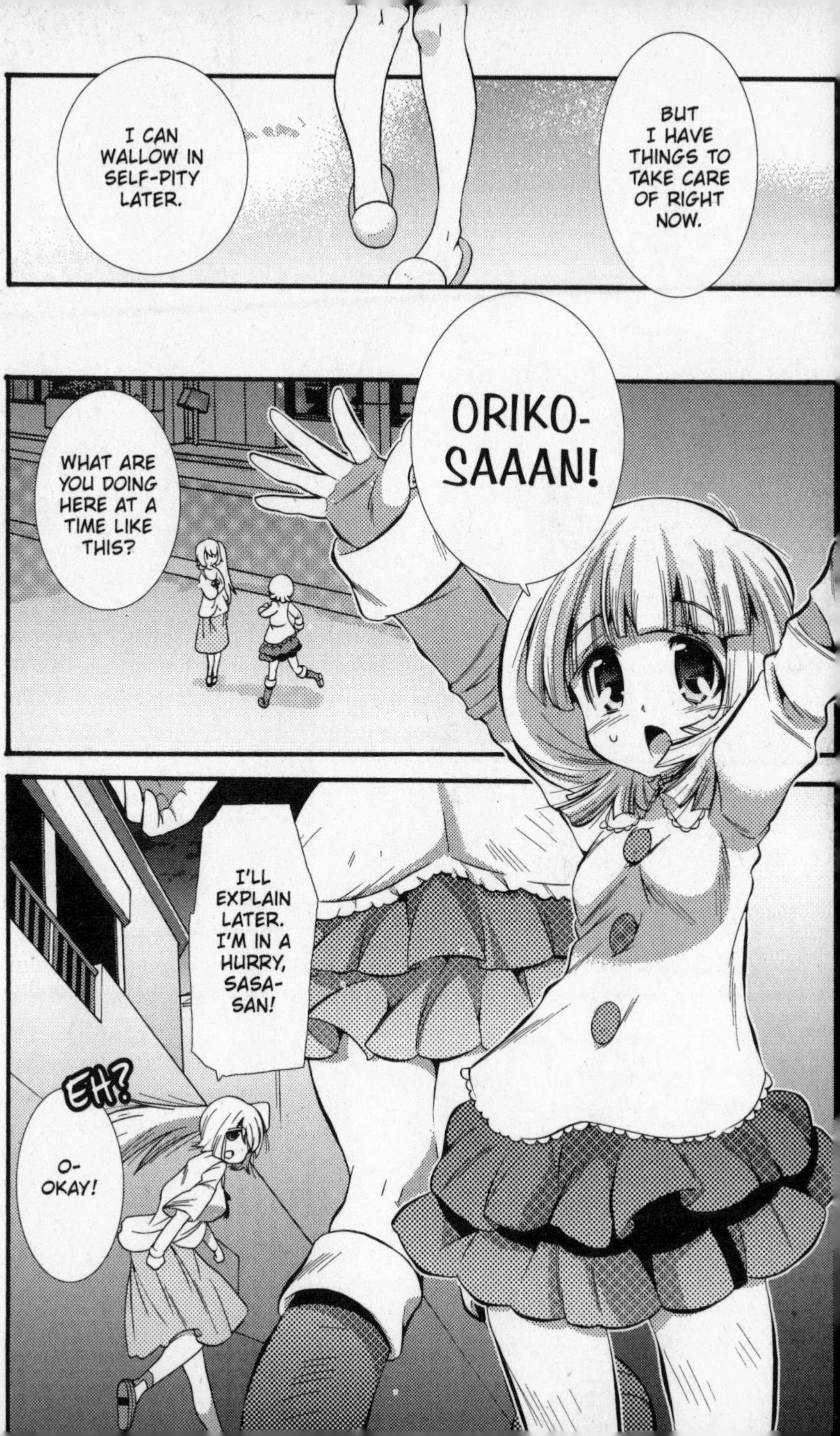
BUT I HAVE THINGS TO TAKE CARE OF RIGHT NOW.
I CAN WALLOW IN SELF-PITY LATER.
ORIKO-SAAAN!
WHAT ARE YOU DOING HERE AT A TIME LIKE THIS?
I'LL EXPLAIN LATER. I'M IN A HURRY, SASA-SAN!
EH?
O-OKAY!

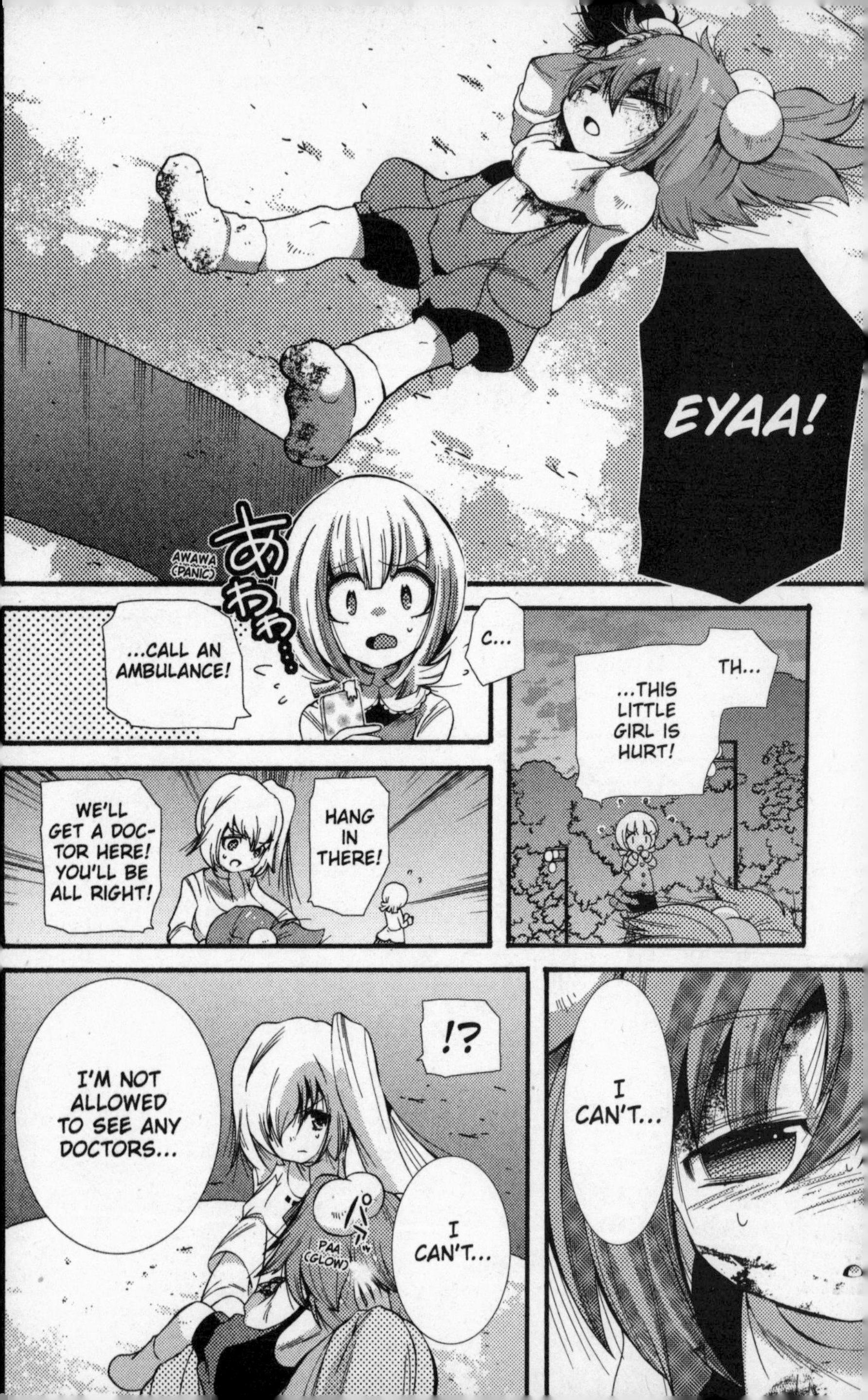
EYAA!
あわゎ…
AWAWA (PANIC)
C…
…CALL AN AMBULANCE!
TH…
…THIS LITTLE GIRL IS HURT!
HANG IN THERE!
WE'LL GET A DOC-TOR HERE! YOU'LL BE ALL RIGHT!
!?
I CAN'T…
I CAN'T…
PAA (GLOW)
I'M NOT ALLOWED TO SEE ANY DOCTORS…

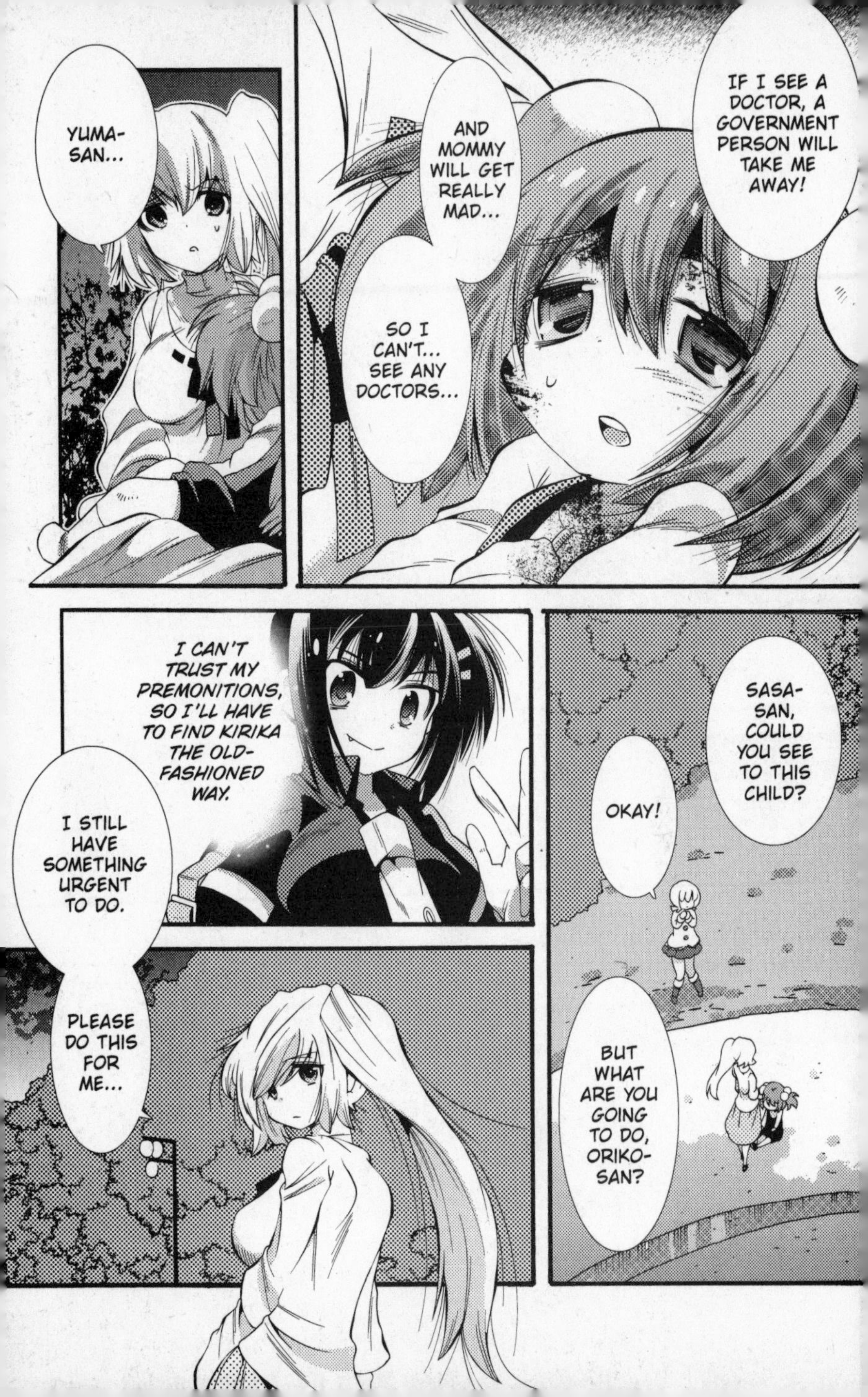
IF I SEE A DOCTOR, A GOVERNMENT PERSON WILL TAKE ME AWAY!
AND MOMMY WILL GET REALLY MAD...
SO I CAN'T... SEE ANY DOCTORS...
YUMA-SAN...
SASA-SAN, COULD YOU SEE TO THIS CHILD?
OKAY!
BUT WHAT ARE YOU GOING TO DO, ORIKO-SAN?
I CAN'T TRUST MY PREMONITIONS, SO I'LL HAVE TO FIND KIRIKA THE OLD-FASHIONED WAY.
I STILL HAVE SOMETHING URGENT TO DO.
PLEASE DO THIS FOR ME...

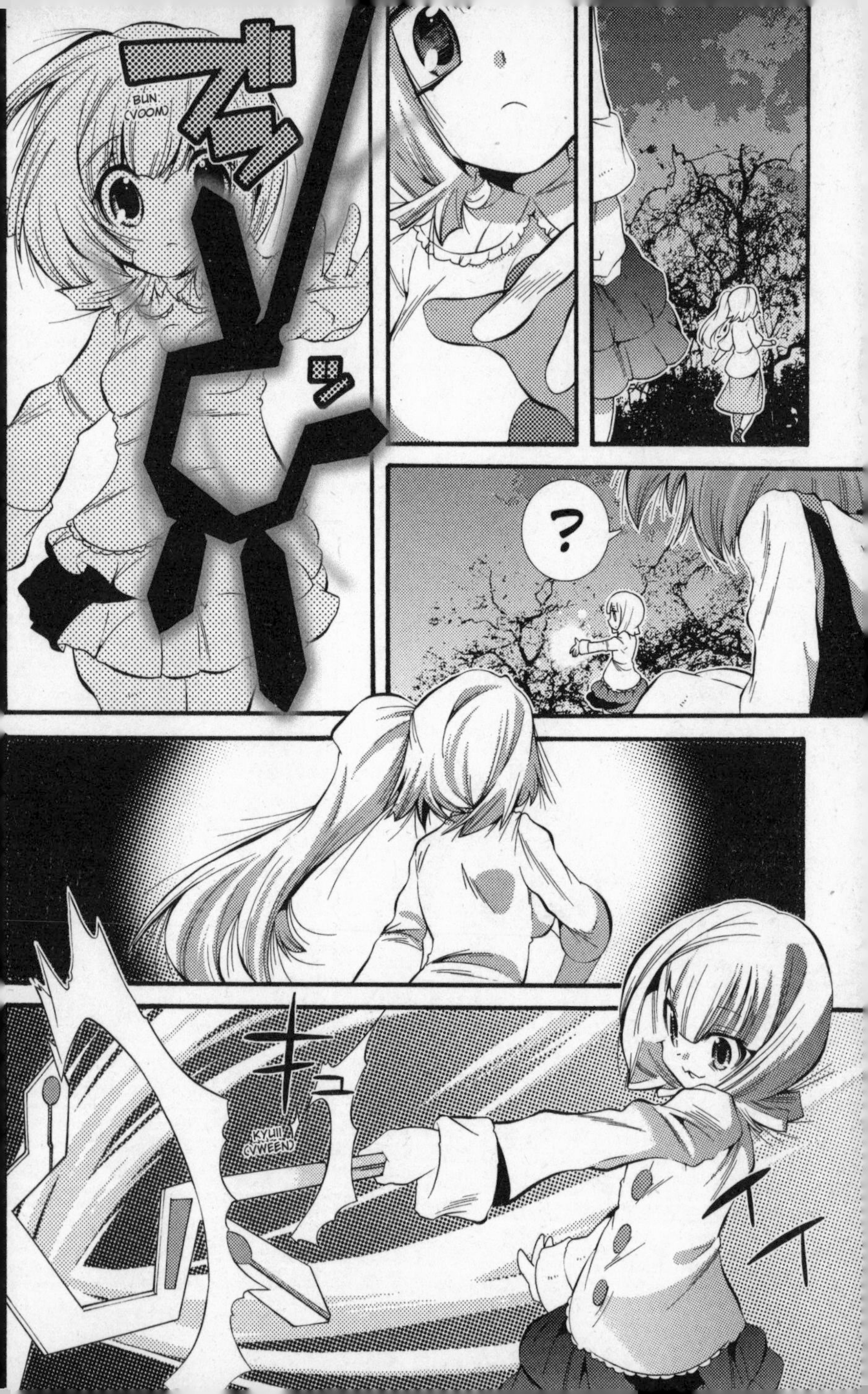
?
BUN (VOOM)
KYUII (VWEEN)

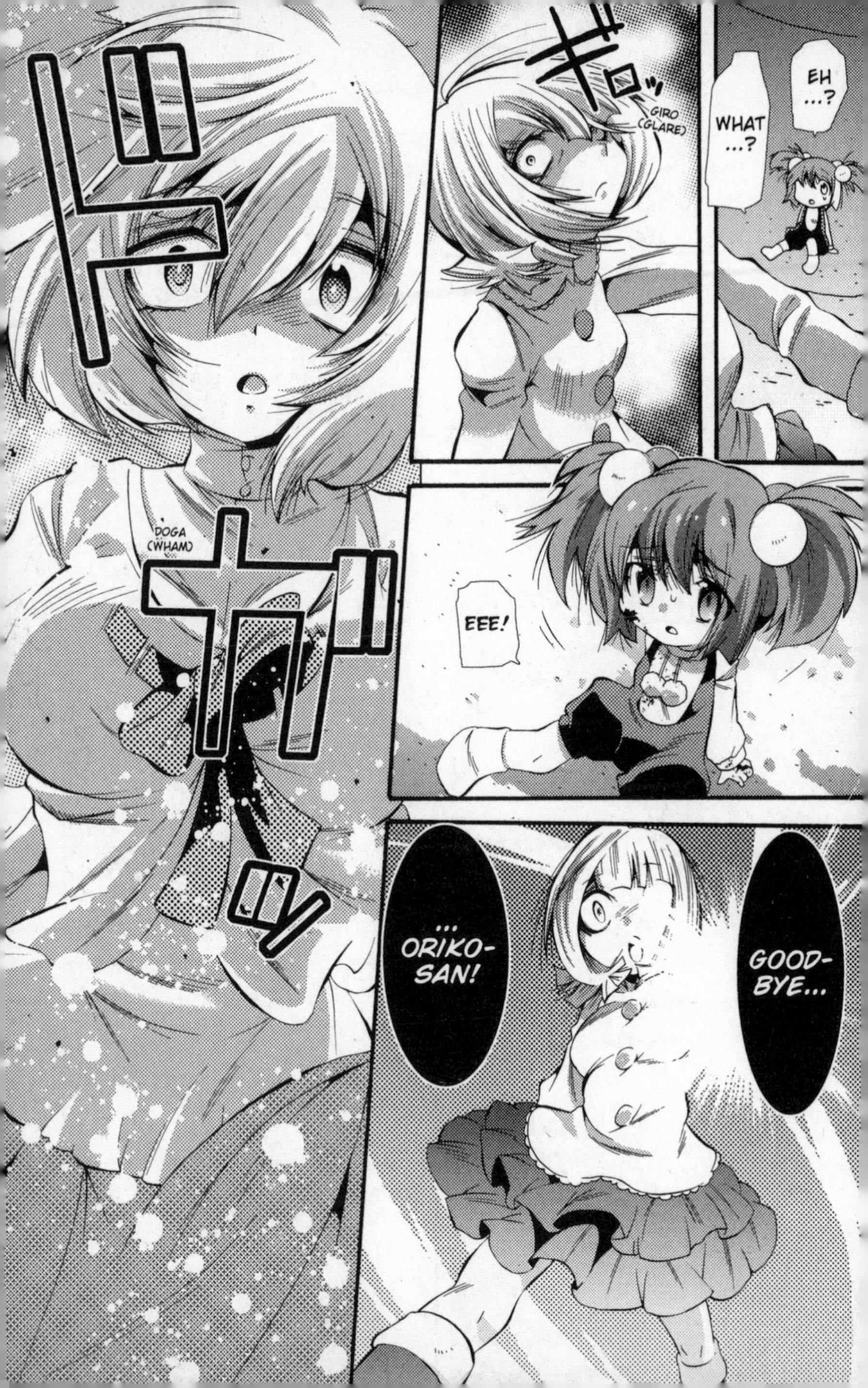
EH ...?
WHAT ...?
GIRO (GLARE)
EEE!
GOOD-BYE...
... ORIKO-SAN!
DOGA (WHAM)

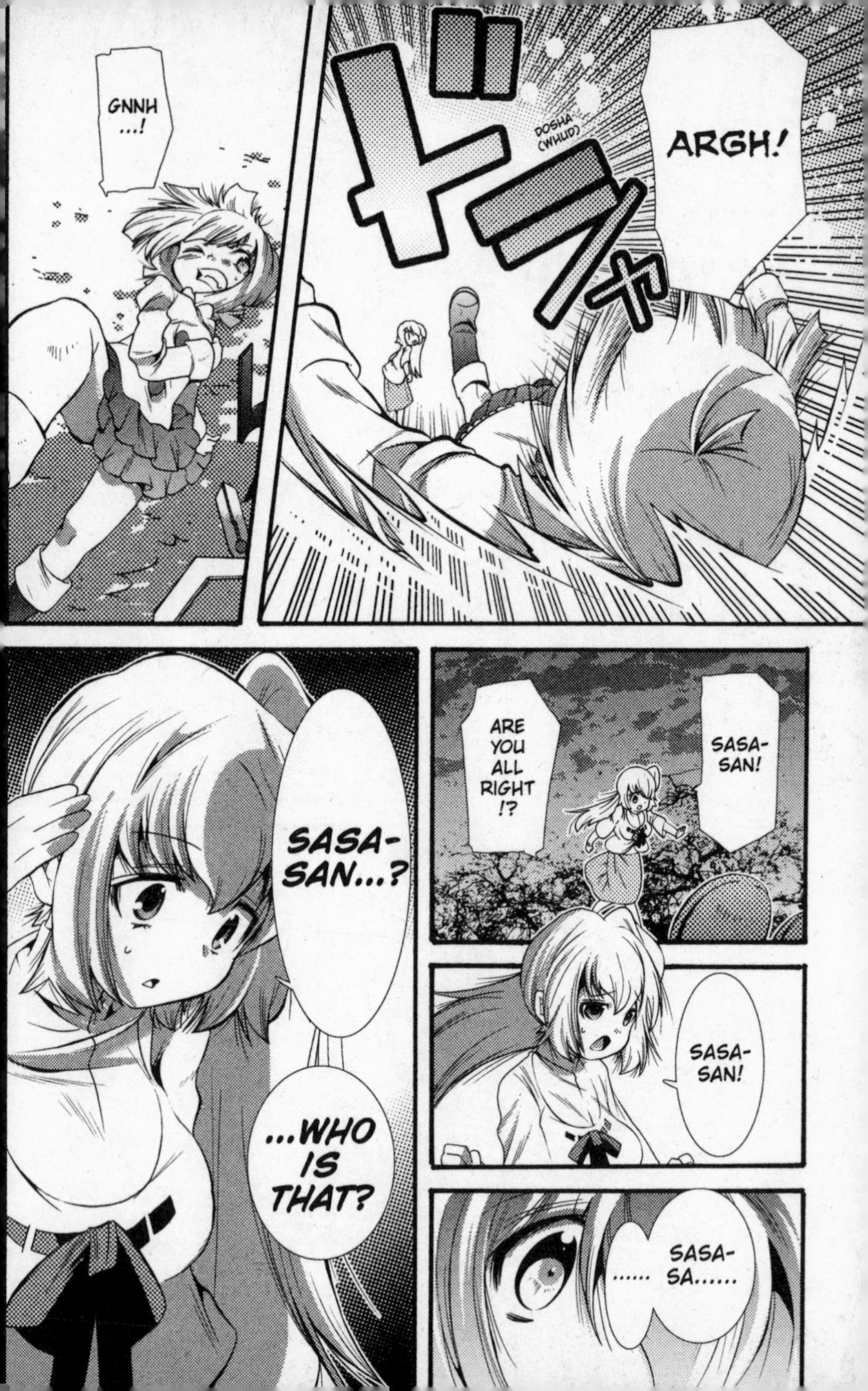
ARGH!
DOSHA (WHUD)
GNNH ...!
SASA-SAN!
ARE YOU ALL RIGHT !?
SASA-SAN!
...... SASA-SA......
SASA-SAN...?
...WHO IS THAT?

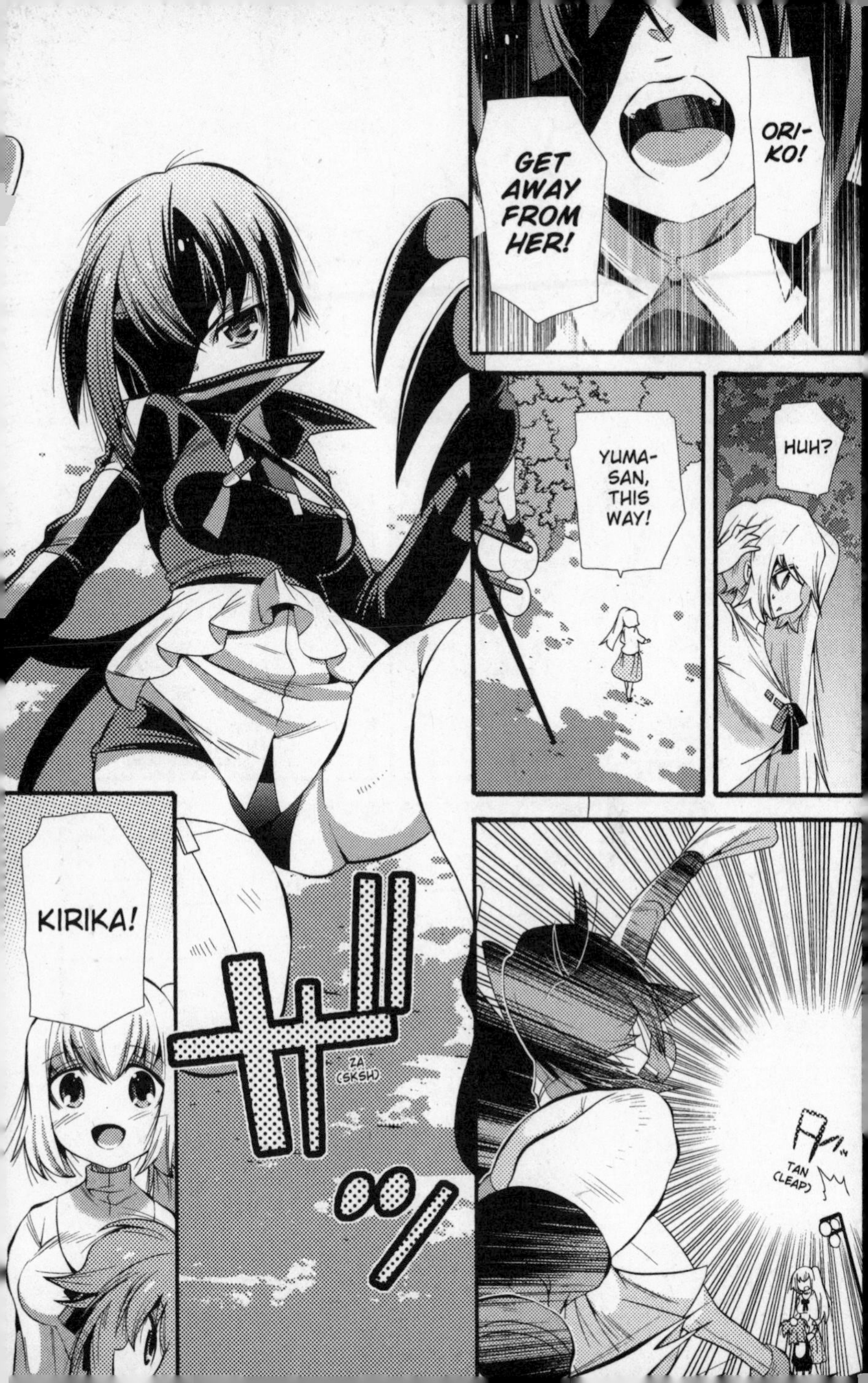

ORI-KO!
GET AWAY FROM HER!
HUH?
YUMA-SAN, THIS WAY!
TAN (LEAP)
KIRIKA!
ZA (SKSH)

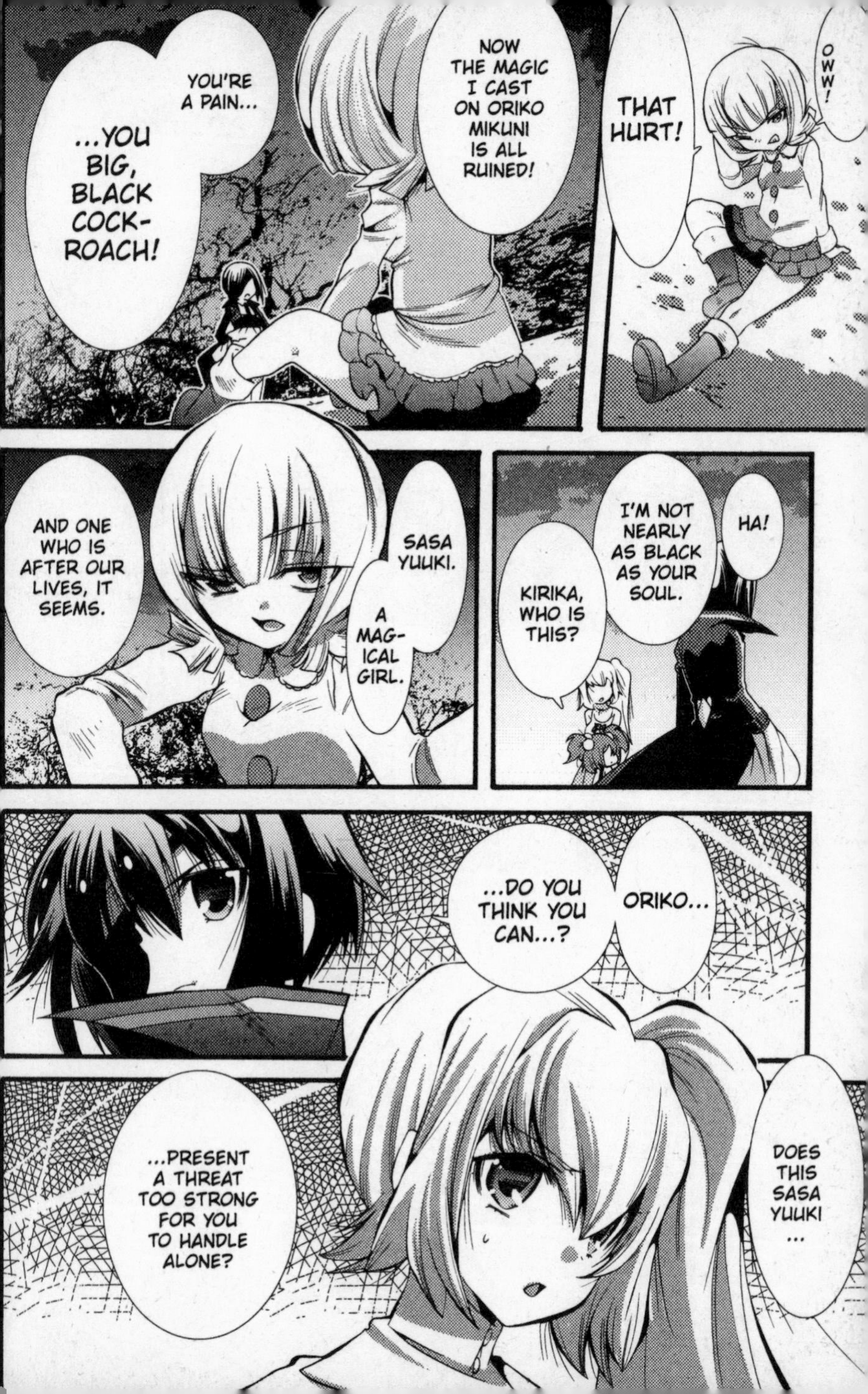
OWW!
THAT HURT!
NOW THE MAGIC I CAST ON ORIKO MIKUNI IS ALL RUINED!
YOU'RE A PAIN...
...YOU BIG, BLACK COCKROACH!
HA!
I'M NOT NEARLY AS BLACK AS YOUR SOUL.
KIRIKA, WHO IS THIS?
SASA YUUKI.
A MAGICAL GIRL.
AND ONE WHO IS AFTER OUR LIVES, IT SEEMS.
ORIKO...
...DO YOU THINK YOU CAN...?
DOES THIS SASA YUUKI...
...PRESENT A THREAT TOO STRONG FOR YOU TO HANDLE ALONE?

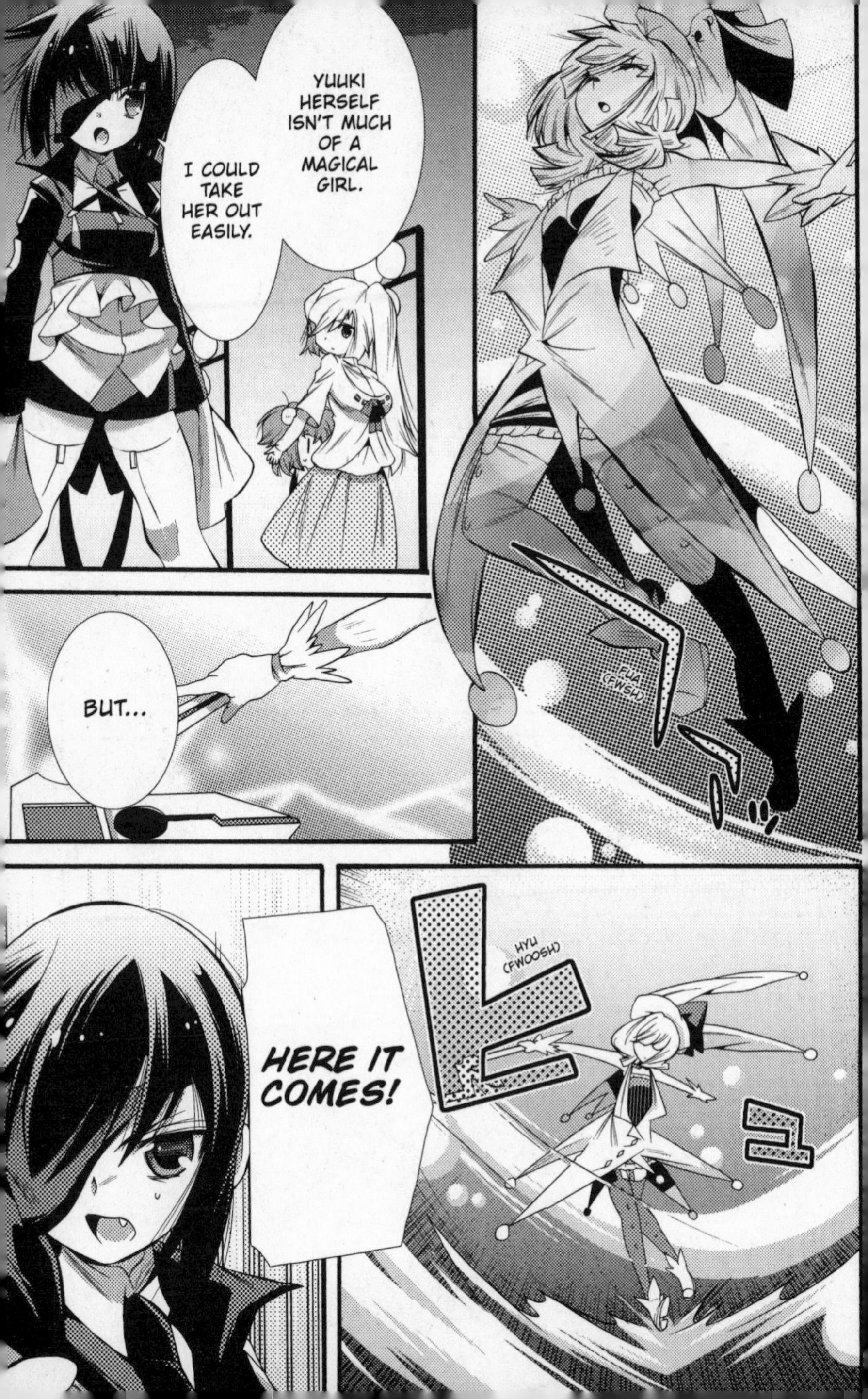
FUA (FWSH)
YUUKI HERSELF ISN'T MUCH OF A MAGICAL GIRL.
I COULD TAKE HER OUT EASILY.
BUT...
HYU (FWOOSH)
HERE IT COMES!

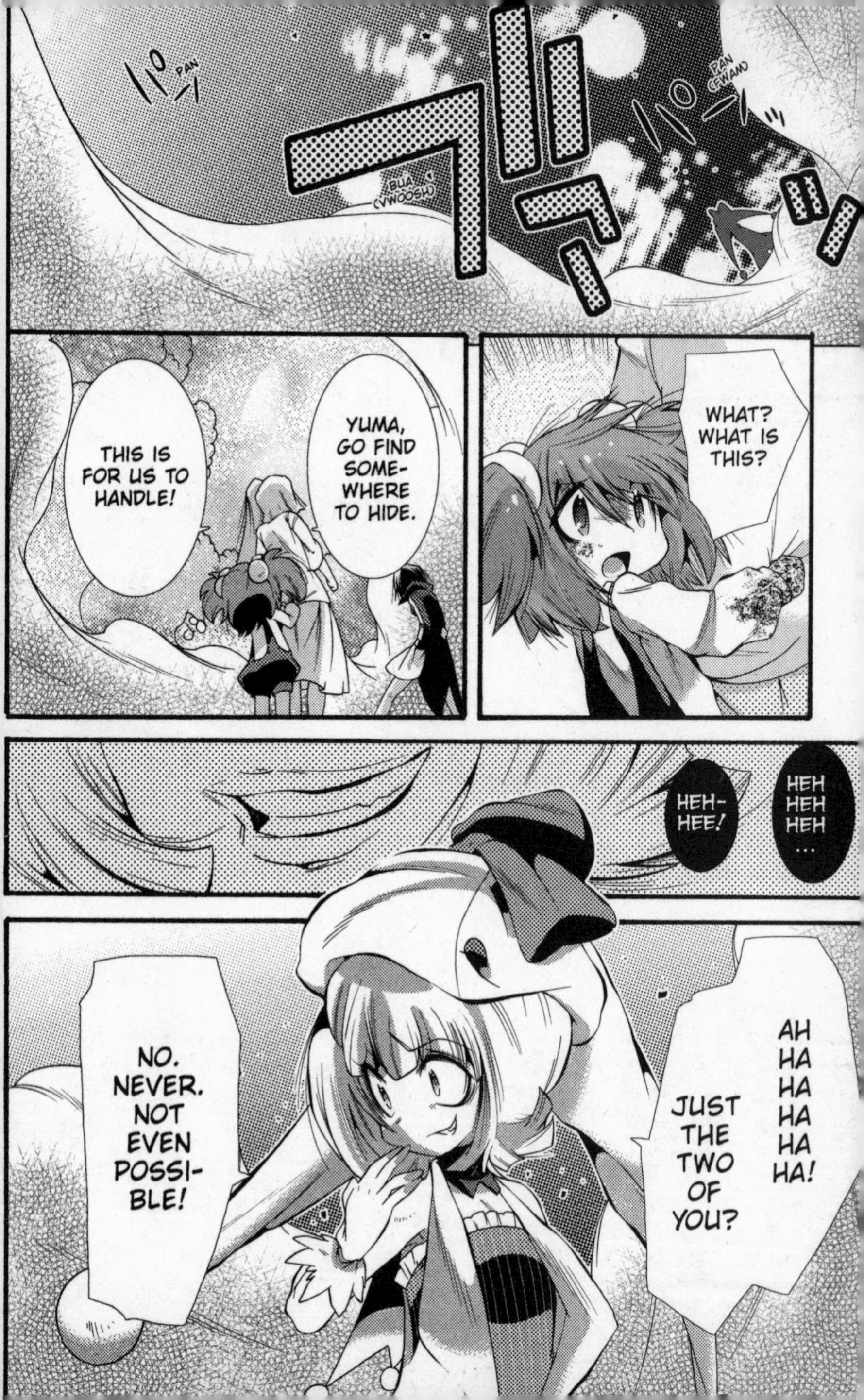
PAN (FWAM)
BUA (VWOOSH)
PAN
WHAT? WHAT IS THIS?
YUMA, GO FIND SOME-WHERE TO HIDE.
THIS IS FOR US TO HANDLE!
HEH HEH HEH …
HEH-HEE!
AH HA HA HA HA HA!
JUST THE TWO OF YOU?
NO. NEVER. NOT EVEN POSSIBLE!

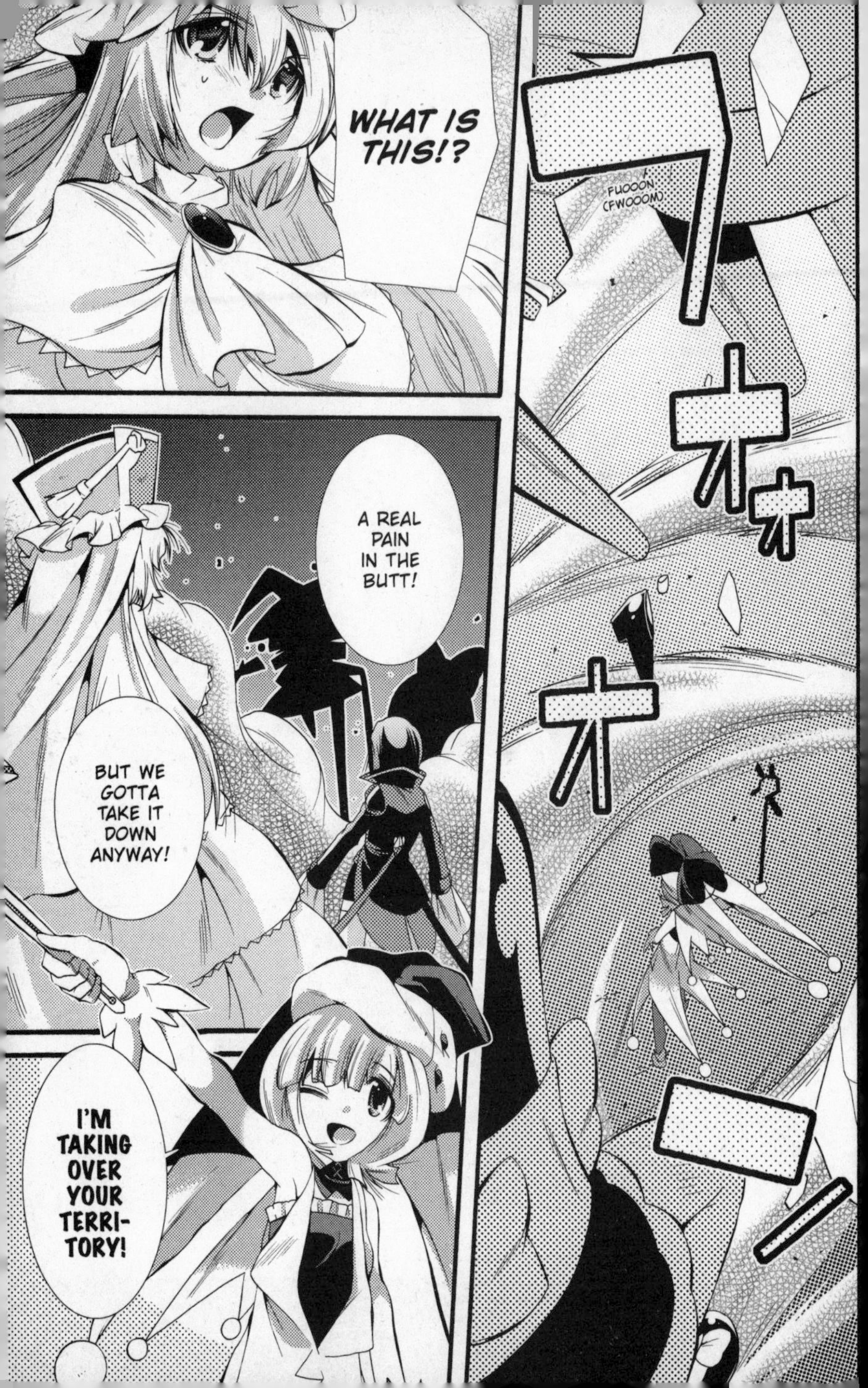
FUOOON (FWOOOM)
WHAT IS THIS!?
A REAL PAIN IN THE BUTT!
BUT WE GOTTA TAKE IT DOWN ANYWAY!
I'M TAKING OVER YOUR TERRITORY!

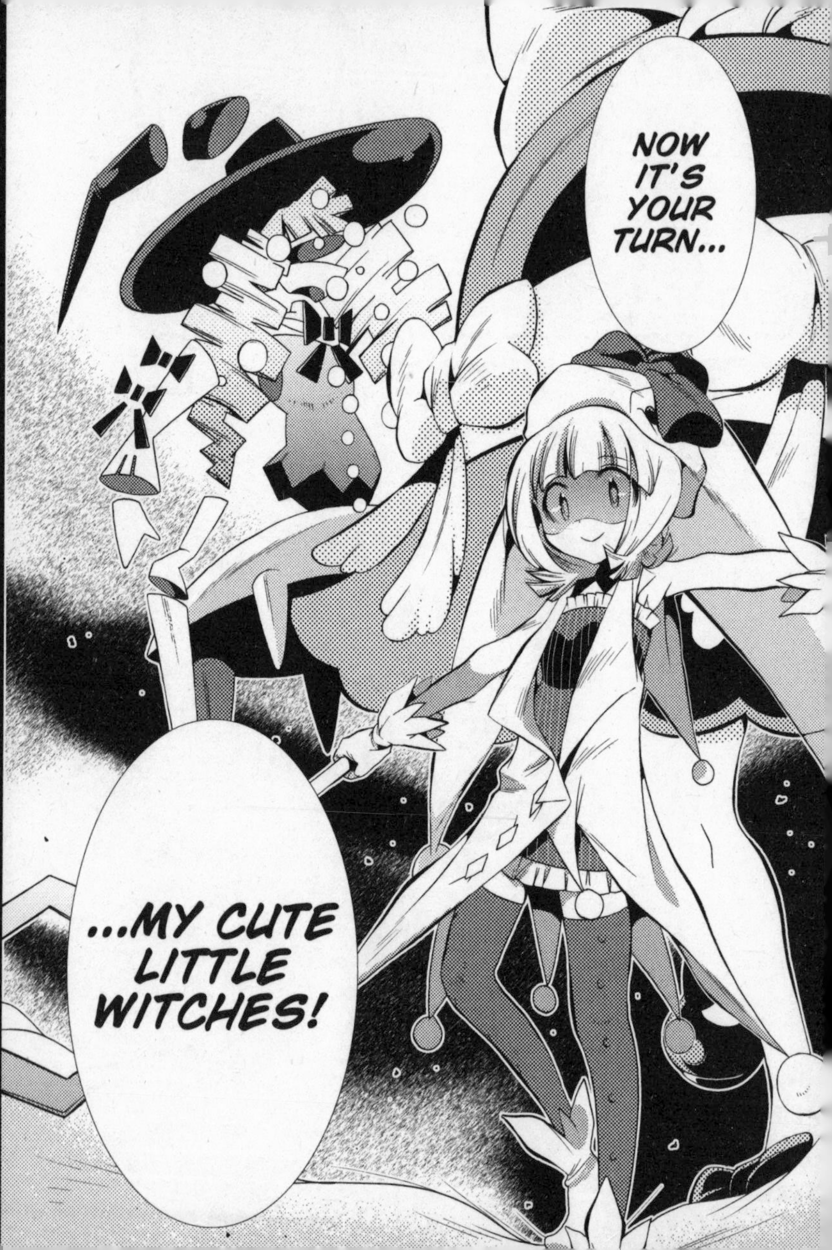
NOW IT'S YOUR TURN...
...MY CUTE LITTLE WITCHES!

PUELLA MAGI
ORIKO ★ MAGICA
[extra story]

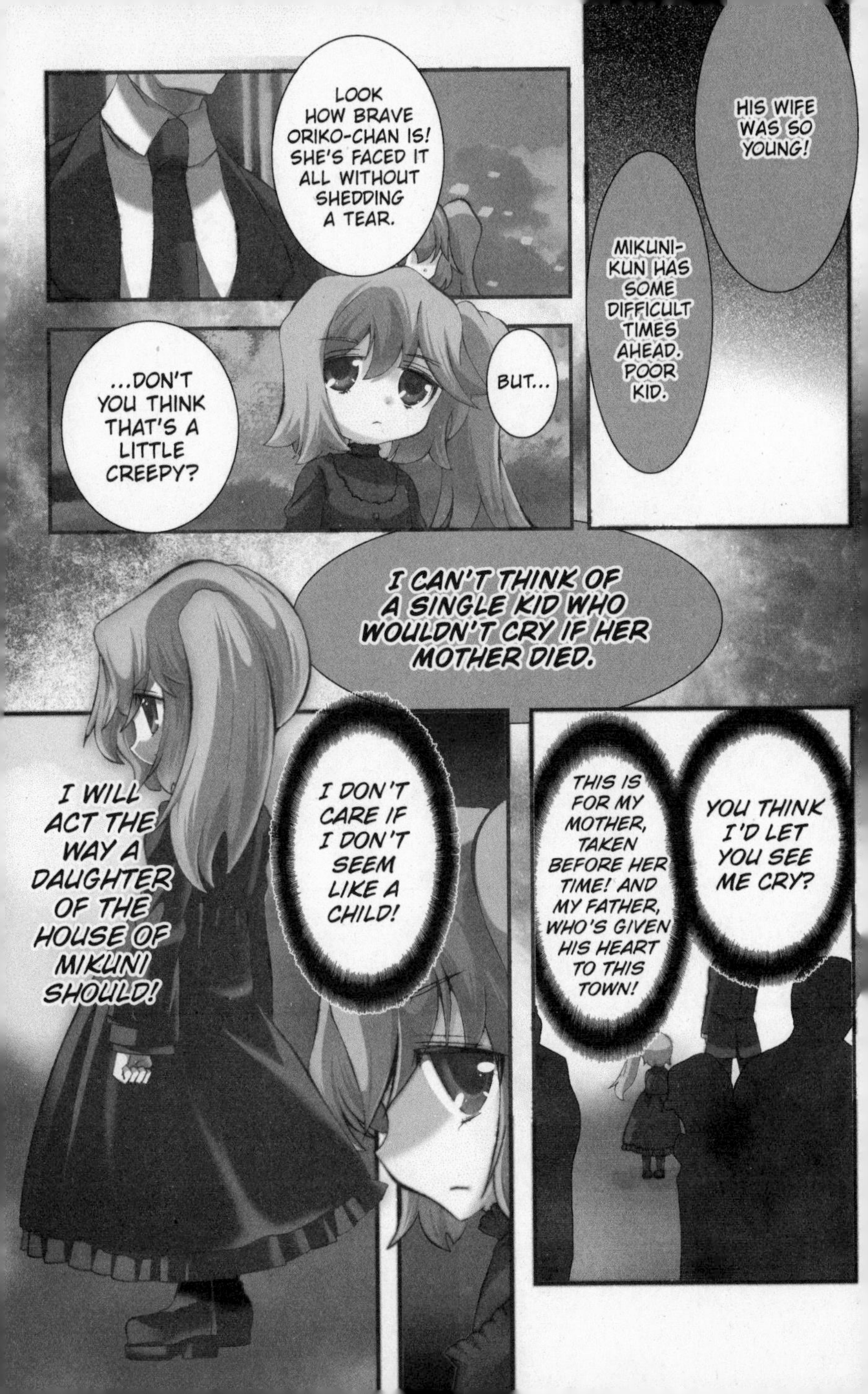
HIS WIFE WAS SO YOUNG!
MIKUNI-KUN HAS SOME DIFFICULT TIMES AHEAD. POOR KID.
LOOK HOW BRAVE ORIKO-CHAN IS! SHE'S FACED IT ALL WITHOUT SHEDDING A TEAR.
BUT...
...DON'T YOU THINK THAT'S A LITTLE CREEPY?
I CAN'T THINK OF A SINGLE KID WHO WOULDN'T CRY IF HER MOTHER DIED.
YOU THINK I'D LET YOU SEE ME CRY?
THIS IS FOR MY MOTHER, TAKEN BEFORE HER TIME! AND MY FATHER, WHO'S GIVEN HIS HEART TO THIS TOWN!
I DON'T CARE IF I DON'T SEEM LIKE A CHILD!
I WILL ACT THE WAY A DAUGHTER OF THE HOUSE OF MIKUNI SHOULD!

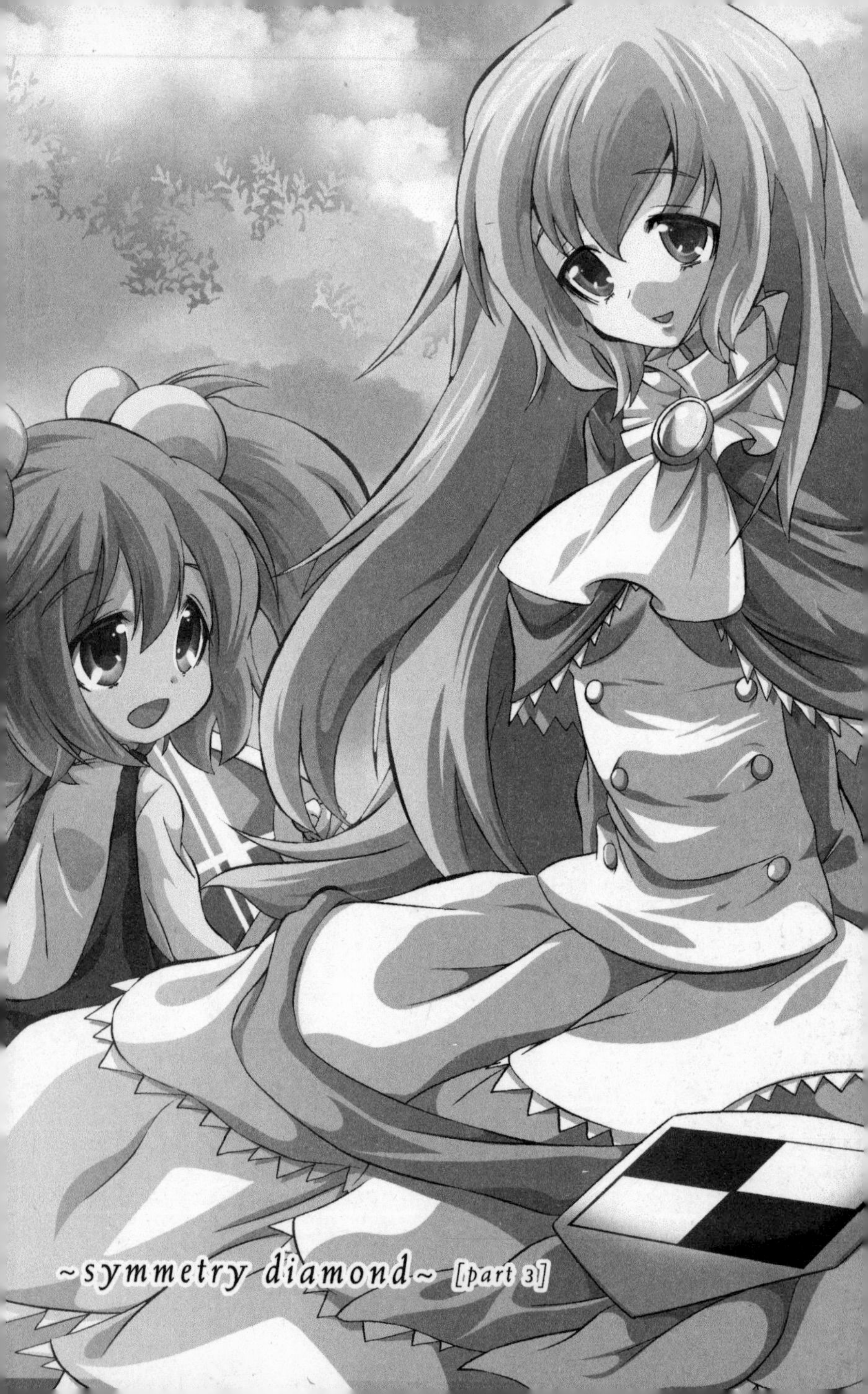
~symmetry diamond~ [part 3]

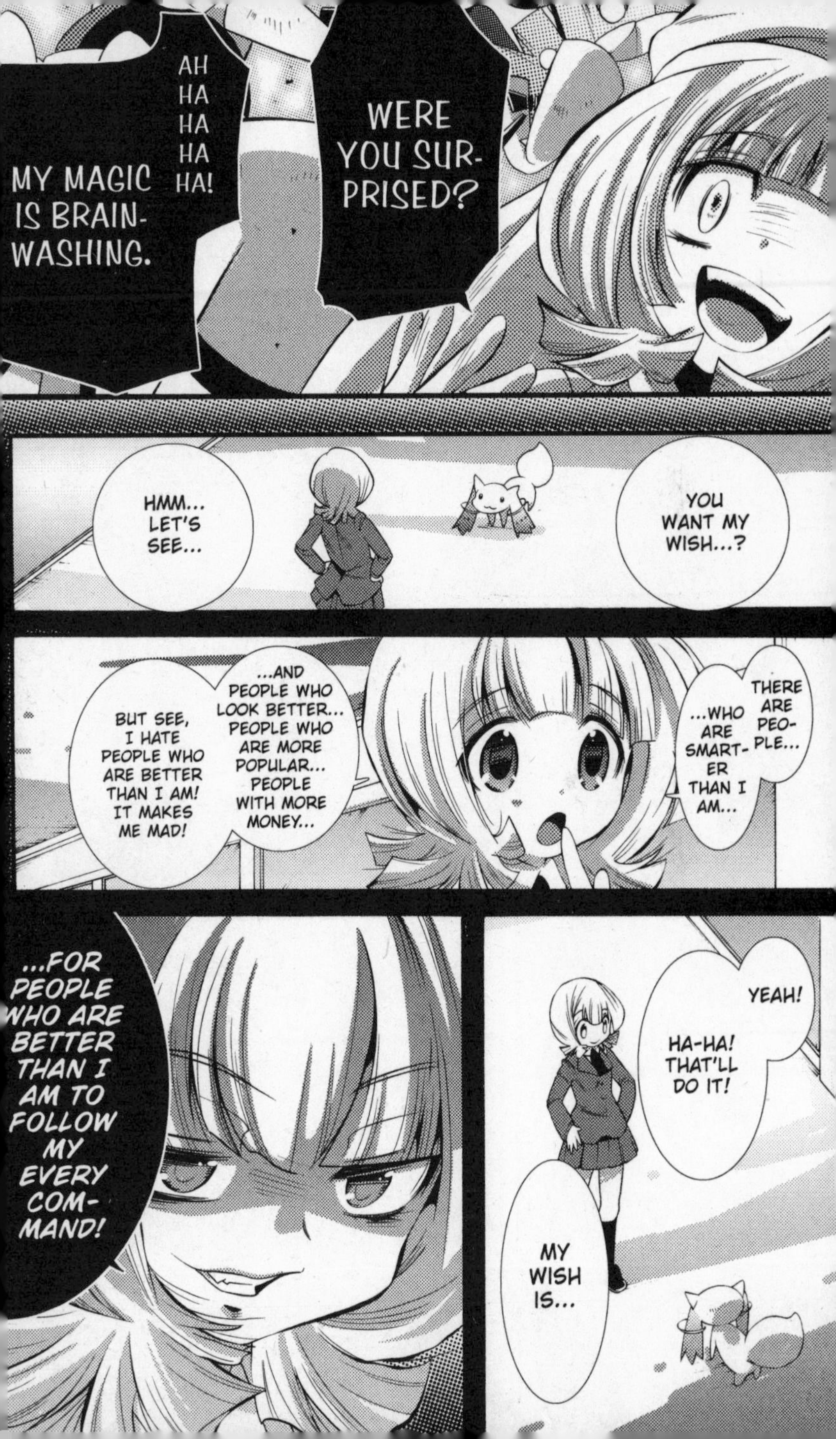
WERE YOU SURPRISED?
AH HA HA HA HA!
MY MAGIC IS BRAINWASHING.
YOU WANT MY WISH...?
HMM... LET'S SEE...
THERE ARE PEOPLE...
...WHO ARE SMARTER THAN I AM...
...AND PEOPLE WHO LOOK BETTER... PEOPLE WHO ARE MORE POPULAR... PEOPLE WITH MORE MONEY...
BUT SEE, I HATE PEOPLE WHO ARE BETTER THAN I AM! IT MAKES ME MAD!
YEAH!
HA-HA! THAT'LL DO IT!
MY WISH IS...
...FOR PEOPLE WHO ARE BETTER THAN I AM TO FOLLOW MY EVERY COMMAND!

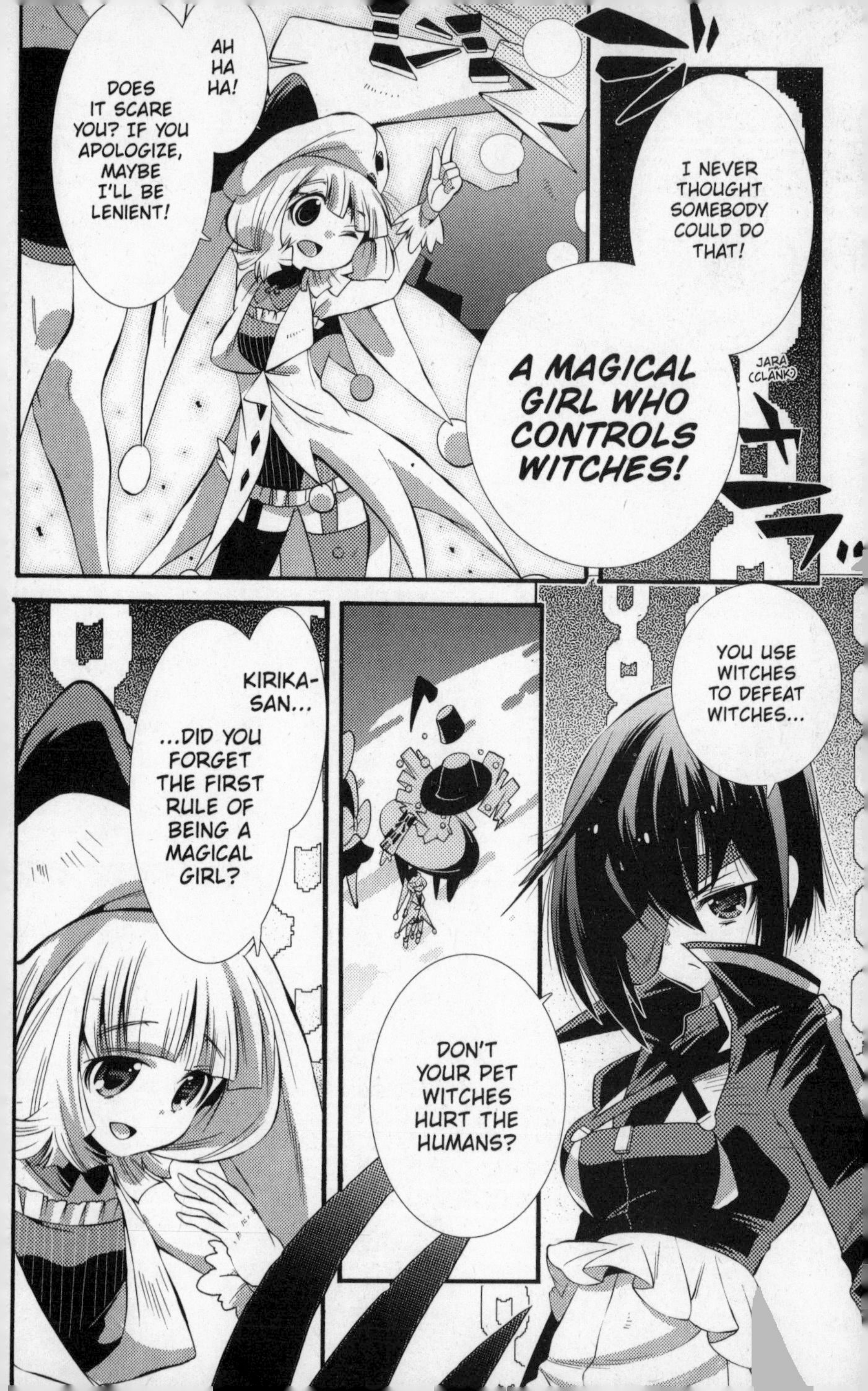
I NEVER THOUGHT SOMEBODY COULD DO THAT!
A MAGICAL GIRL WHO CONTROLS WITCHES!
JARA (CLANK)
AH HA HA!
DOES IT SCARE YOU? IF YOU APOLOGIZE, MAYBE I'LL BE LENIENT!
YOU USE WITCHES TO DEFEAT WITCHES...
DON'T YOUR PET WITCHES HURT THE HUMANS?
KIRIKA-SAN...
...DID YOU FORGET THE FIRST RULE OF BEING A MAGICAL GIRL?

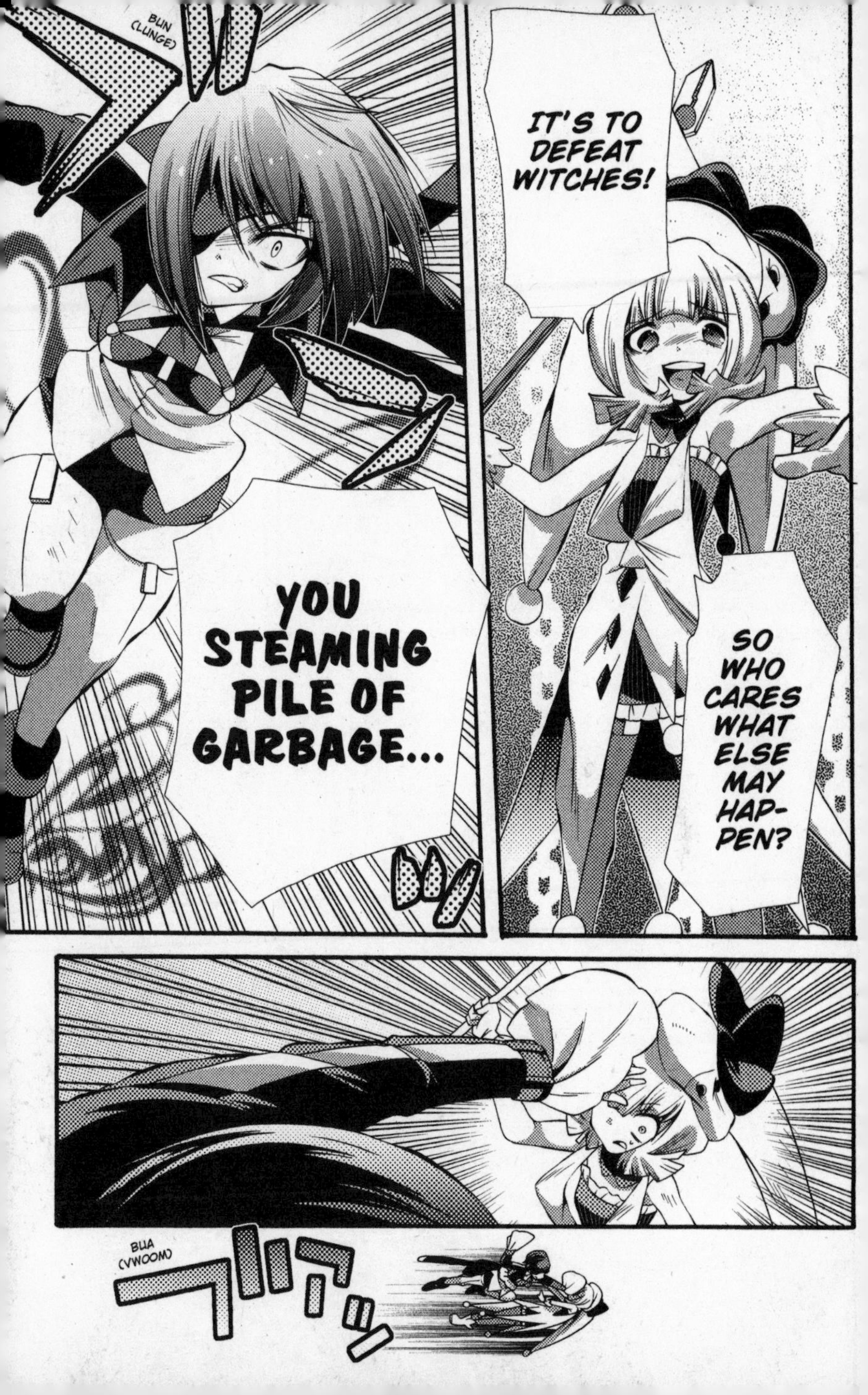
IT'S TO DEFEAT WITCHES!
SO WHO CARES WHAT ELSE MAY HAP-PEN?
BUN (LUNGE)
YOU STEAMING PILE OF GARBAGE...
BUA (VWOOM)

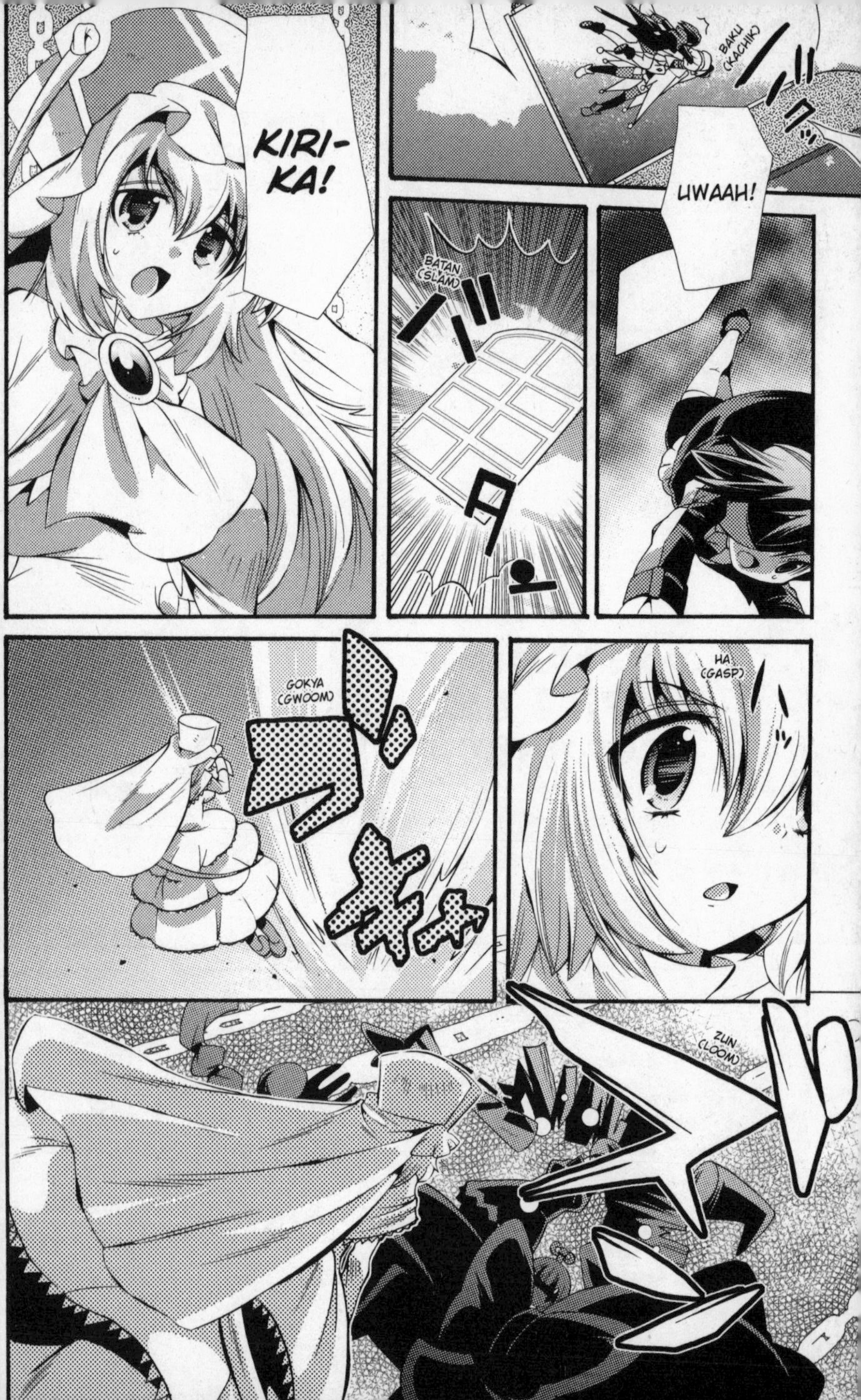
BAKU (KACHIK)
UWAAH!
BATAN (SLAM)
KIRI-KA!
HA (GASP)
GOKYA (GWOOM)
ZUN (LOOM)

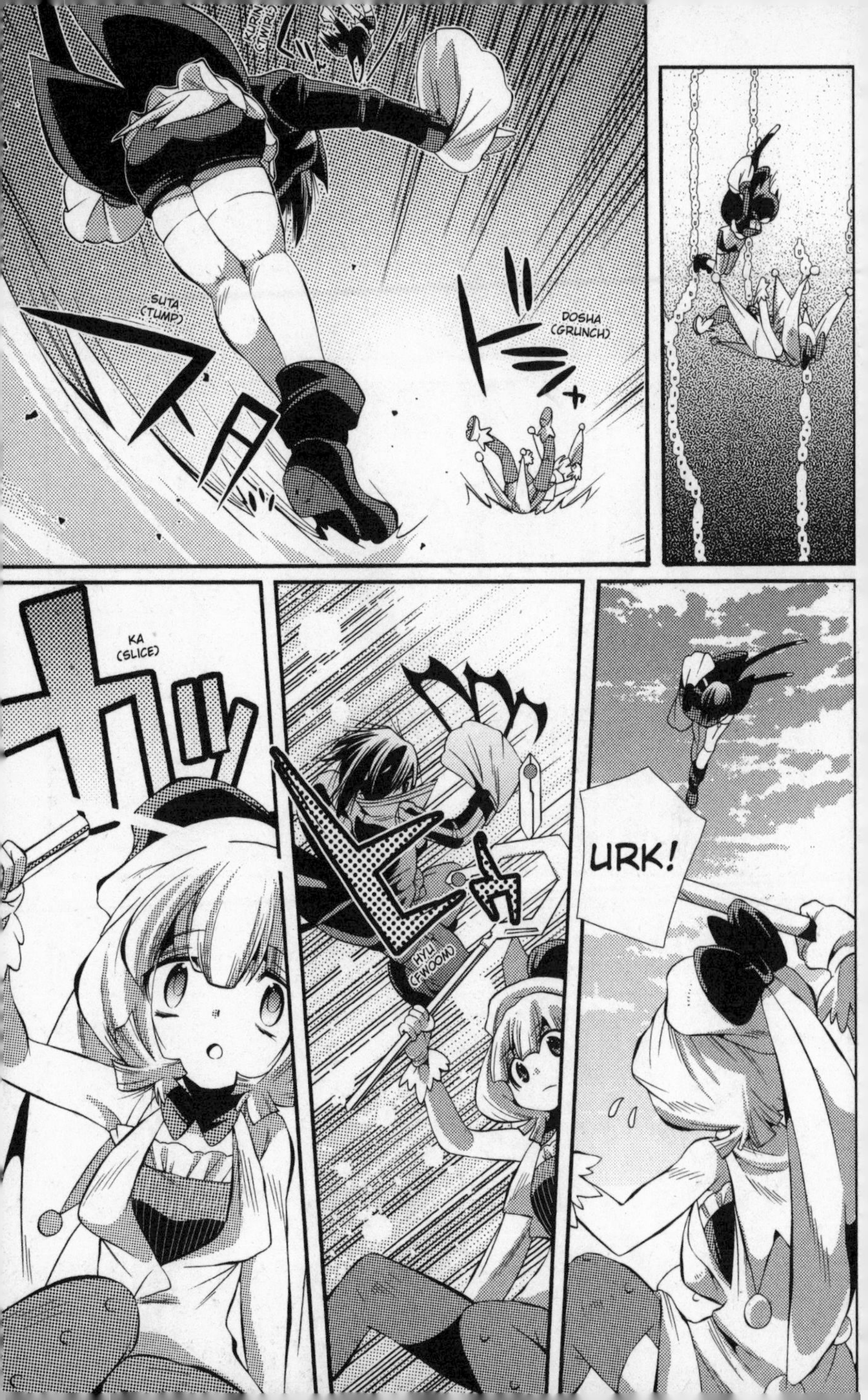
KURIN (TWIRL)
DOSHA (GRUNCH)
SUTA (TUMP)
URK!
HYU (FWOOM)
KA (SLICE)

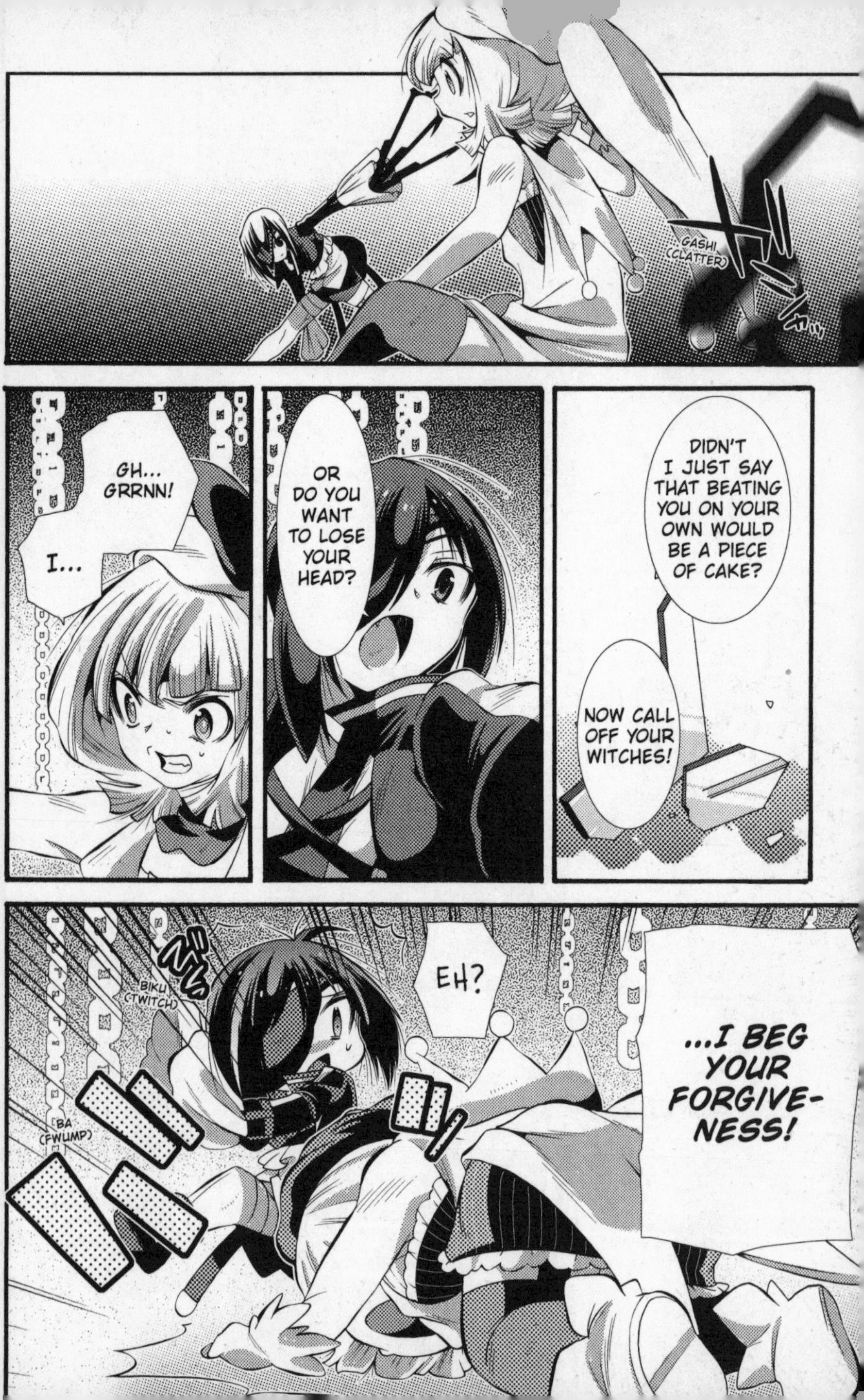
GASHI
(CLATTER)
DIDN'T I JUST SAY THAT BEATING YOU ON YOUR OWN WOULD BE A PIECE OF CAKE?
NOW CALL OFF YOUR WITCHES!
OR DO YOU WANT TO LOSE YOUR HEAD?
GH... GRRNN!
I...
...I BEG YOUR FORGIVE-NESS!
EH?
BIKU
(TWITCH)
BA
(FWUMP)

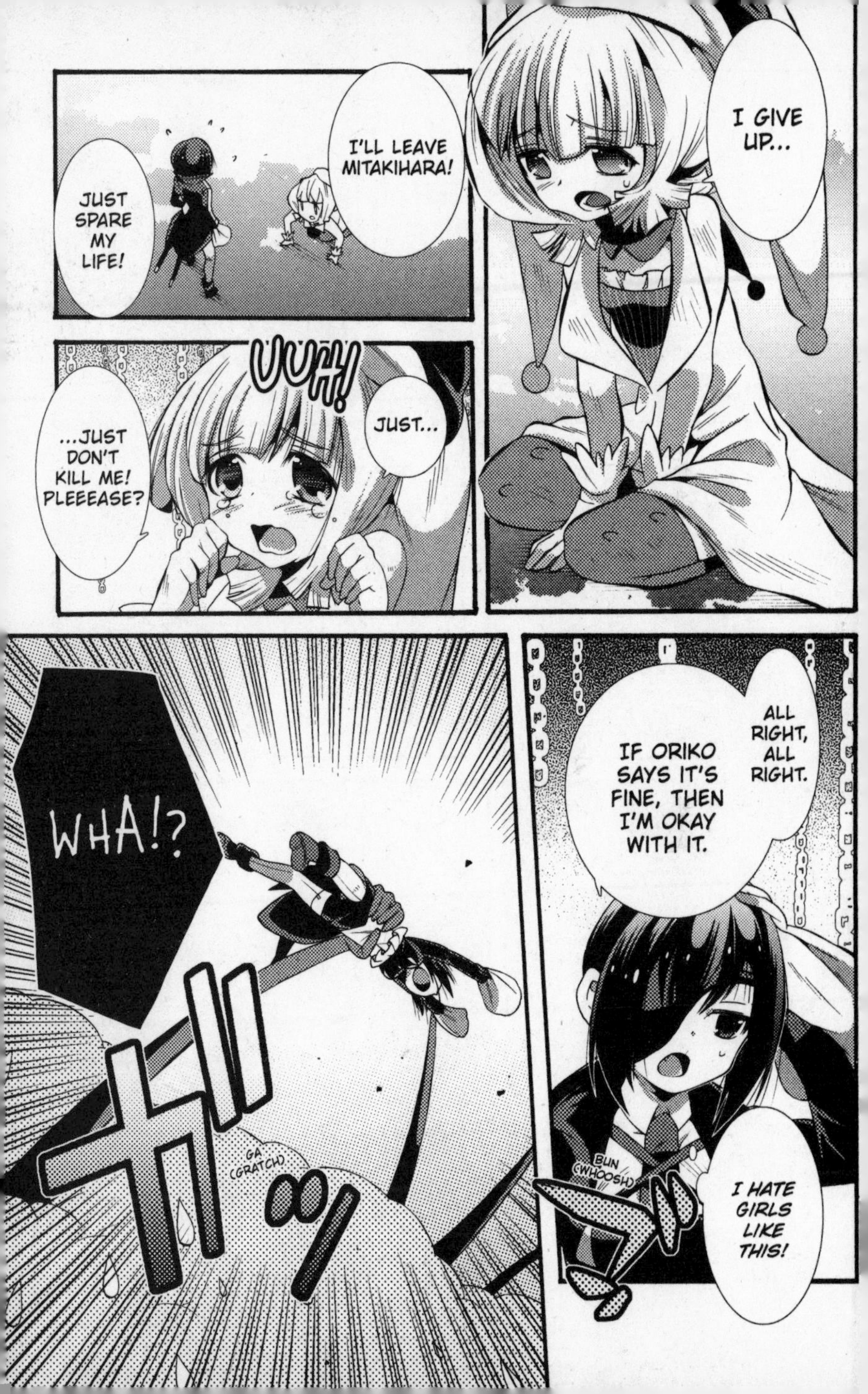
I GIVE UP...
I'LL LEAVE MITAKIHARA!
JUST SPARE MY LIFE!
UUH!
JUST...
...JUST DON'T KILL ME! PLEEEASE?
ALL RIGHT, ALL RIGHT.
IF ORIKO SAYS IT'S FINE, THEN I'M OKAY WITH IT.
BUN (WHOOSH)
I HATE GIRLS LIKE THIS!
WHA!?
GA (GRATCH)

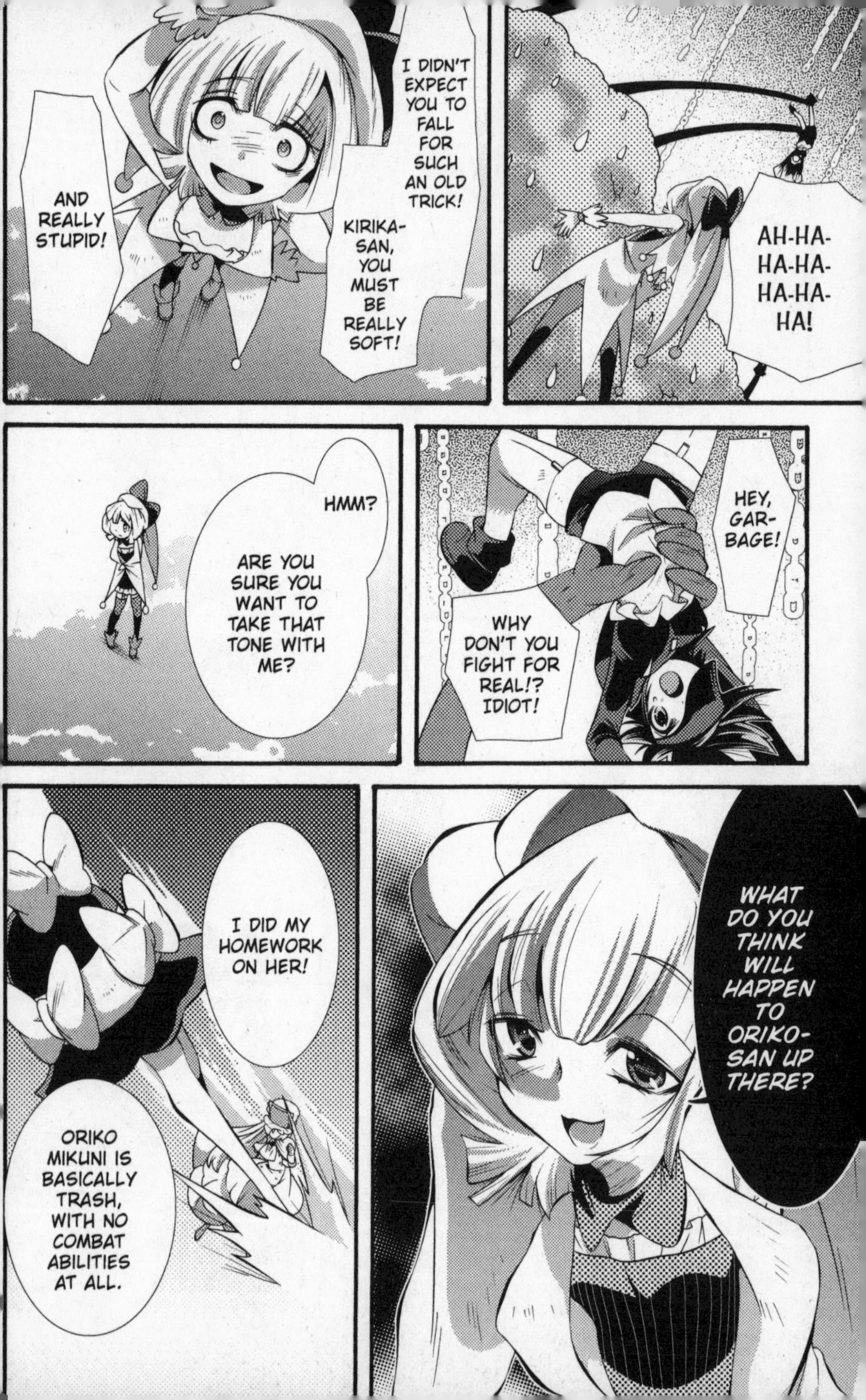
AH-HA-HA-HA-HA-HA-HA!
I DIDN'T EXPECT YOU TO FALL FOR SUCH AN OLD TRICK!
KIRIKA-SAN, YOU MUST BE REALLY SOFT!
AND REALLY STUPID!
HEY, GARBAGE!
WHY DON'T YOU FIGHT FOR REAL!? IDIOT!
HMM?
ARE YOU SURE YOU WANT TO TAKE THAT TONE WITH ME?
WHAT DO YOU THINK WILL HAPPEN TO ORIKO-SAN UP THERE?
I DID MY HOMEWORK ON HER!
ORIKO MIKUNI IS BASICALLY TRASH, WITH NO COMBAT ABILITIES AT ALL.

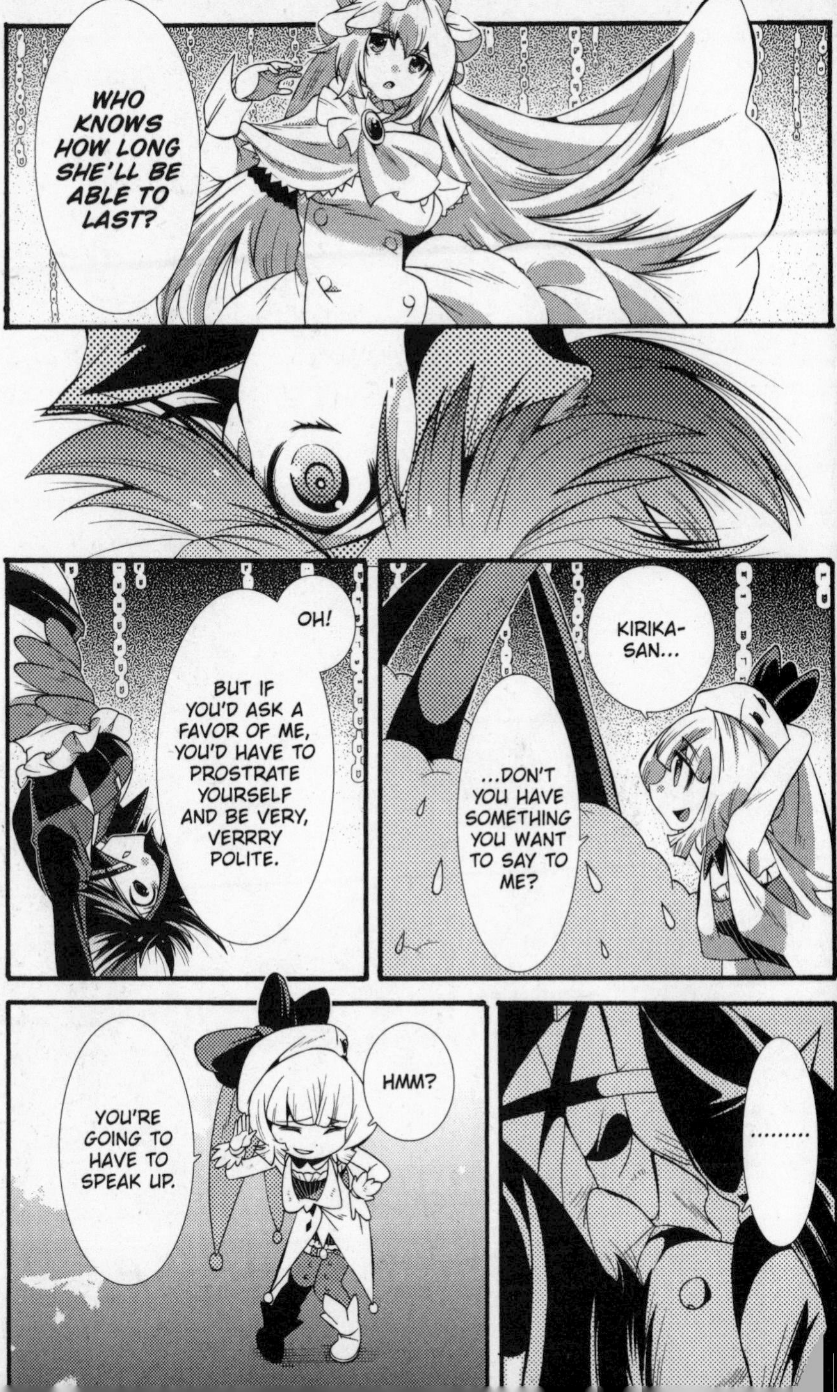
WHO KNOWS HOW LONG SHE'LL BE ABLE TO LAST?
KIRIKA-SAN...
...DON'T YOU HAVE SOMETHING YOU WANT TO SAY TO ME?
OH!
BUT IF YOU'D ASK A FAVOR OF ME, YOU'D HAVE TO PROSTRATE YOURSELF AND BE VERY, VERRRY POLITE.
....
HMM?
YOU'RE GOING TO HAVE TO SPEAK UP.

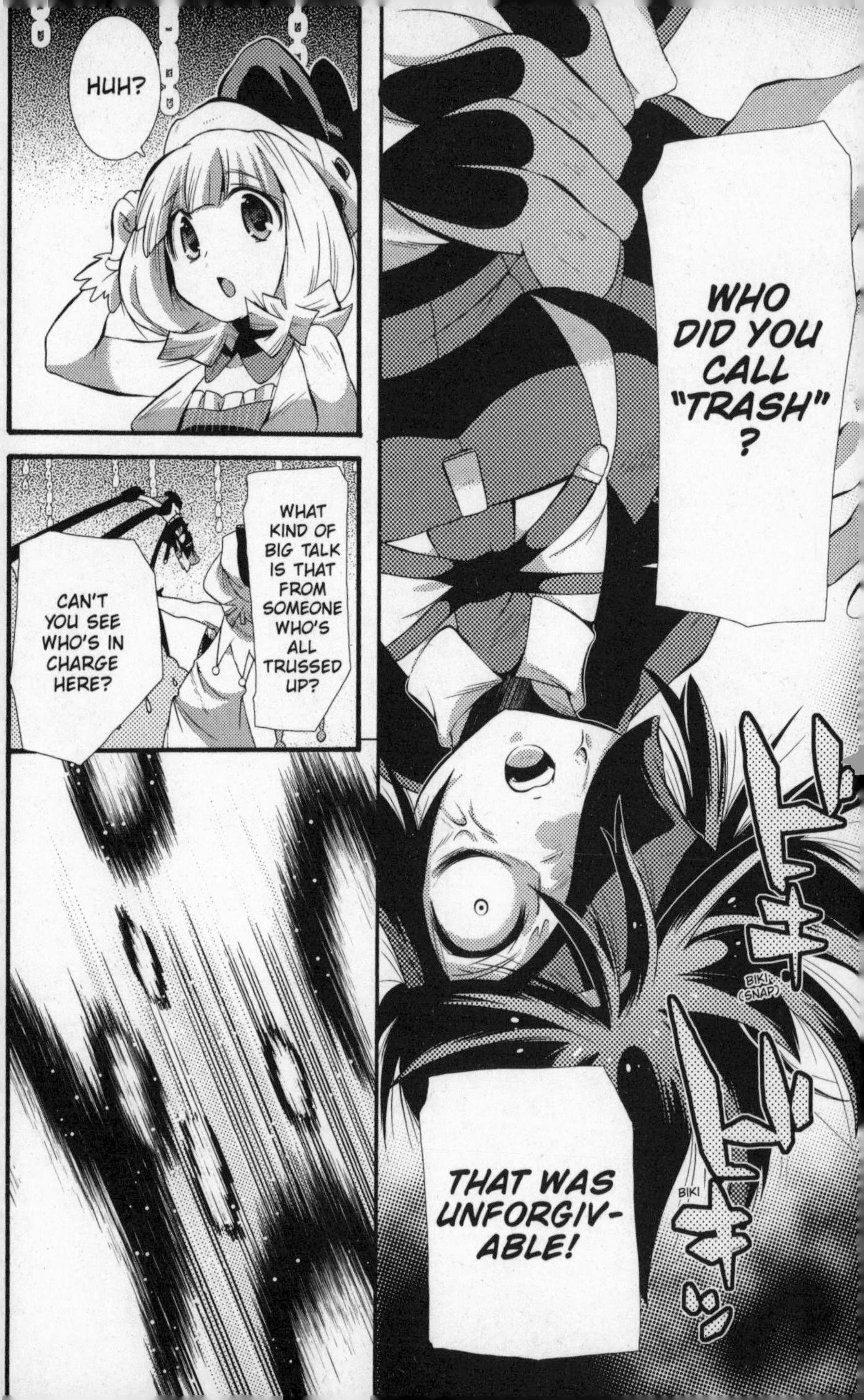
WHO DID YOU CALL "TRASH"?
BIKI (SNAP)
BIKI
THAT WAS UNFORGIV-ABLE!
HUH?
WHAT KIND OF BIG TALK IS THAT FROM SOMEONE WHO'S ALL TRUSSED UP?
CAN'T YOU SEE WHO'S IN CHARGE HERE?

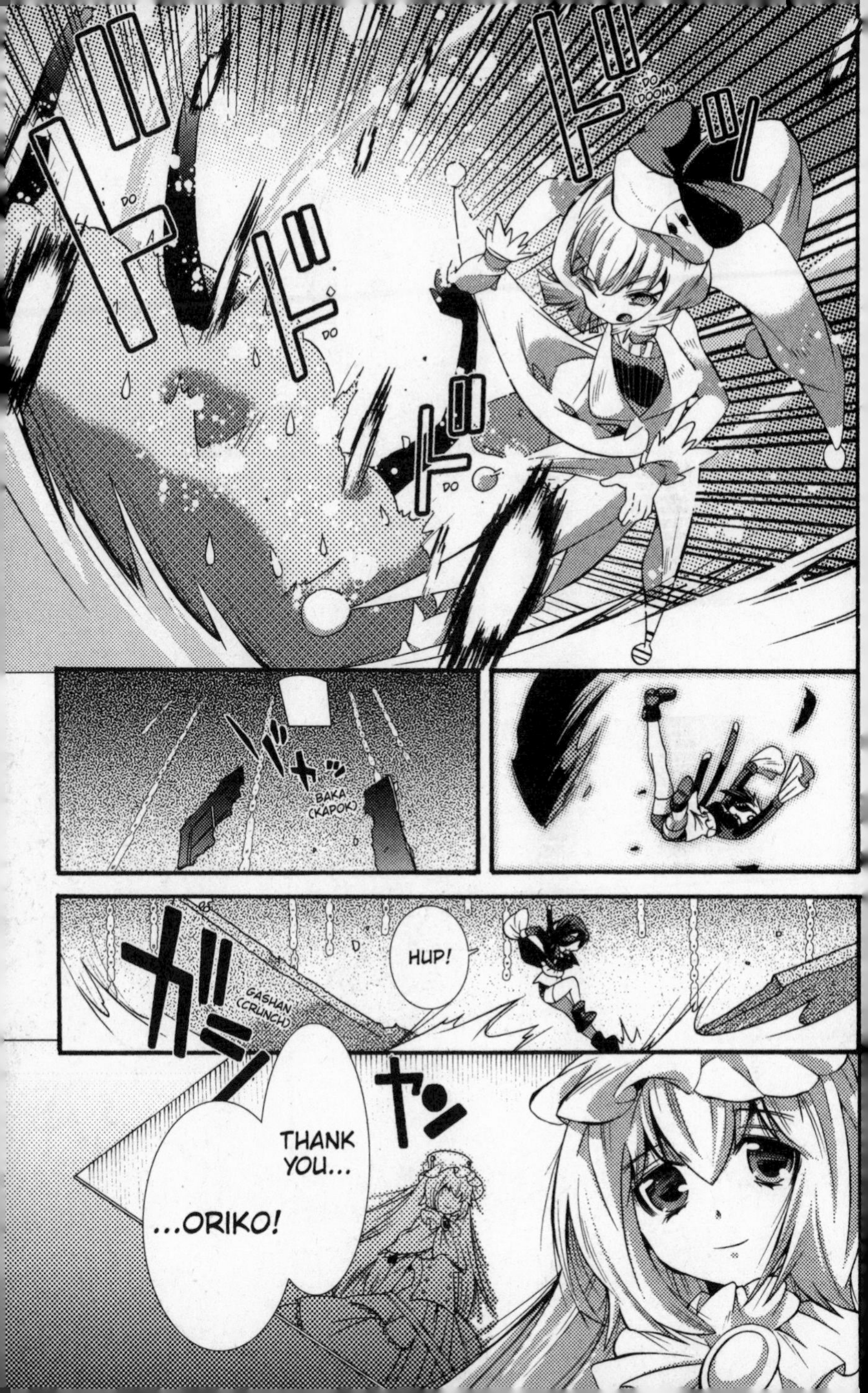
DO (DOOM)
DO
DO
DO
BAKA (KAPOK)
HUP!
GASHAN (CRUNCH)
THANK YOU...
...ORIKO!

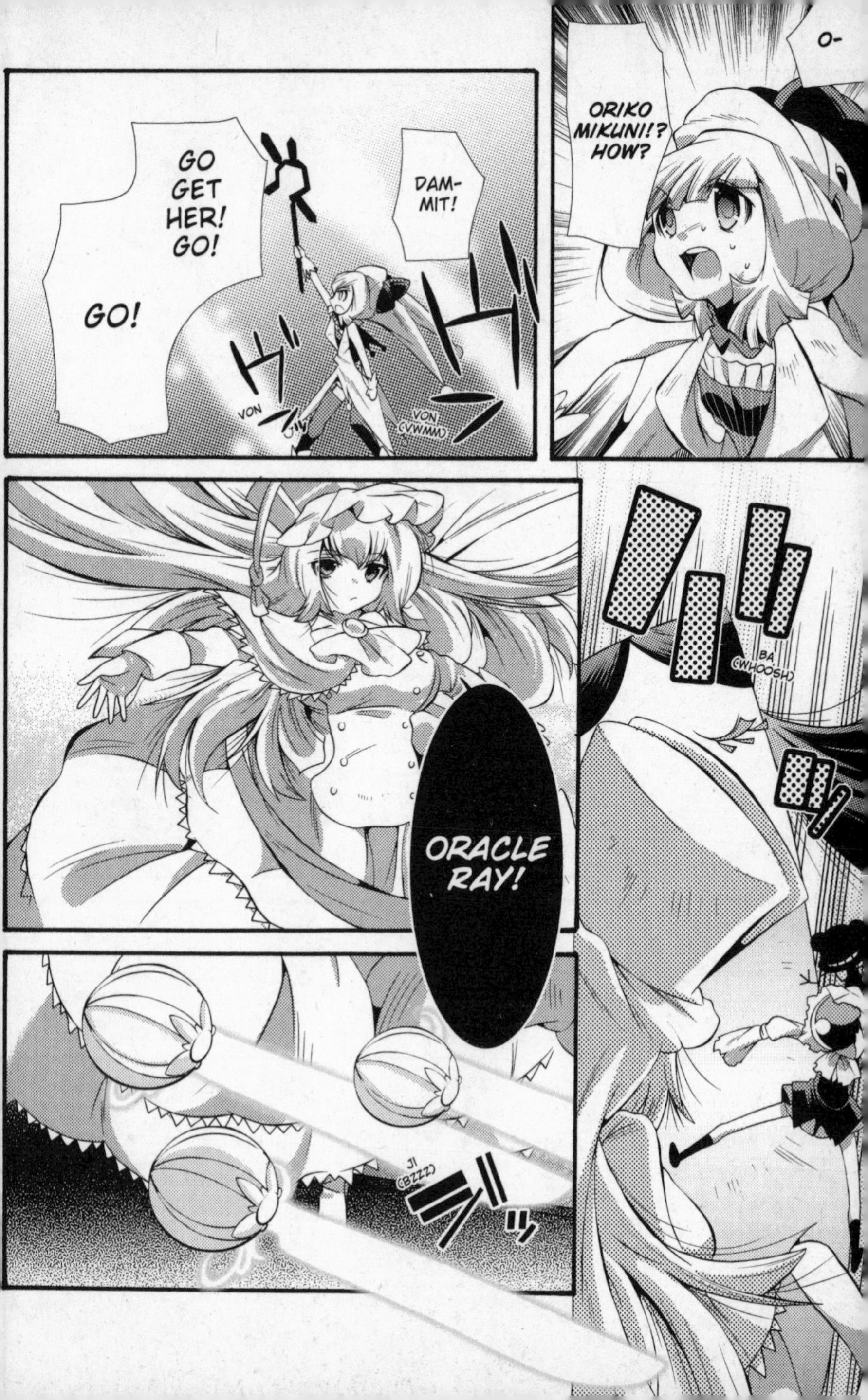
O-
ORIKO MIKUNI!? HOW?
DAM-MIT!
GO GET HER! GO!
GO!
VON
VON (VWMM)
BA (WHOOSH)
ORACLE RAY!
JI (BZZZ)

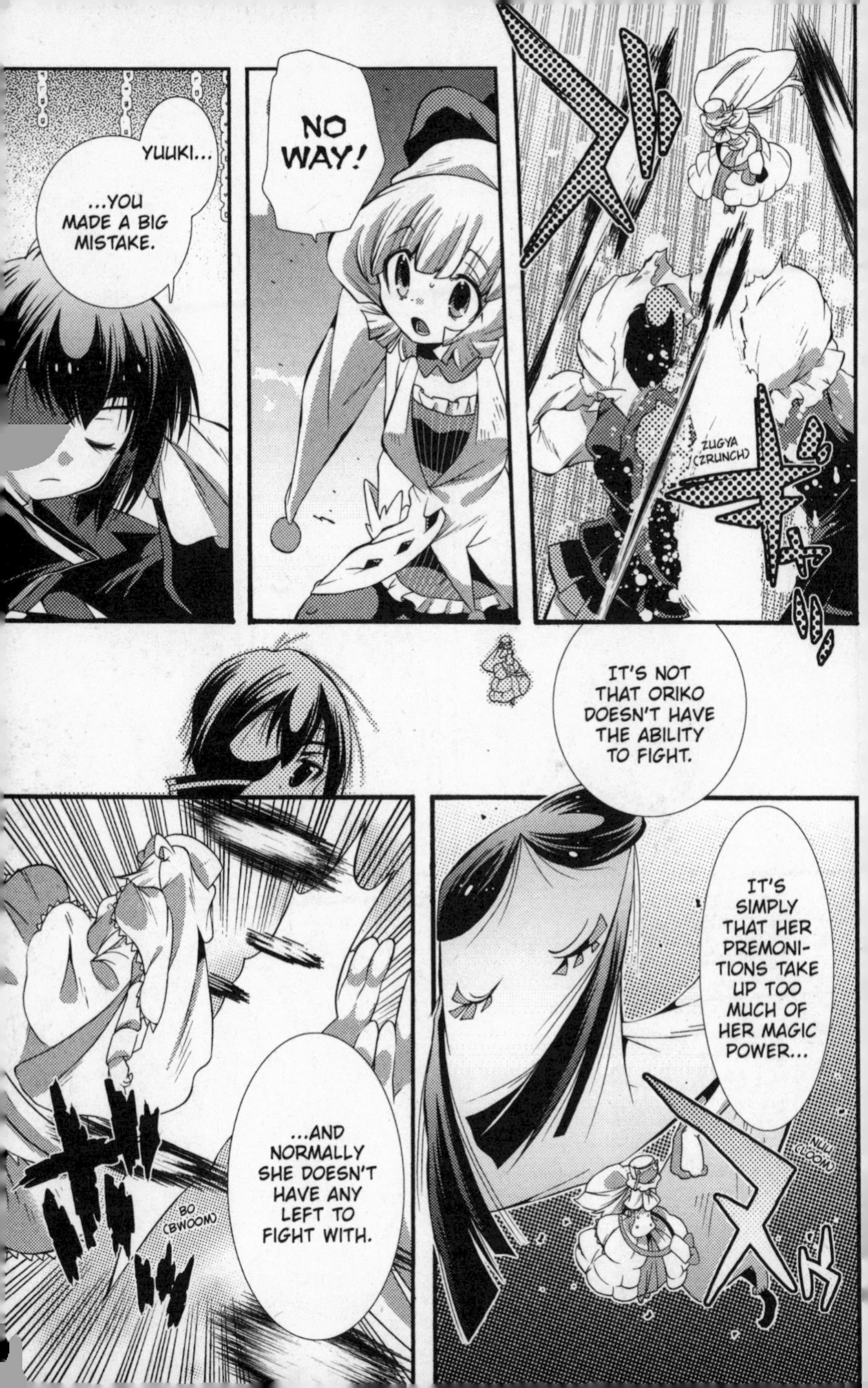
ZUGYA (ZRUNCH)
NO WAY!
YUUKI...
...YOU MADE A BIG MISTAKE.
IT'S NOT THAT ORIKO DOESN'T HAVE THE ABILITY TO FIGHT.
IT'S SIMPLY THAT HER PREMONITIONS TAKE UP TOO MUCH OF HER MAGIC POWER...
NUU (LOOM)
...AND NORMALLY SHE DOESN'T HAVE ANY LEFT TO FIGHT WITH.
BO (BWOOM)

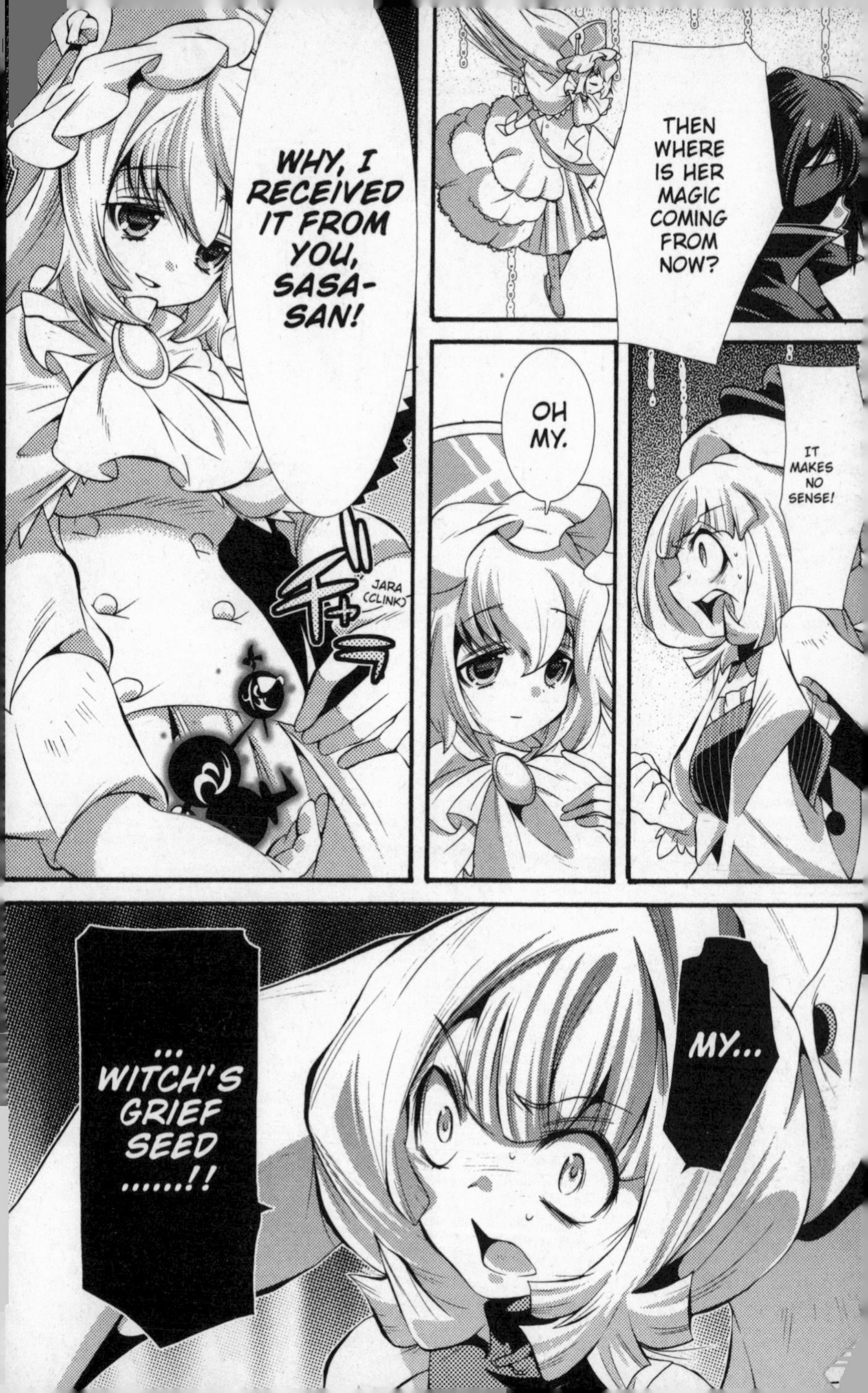
THEN WHERE IS HER MAGIC COMING FROM NOW?
IT MAKES NO SENSE!
OH MY.
WHY, I RECEIVED IT FROM YOU, SASA-SAN!
JARA (CLINK)
MY...
...WITCH'S GRIEF SEED......!!

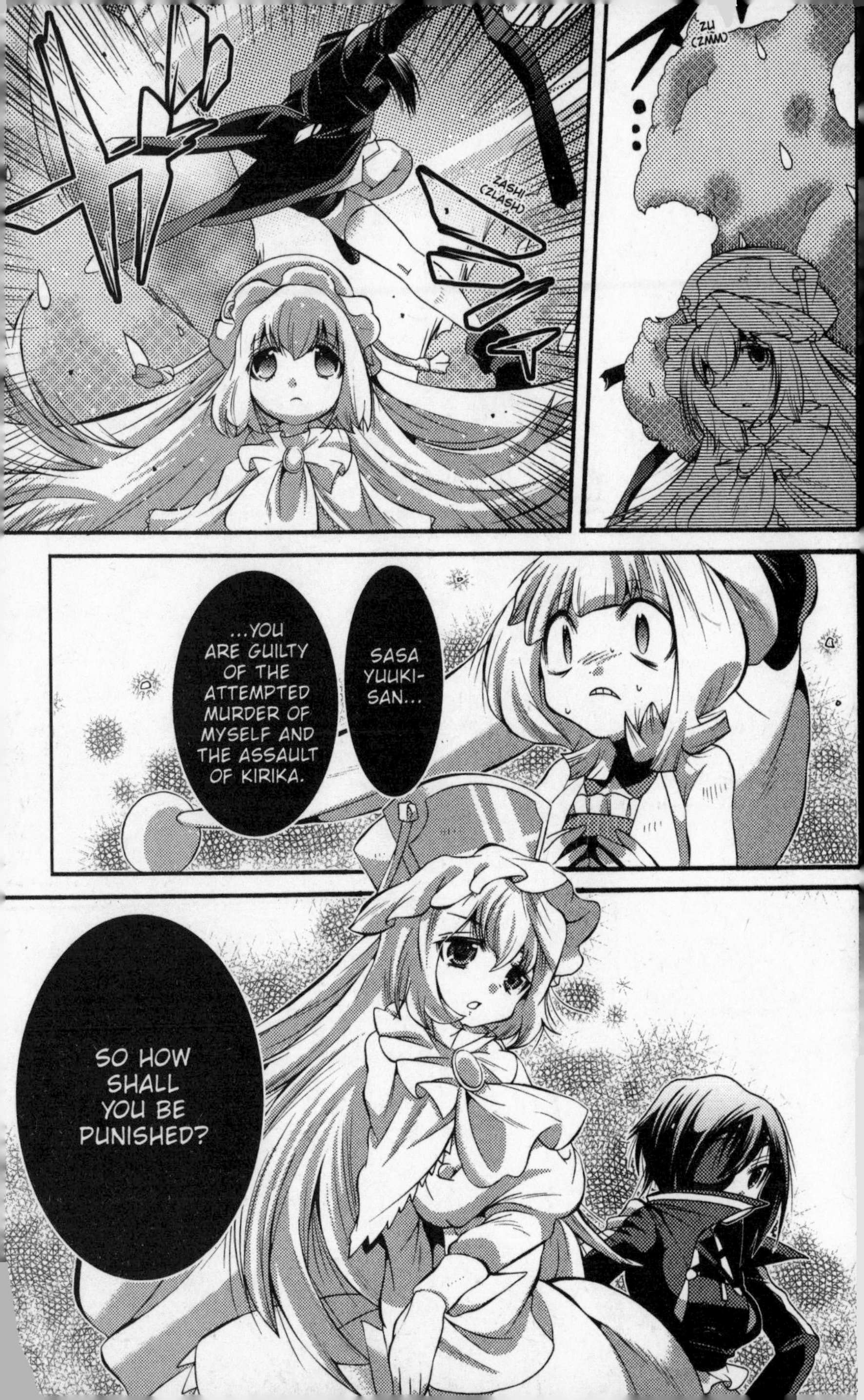
ZU (ZMM)
ZASHI (ZLASH)
SASA YUUKI-SAN...
...YOU ARE GUILTY OF THE ATTEMPTED MURDER OF MYSELF AND THE ASSAULT OF KIRIKA.
SO HOW SHALL YOU BE PUNISHED?

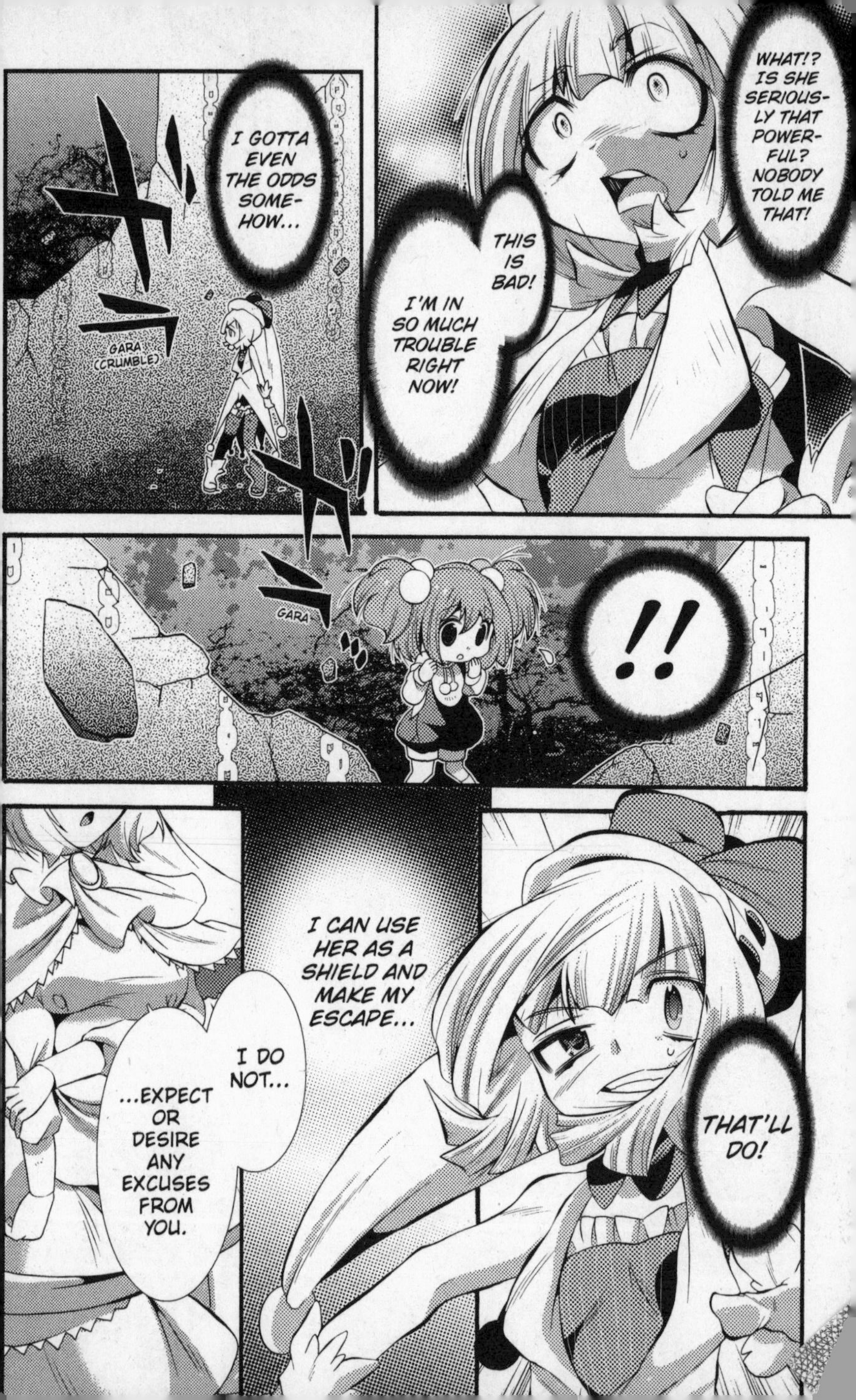
WHAT!? IS SHE SERIOUSLY THAT POWERFUL? NOBODY TOLD ME THAT!
THIS IS BAD!
I'M IN SO MUCH TROUBLE RIGHT NOW!
I GOTTA EVEN THE ODDS SOMEHOW...
GARA (CRUMBLE)
!!
GARA
THAT'LL DO!
I CAN USE HER AS A SHIELD AND MAKE MY ESCAPE...
I DO NOT...
...EXPECT OR DESIRE ANY EXCUSES FROM YOU.

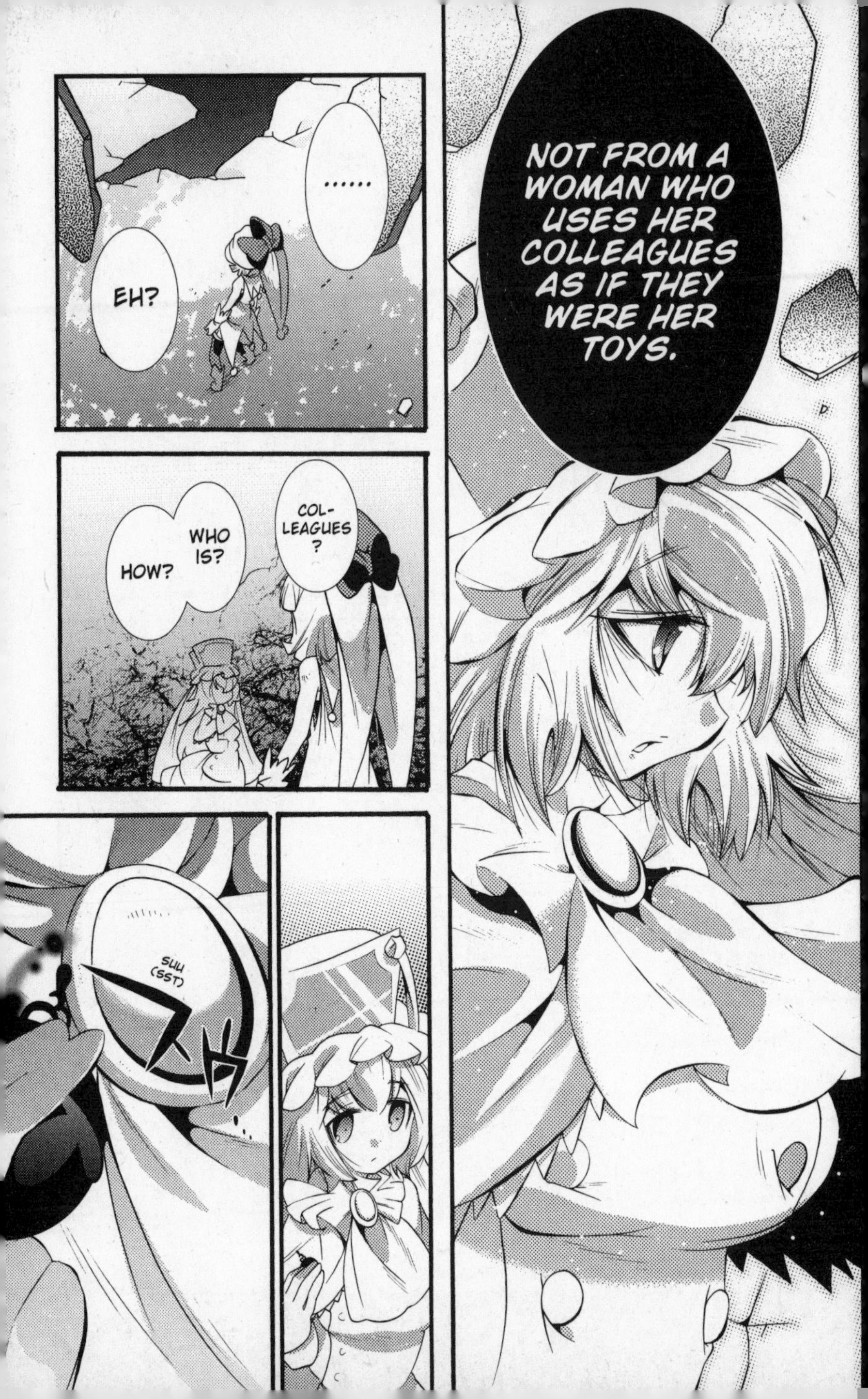
NOT FROM A WOMAN WHO USES HER COLLEAGUES AS IF THEY WERE HER TOYS.
......
EH?
COL-LEAGUES?
WHO IS?
HOW?
SUU (SST)

!!!!!

......

YOU'RE KIDDING ME, RIGHT?

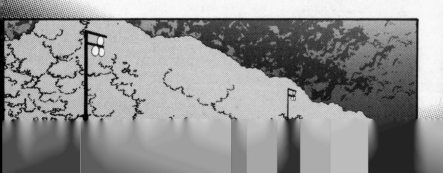

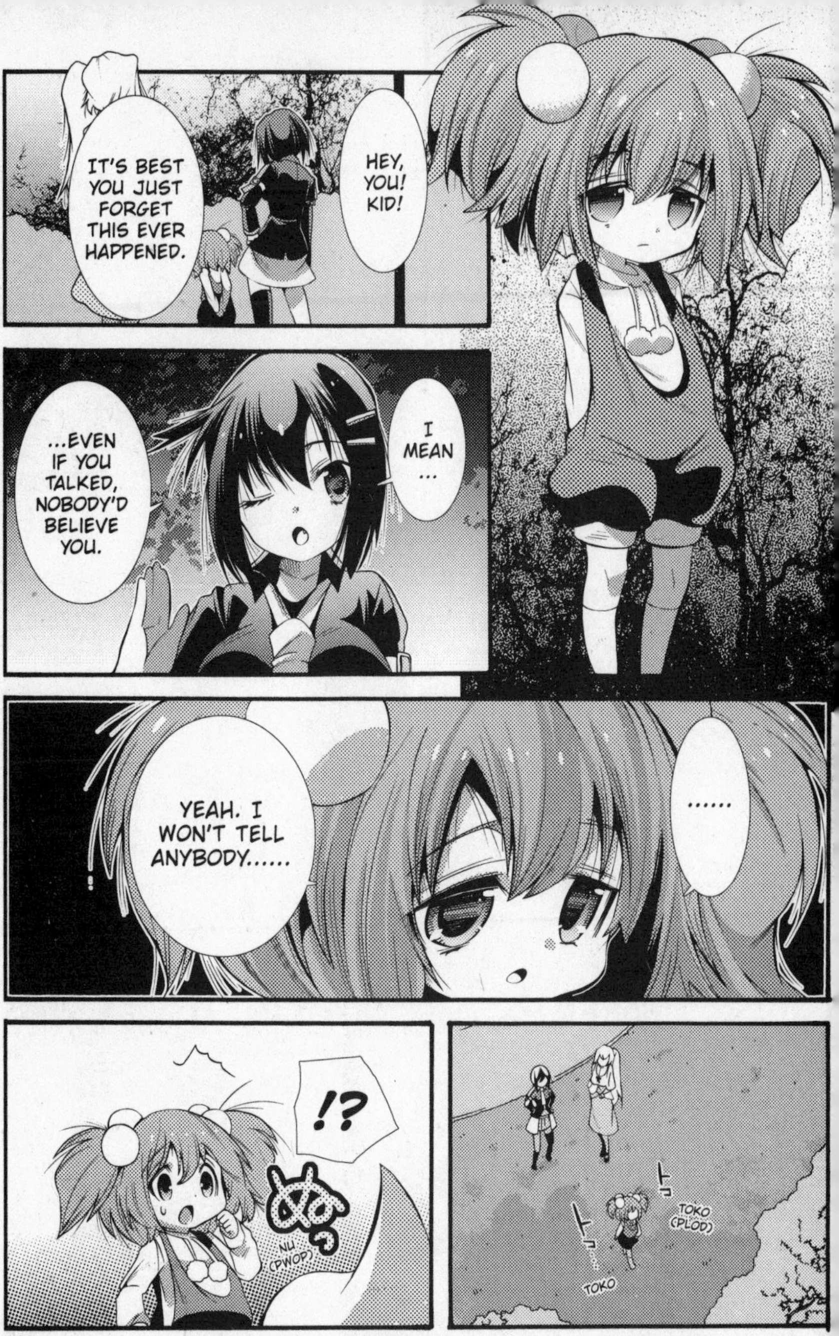
HEY, YOU! KID!
IT'S BEST YOU JUST FORGET THIS EVER HAPPENED.
I MEAN ...
...EVEN IF YOU TALKED, NOBODY'D BELIEVE YOU.
......
YEAH. I WON'T TELL ANYBODY......
TOKO (PLOD)
TOKO
!?
NU (PWOP)

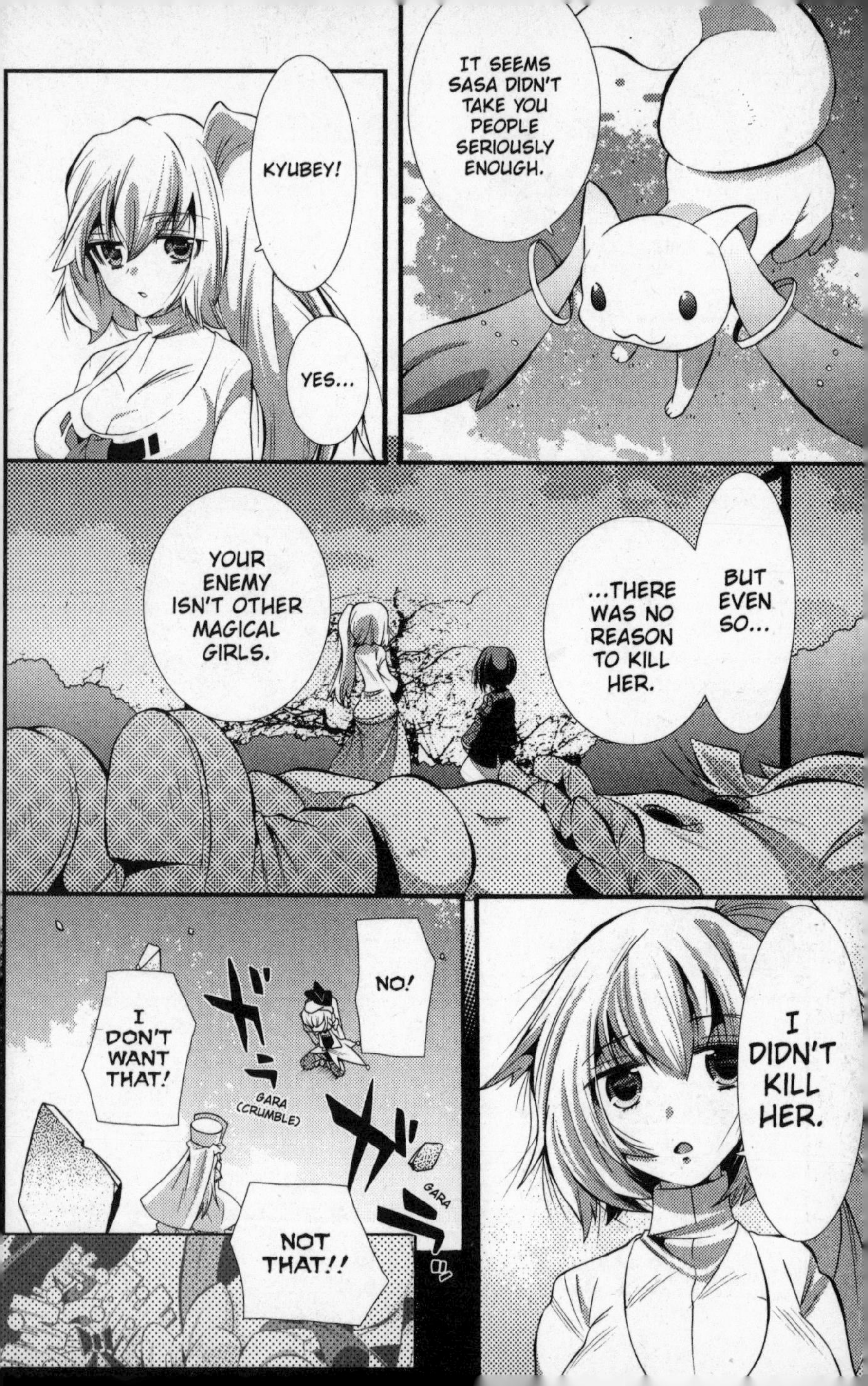
IT SEEMS SASA DIDN'T TAKE YOU PEOPLE SERIOUSLY ENOUGH.
KYUBEY!
YES...
BUT EVEN SO...
...THERE WAS NO REASON TO KILL HER.
YOUR ENEMY ISN'T OTHER MAGICAL GIRLS.
I DIDN'T KILL HER.
NO!
I DON'T WANT THAT!
GARA (CRUMBLE)
GARA
NOT THAT!!

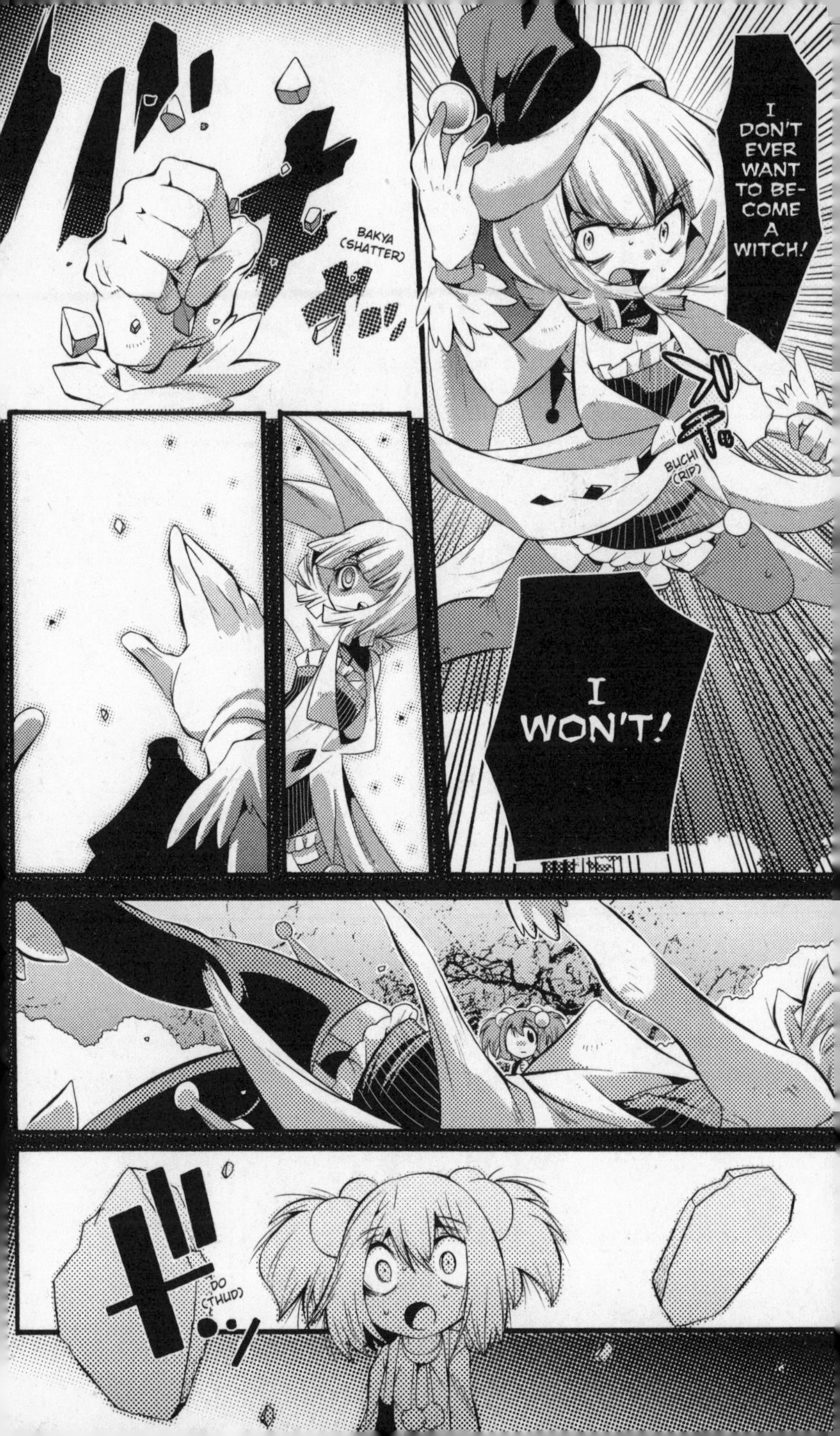

I DON'T EVER WANT TO BE-COME A WITCH!
BAKYA (SHATTER)
BUCHI (RIP)
I WON'T!
DO (THUD)

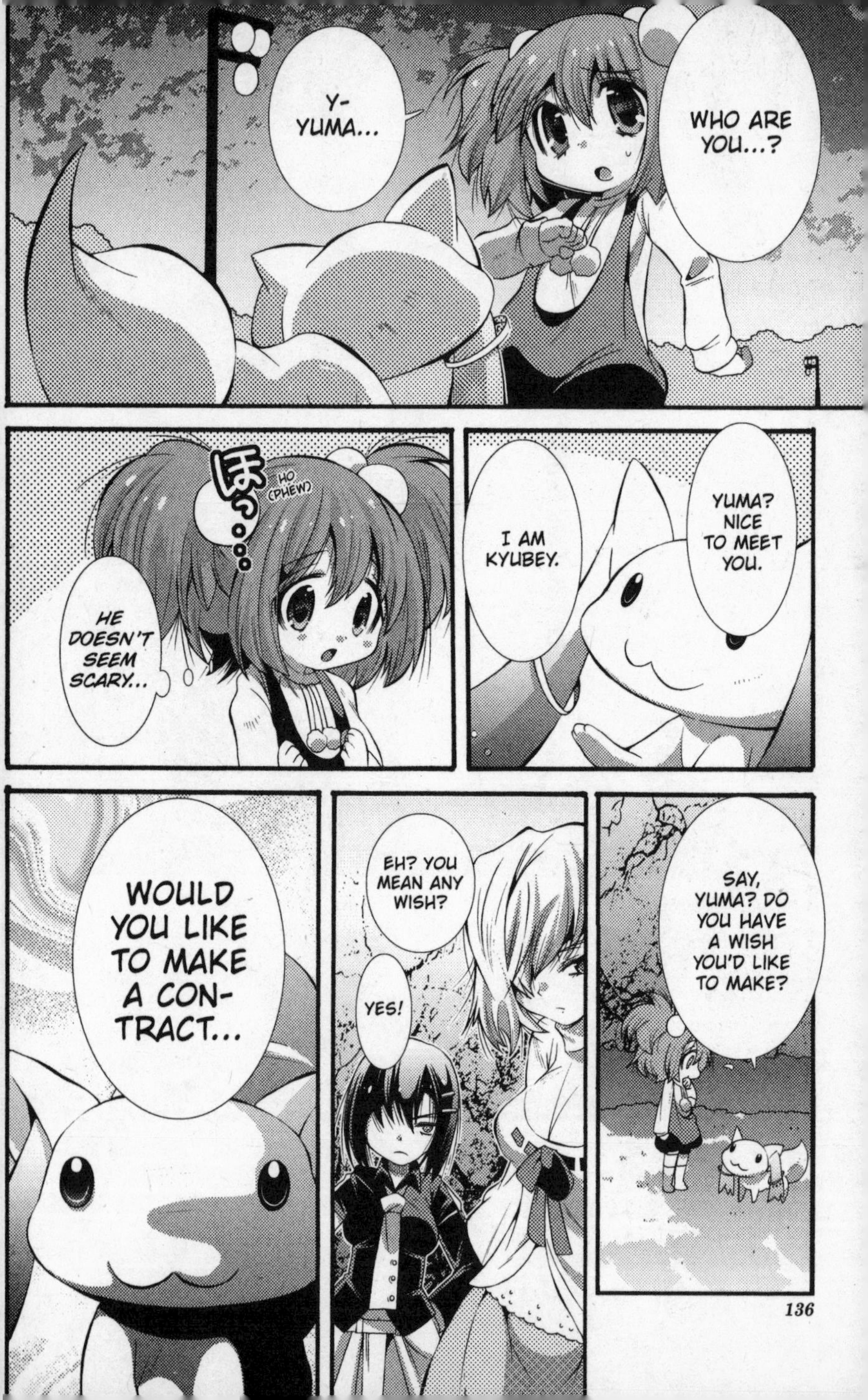
WHO ARE YOU...?
Y-YUMA...
YUMA? NICE TO MEET YOU.
I AM KYUBEY.
ほっ。。。
HO (PHEW)
HE DOESN'T SEEM SCARY...
SAY, YUMA? DO YOU HAVE A WISH YOU'D LIKE TO MAKE?
EH? YOU MEAN ANY WISH?
YES!
WOULD YOU LIKE TO MAKE A CONTRACT...

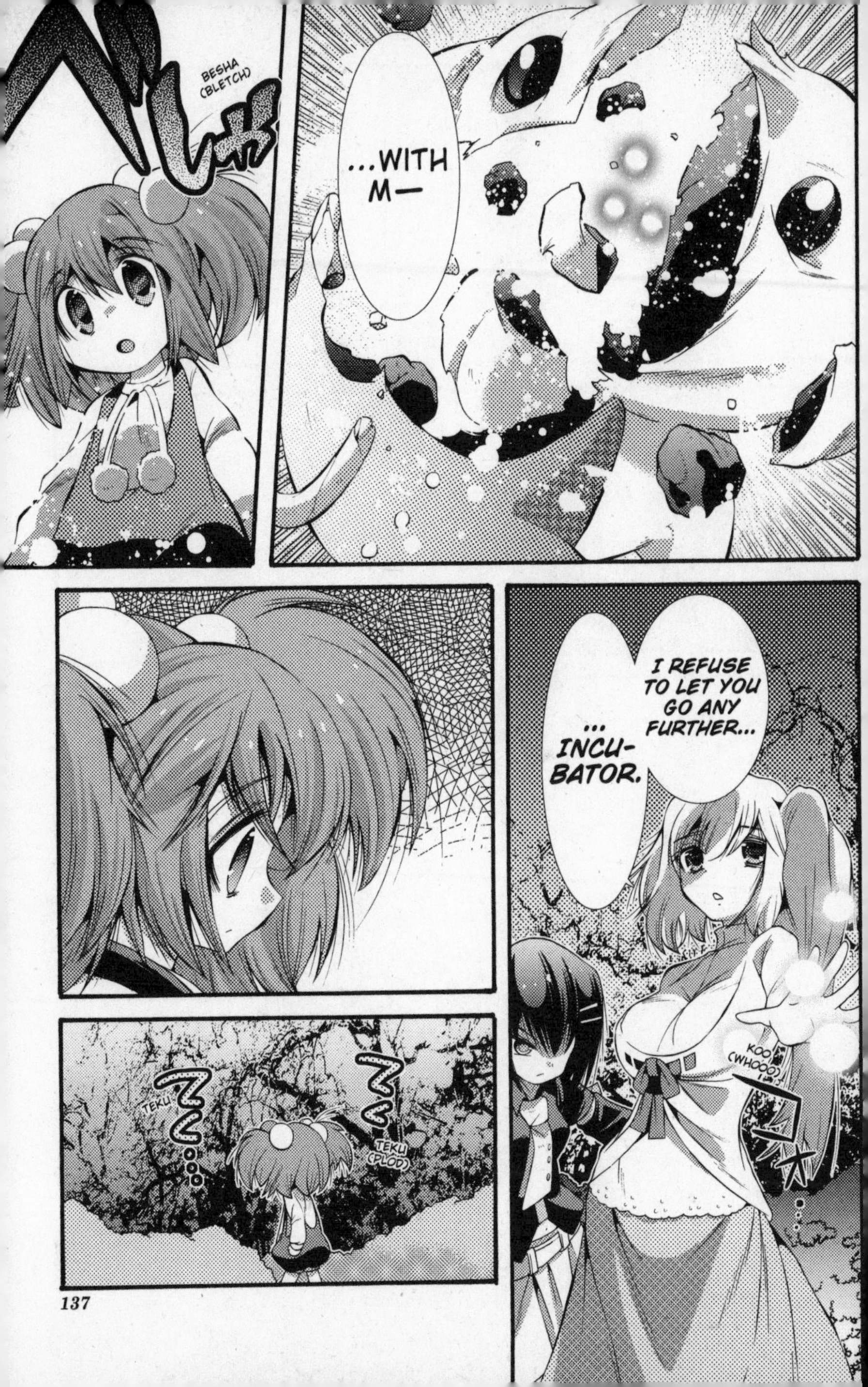
...WITH M—
BESHA (BLETCH)
I REFUSE TO LET YOU GO ANY FURTHER...
... INCUBATOR.
KOO (WHOOO)
TEKU
TEKU (PLOD)

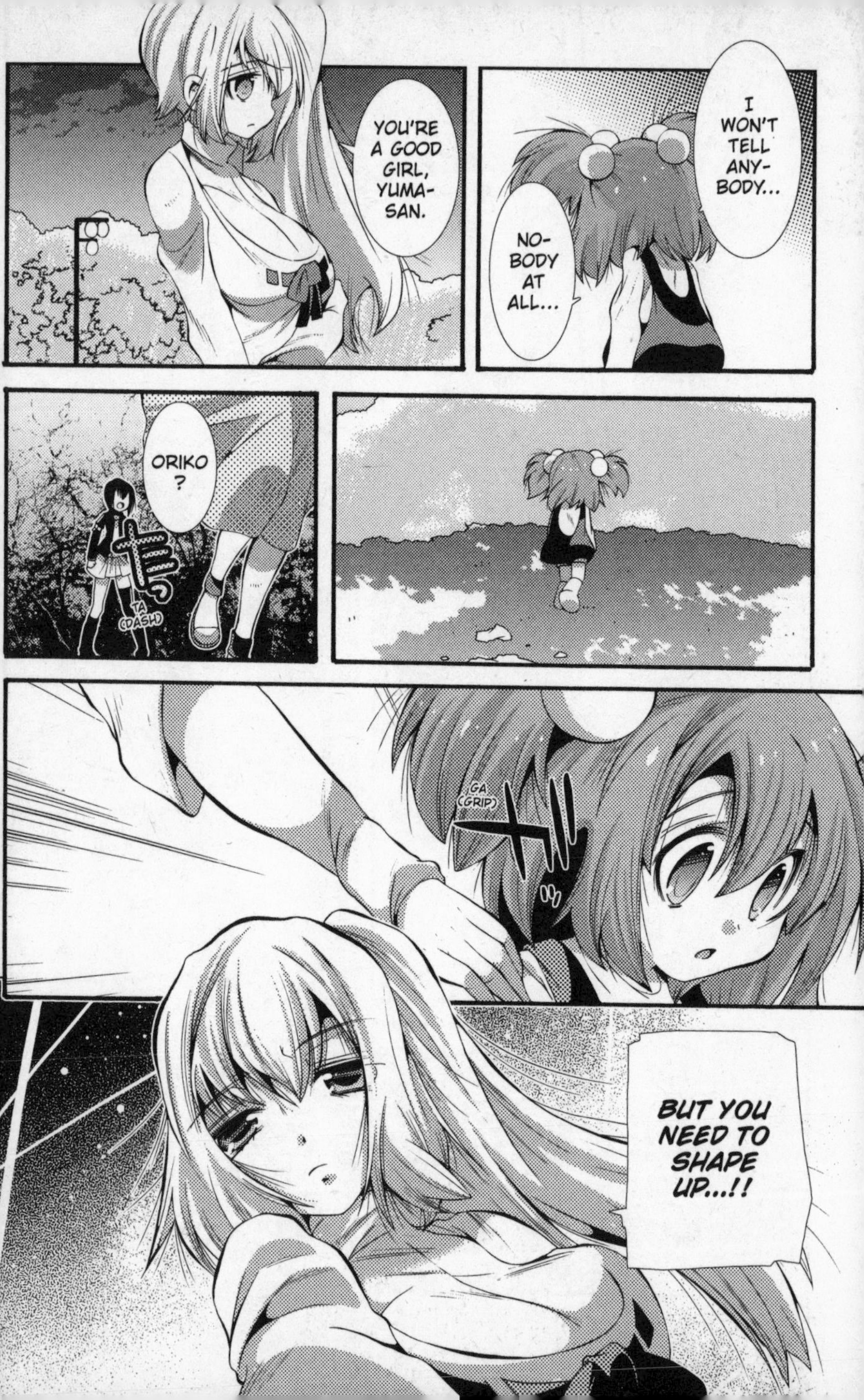
I WON'T TELL ANY-BODY...
NO-BODY AT ALL...
YOU'RE A GOOD GIRL, YUMA-SAN.
ORIKO ?
TA (DASH)
GA (GRIP)
BUT YOU NEED TO SHAPE UP...!!

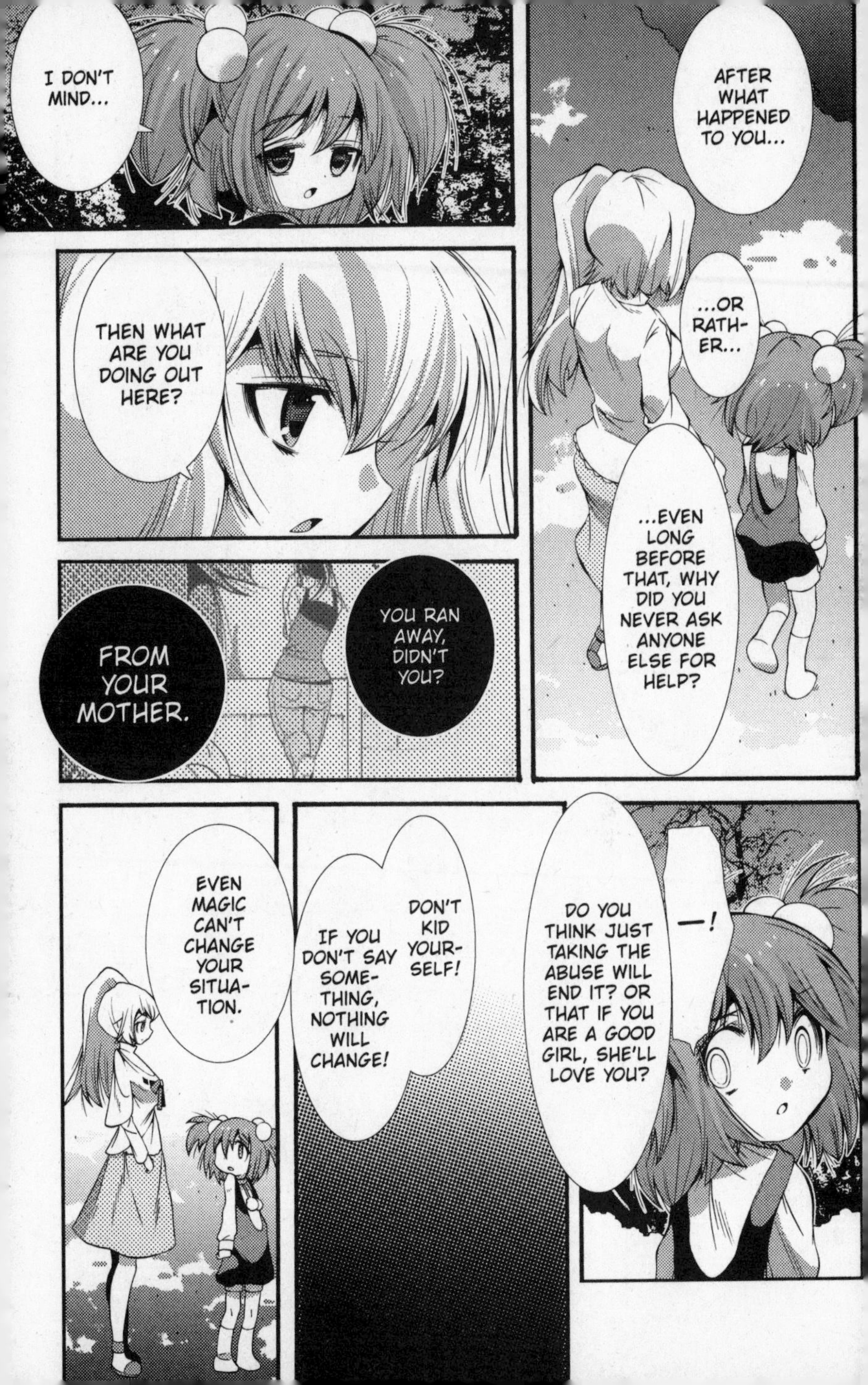
AFTER WHAT HAPPENED TO YOU...
...OR RATHER...
...EVEN LONG BEFORE THAT, WHY DID YOU NEVER ASK ANYONE ELSE FOR HELP?
I DON'T MIND...
THEN WHAT ARE YOU DOING OUT HERE?
YOU RAN AWAY, DIDN'T YOU?
FROM YOUR MOTHER.
DO YOU THINK JUST TAKING THE ABUSE WILL END IT? OR THAT IF YOU ARE A GOOD GIRL, SHE'LL LOVE YOU?
—!
DON'T KID YOURSELF!
IF YOU DON'T SAY SOMETHING, NOTHING WILL CHANGE!
EVEN MAGIC CAN'T CHANGE YOUR SITUATION.

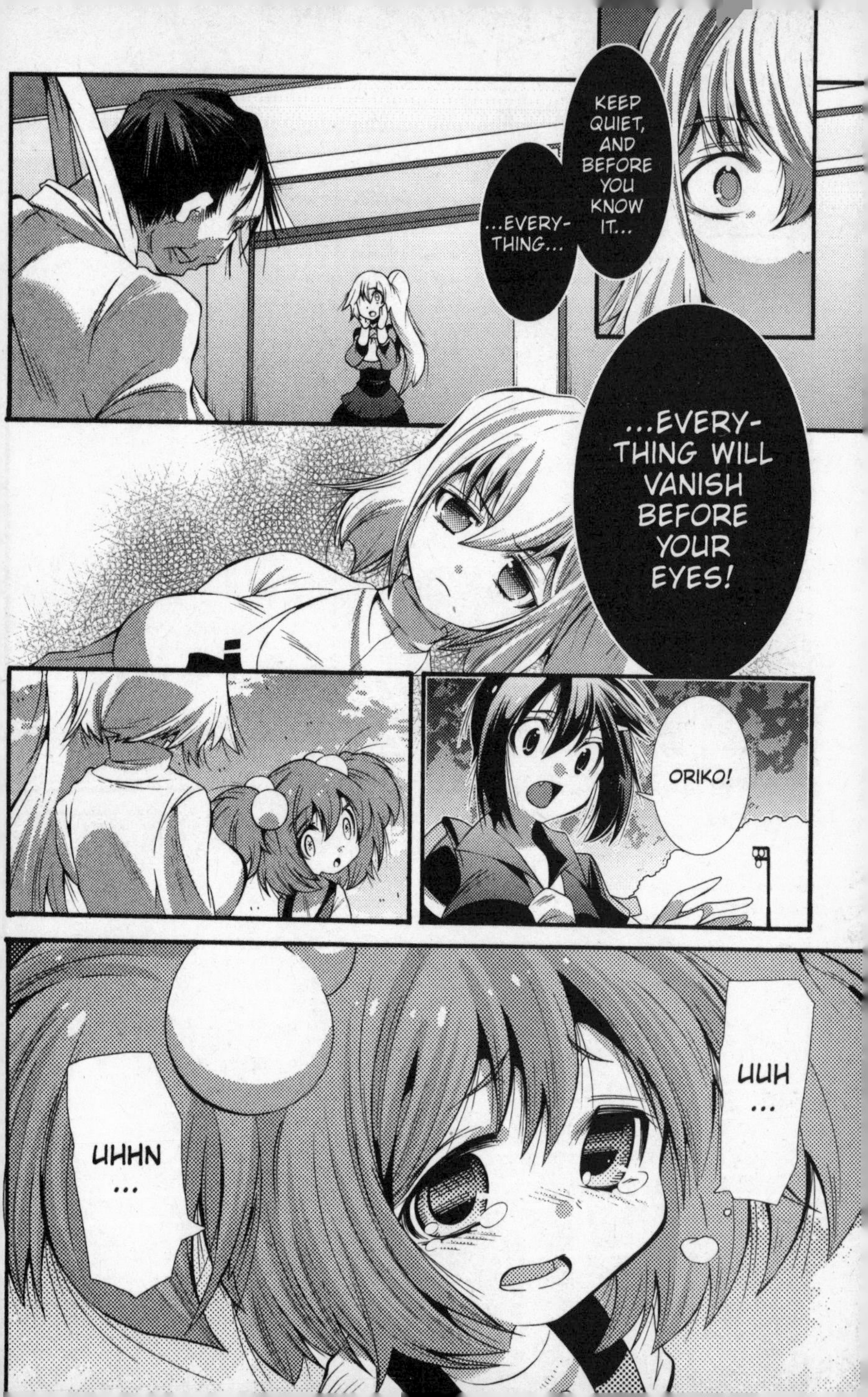
KEEP QUIET, AND BEFORE YOU KNOW IT...
...EVERY-THING...
...EVERY-THING WILL VANISH BEFORE YOUR EYES!
ORIKO!
UUH...
UHHN...

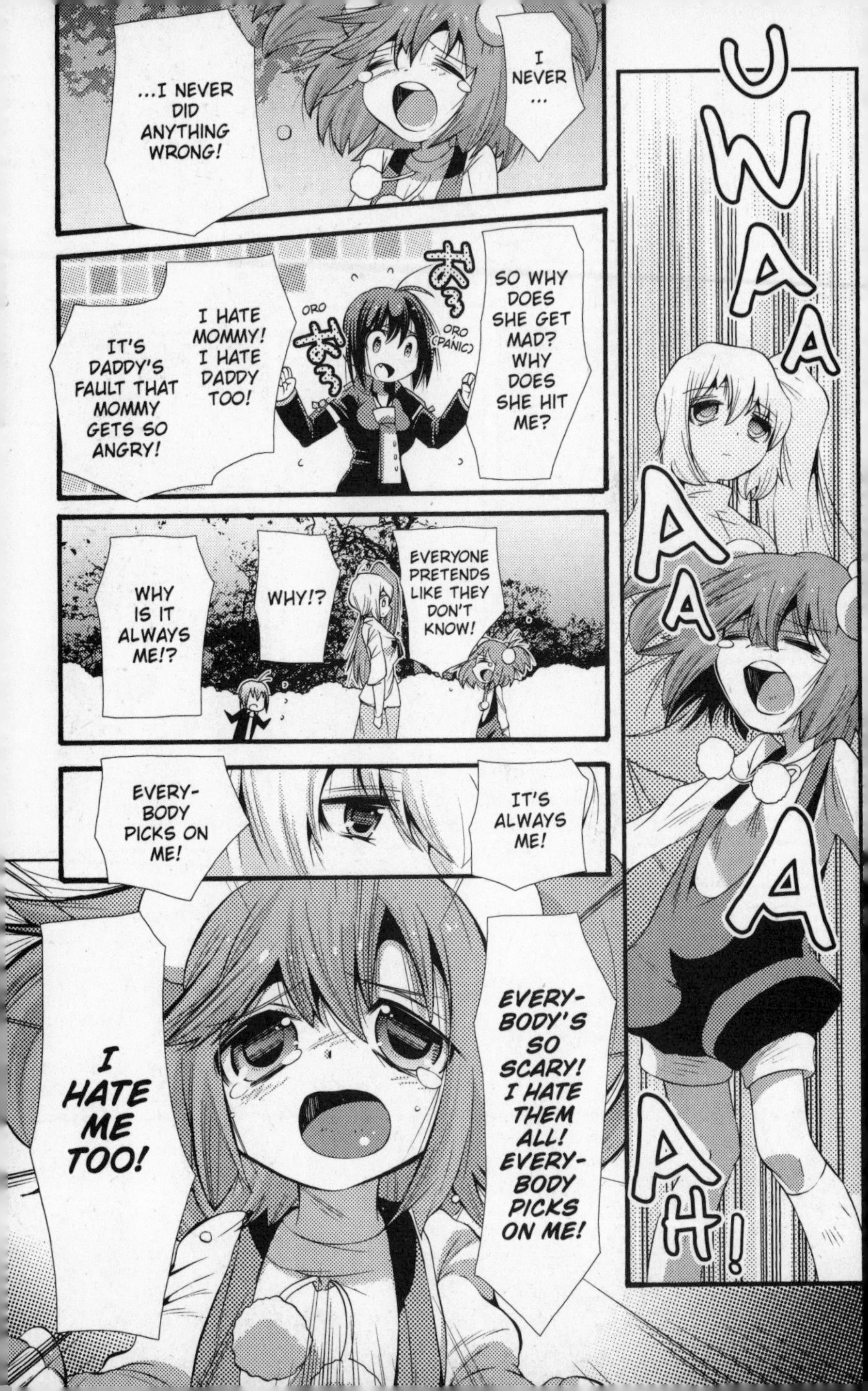
UWAAAAAH!
I NEVER ...
...I NEVER DID ANYTHING WRONG!
SO WHY DOES SHE GET MAD? WHY DOES SHE HIT ME?
ORO (PANIC)
ORO
I HATE MOMMY! I HATE DADDY TOO!
IT'S DADDY'S FAULT THAT MOMMY GETS SO ANGRY!
EVERYONE PRETENDS LIKE THEY DON'T KNOW!
WHY!?
WHY IS IT ALWAYS ME!?
IT'S ALWAYS ME!
EVERY-BODY PICKS ON ME!
EVERY-BODY'S SO SCARY! I HATE THEM ALL! EVERY-BODY PICKS ON ME!
I HATE ME TOO!

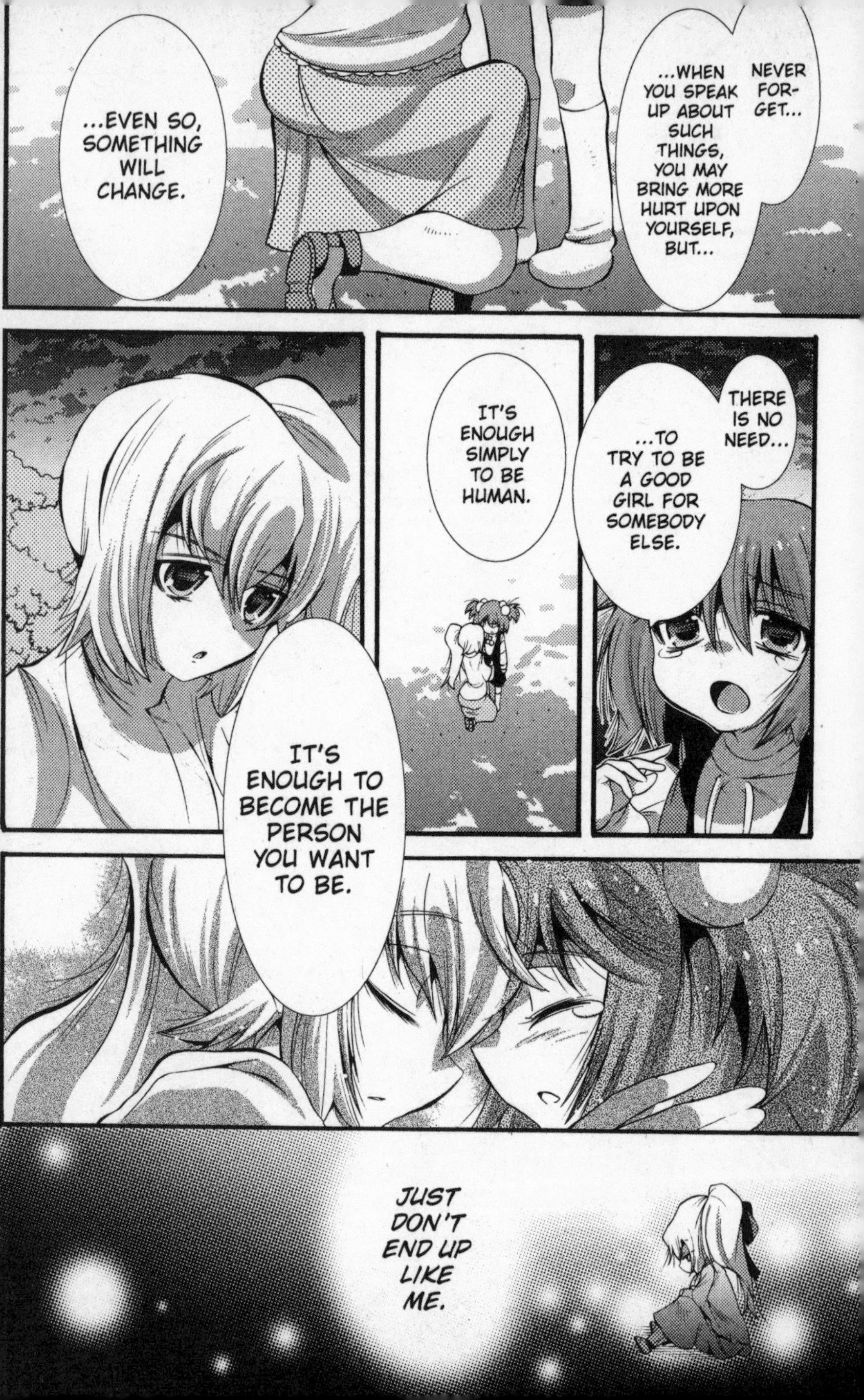
NEVER FORGET...
...WHEN YOU SPEAK UP ABOUT SUCH THINGS, YOU MAY BRING MORE HURT UPON YOURSELF, BUT...
...EVEN SO, SOMETHING WILL CHANGE.
THERE IS NO NEED...
...TO TRY TO BE A GOOD GIRL FOR SOMEBODY ELSE.
IT'S ENOUGH SIMPLY TO BE HUMAN.
IT'S ENOUGH TO BECOME THE PERSON YOU WANT TO BE.
JUST DON'T END UP LIKE ME.

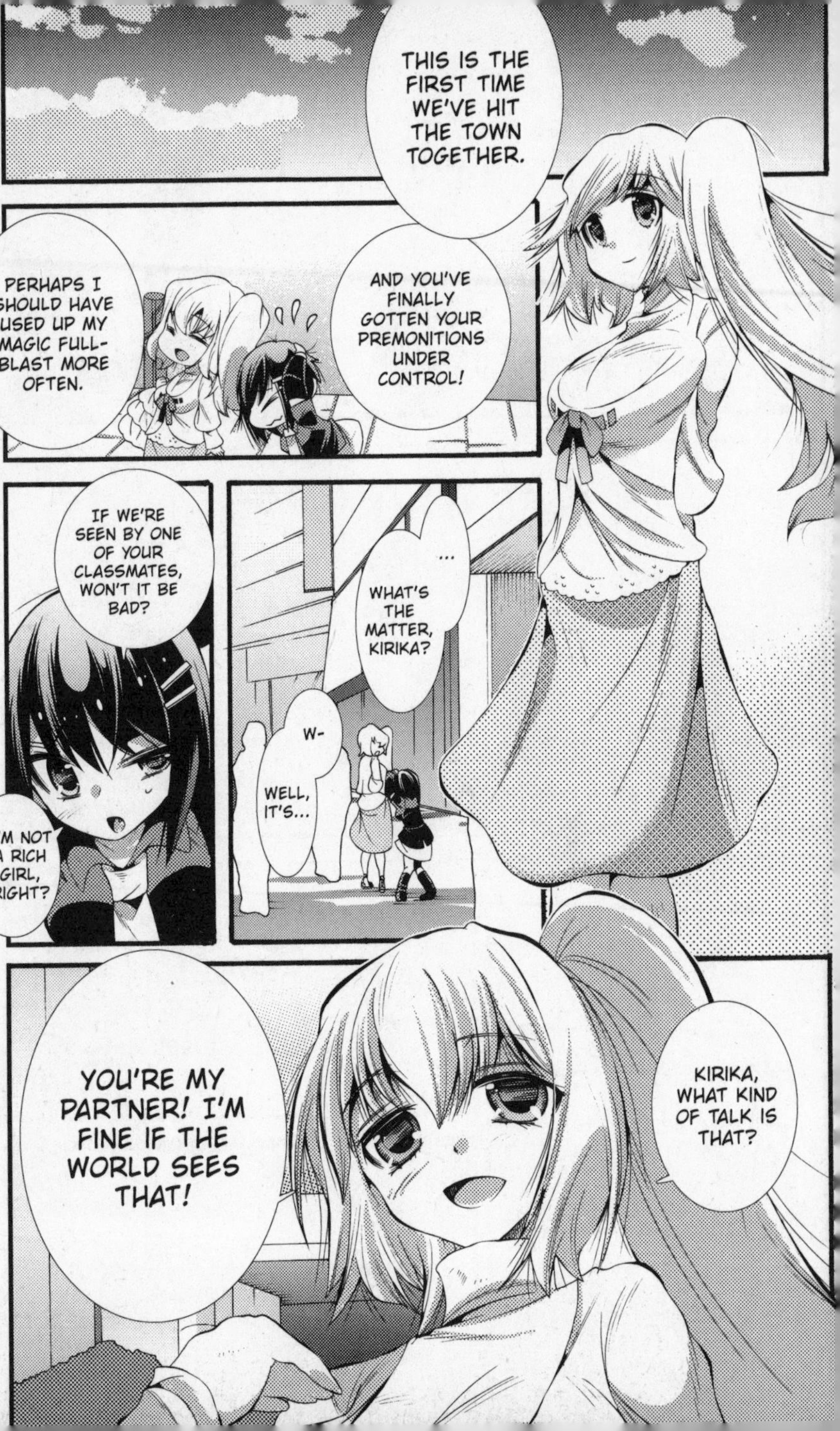
THIS IS THE FIRST TIME WE'VE HIT THE TOWN TOGETHER.
AND YOU'VE FINALLY GOTTEN YOUR PREMONITIONS UNDER CONTROL!
PERHAPS I SHOULD HAVE USED UP MY MAGIC FULL-BLAST MORE OFTEN.
...
WHAT'S THE MATTER, KIRIKA?
W-
WELL, IT'S...
IF WE'RE SEEN BY ONE OF YOUR CLASSMATES, WON'T IT BE BAD?
I'M NOT A RICH GIRL, RIGHT?
KIRIKA, WHAT KIND OF TALK IS THAT?
YOU'RE MY PARTNER! I'M FINE IF THE WORLD SEES THAT!

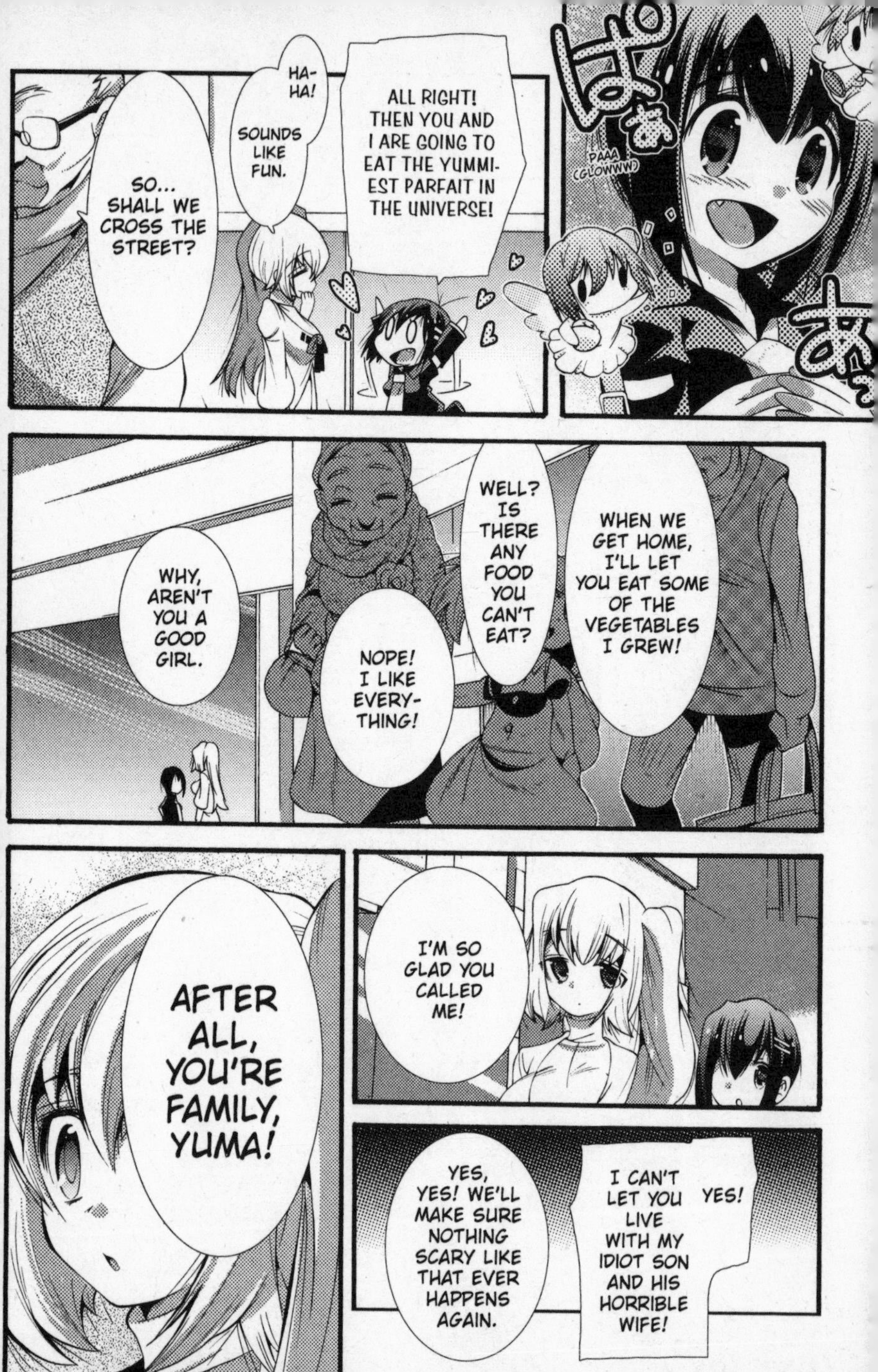
ぱぁ
PAAA (GLOWWW)
ALL RIGHT! THEN YOU AND I ARE GOING TO EAT THE YUMMIEST PARFAIT IN THE UNIVERSE!
HA-HA! SOUNDS LIKE FUN.
SO... SHALL WE CROSS THE STREET?
WHEN WE GET HOME, I'LL LET YOU EAT SOME OF THE VEGETABLES I GREW!
WELL? IS THERE ANY FOOD YOU CAN'T EAT?
NOPE! I LIKE EVERYTHING!
WHY, AREN'T YOU A GOOD GIRL.
I'M SO GLAD YOU CALLED ME!
YES!
I CAN'T LET YOU LIVE WITH MY IDIOT SON AND HIS HORRIBLE WIFE!
YES, YES! WE'LL MAKE SURE NOTHING SCARY LIKE THAT EVER HAPPENS AGAIN.
AFTER ALL, YOU'RE FAMILY, YUMA!

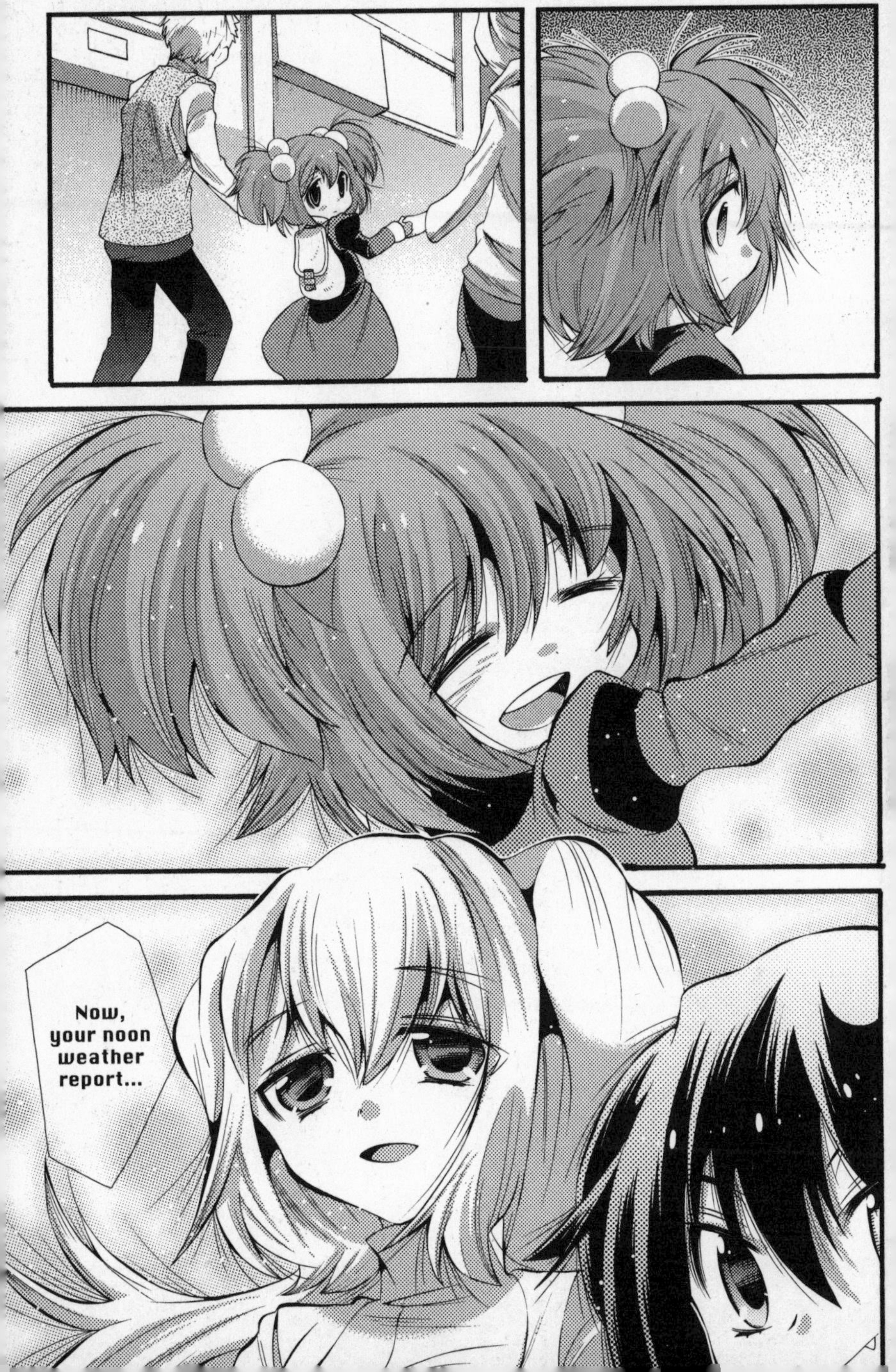
Now, your noon weather report...

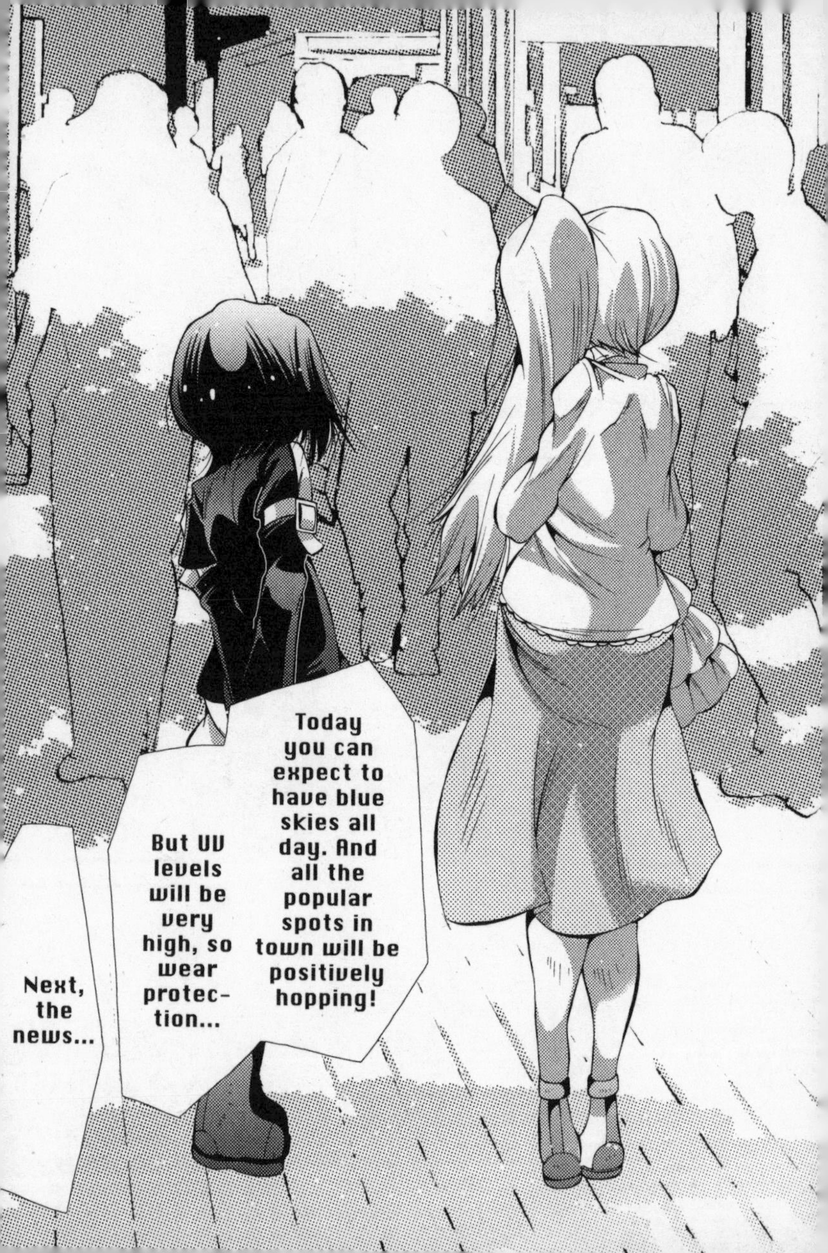
Today you can expect to have blue skies all day. And all the popular spots in town will be positively hopping!
But UV levels will be very high, so wear protec-tion...
Next, the news...

PUELLA MAGI
ORIKO ★ MAGICA
[extra story]

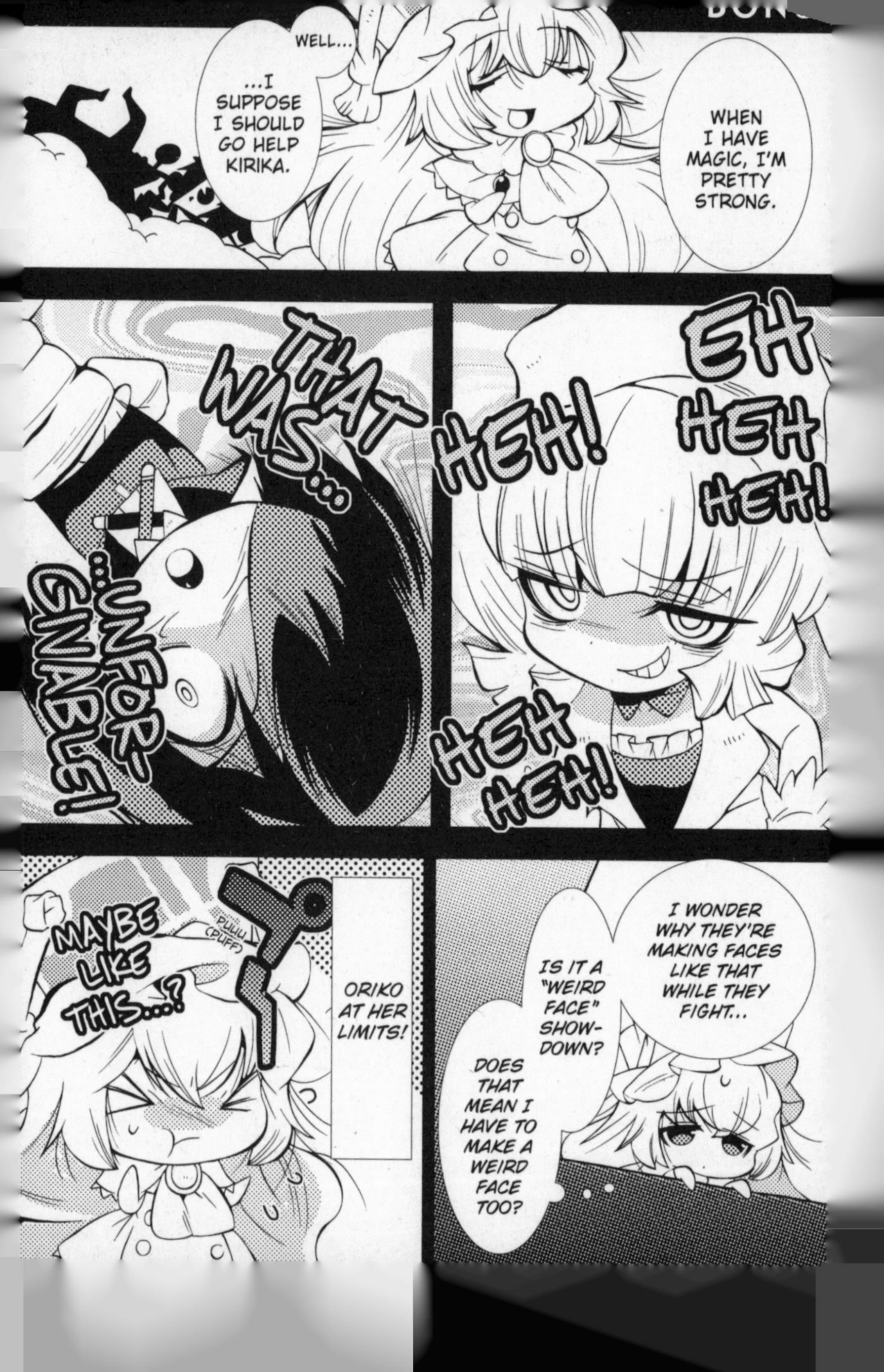
WHEN I HAVE MAGIC, I'M PRETTY STRONG.
WELL...
...I SUPPOSE I SHOULD GO HELP KIRIKA.
EH HEH HEH!
HEH!
HEH HEH!
THAT WAS...
...UNFORGIVABLE!
I WONDER WHY THEY'RE MAKING FACES LIKE THAT WHILE THEY FIGHT...
IS IT A "WEIRD FACE" SHOW-DOWN?
DOES THAT MEAN I HAVE TO MAKE A WEIRD FACE TOO?
ORIKO AT HER LIMITS!
PUUU (PUFF)
MAYBE LIKE THIS...?

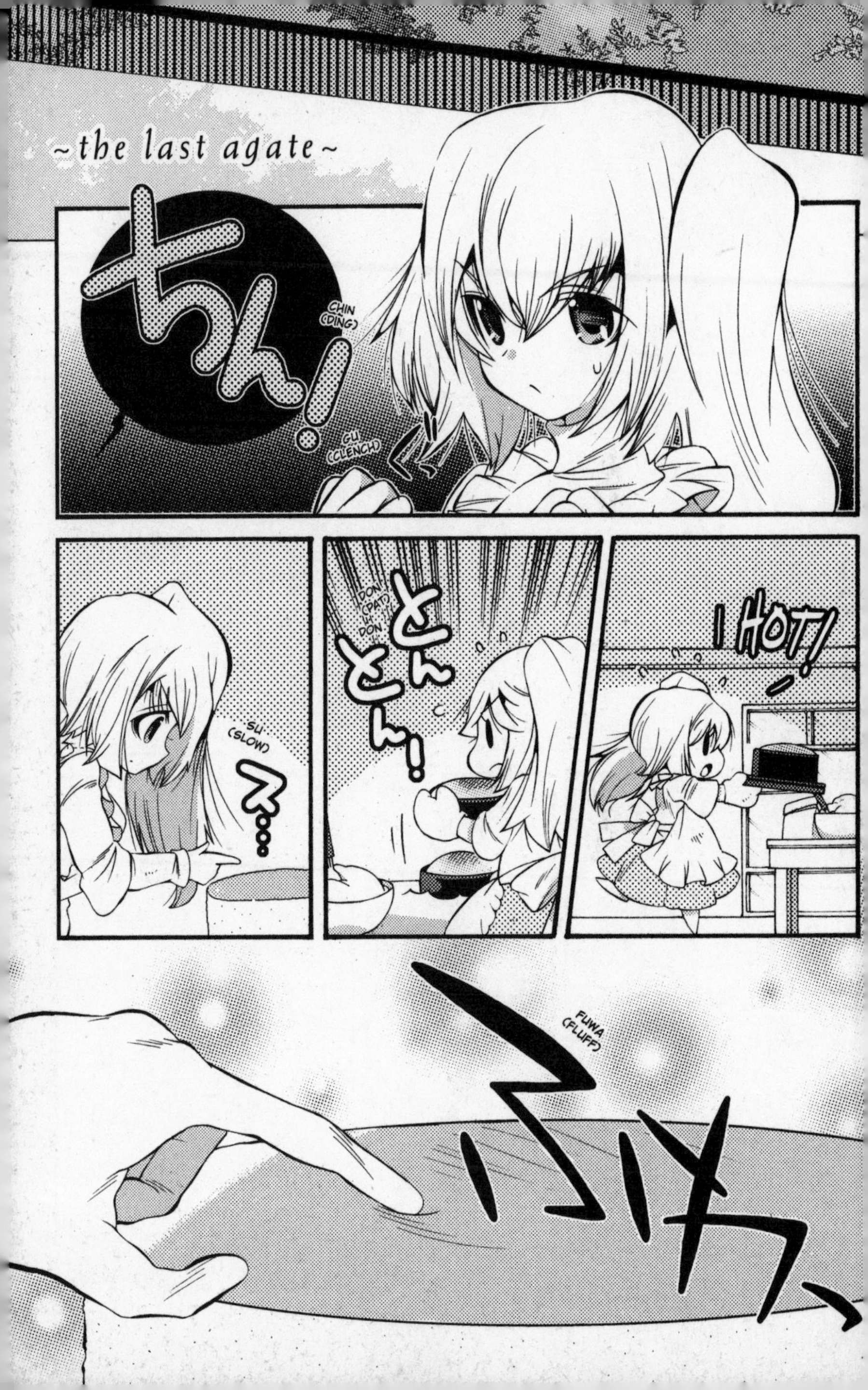
~the last agate~
ちん!
CHIN (DING)
GU (CLENCH)
HOT!
とんとん!
DON (PAT) DON
す…
SU (SLOW)
ふわっ
FUWA (FLUFF)

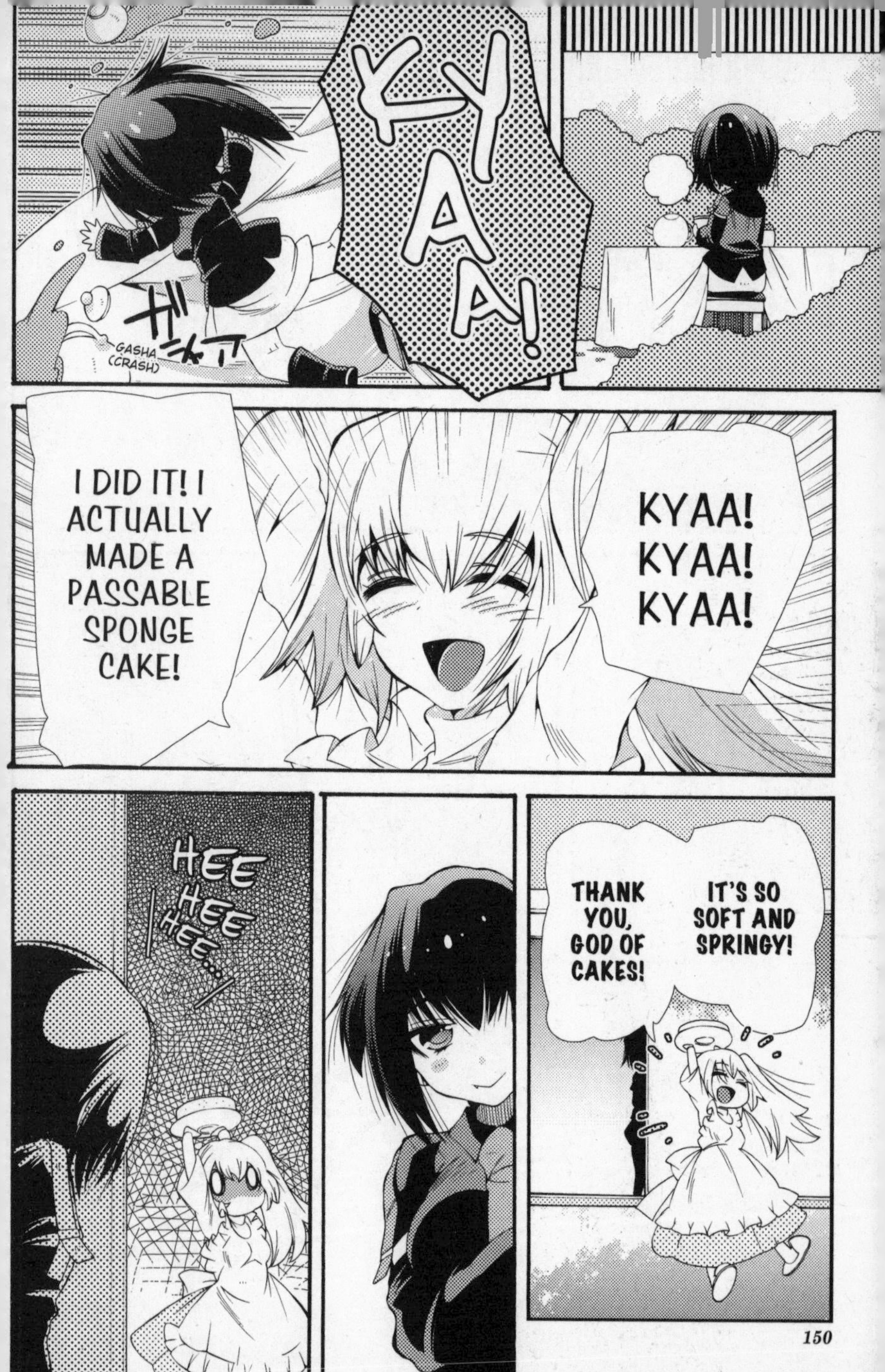
KYAAA!
GASHA
(CRASH)
KYAA! KYAA! KYAA!
I DID IT! I ACTUALLY MADE A PASSABLE SPONGE CAKE!
THANK YOU, GOD OF CAKES!
IT'S SO SOFT AND SPRINGY!
HEE HEE HEE...

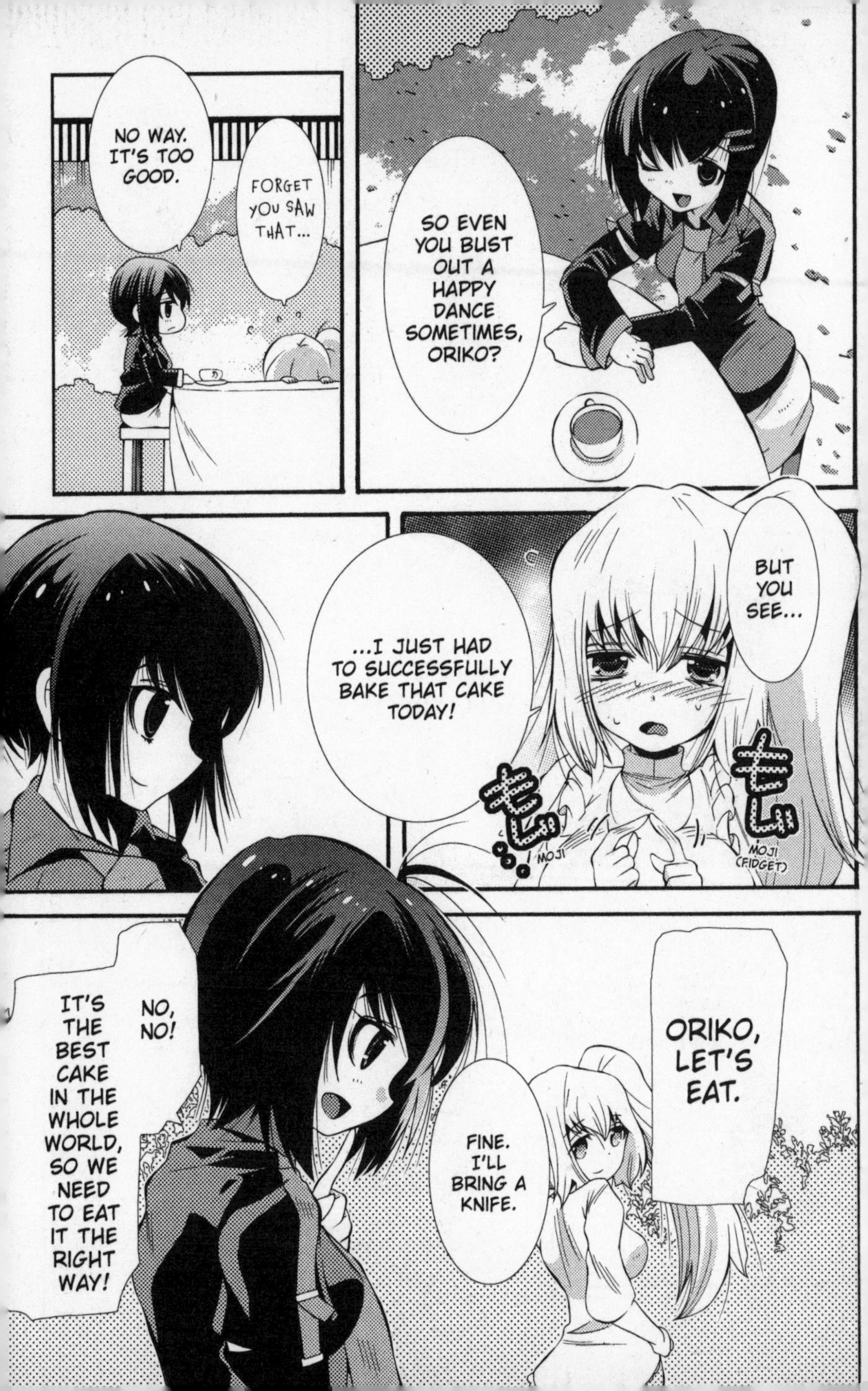
SO EVEN YOU BUST OUT A HAPPY DANCE SOMETIMES, ORIKO?
FORGET YOU SAW THAT...
NO WAY. IT'S TOO GOOD.
BUT YOU SEE...
...I JUST HAD TO SUCCESSFULLY BAKE THAT CAKE TODAY!
MOJI (FIDGET)
MOJI
ORIKO, LET'S EAT.
FINE. I'LL BRING A KNIFE.
NO, NO!
IT'S THE BEST CAKE IN THE WHOLE WORLD, SO WE NEED TO EAT IT THE RIGHT WAY!

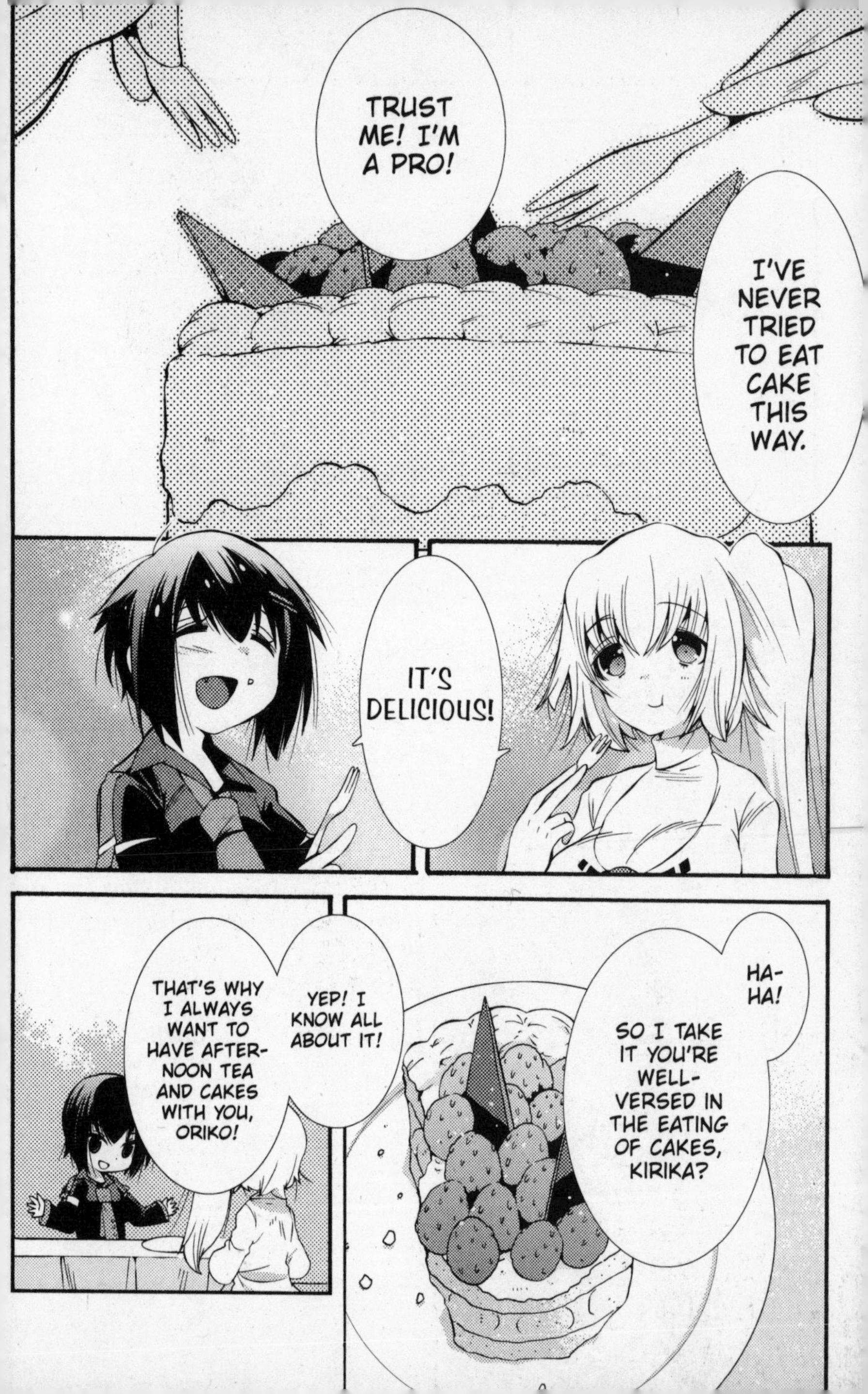
I'VE NEVER TRIED TO EAT CAKE THIS WAY.
TRUST ME! I'M A PRO!
IT'S DELICIOUS!
HA-HA!
SO I TAKE IT YOU'RE WELL-VERSED IN THE EATING OF CAKES, KIRIKA?
YEP! I KNOW ALL ABOUT IT!
THAT'S WHY I ALWAYS WANT TO HAVE AFTER-NOON TEA AND CAKES WITH YOU, ORIKO!

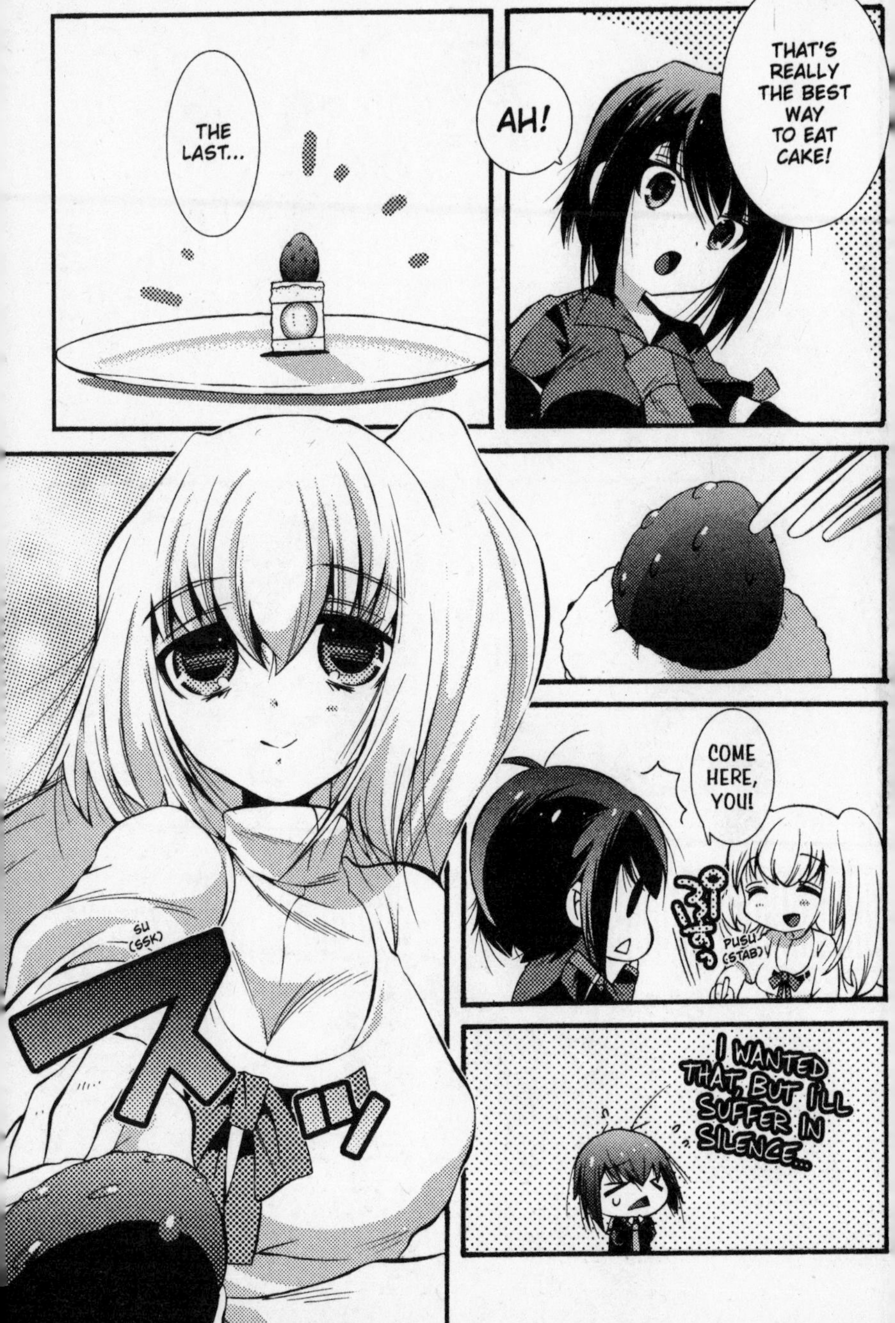
THAT'S REALLY THE BEST WAY TO EAT CAKE!
AH!
THE LAST...
COME HERE, YOU!
PUSU (STAB)
I WANTED THAT, BUT I'LL SUFFER IN SILENCE...
SU (SSK)

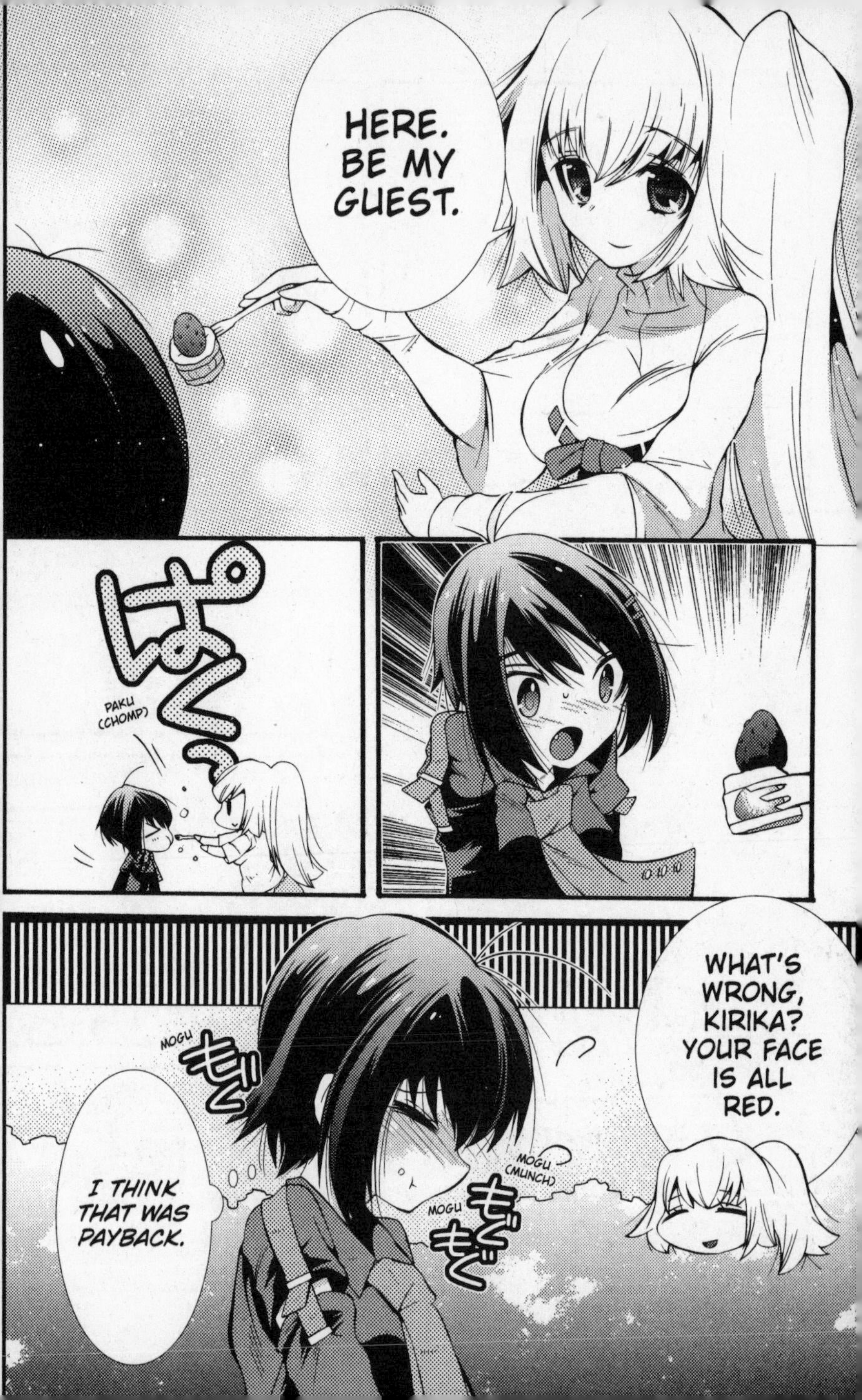
HERE. BE MY GUEST.
ぱくっ
PAKU (CHOMP)
WHAT'S WRONG, KIRIKA? YOUR FACE IS ALL RED.
MOGU
もぐ
MOGU (MUNCH)
もぐもぐ
MOGU
I THINK THAT WAS PAYBACK.

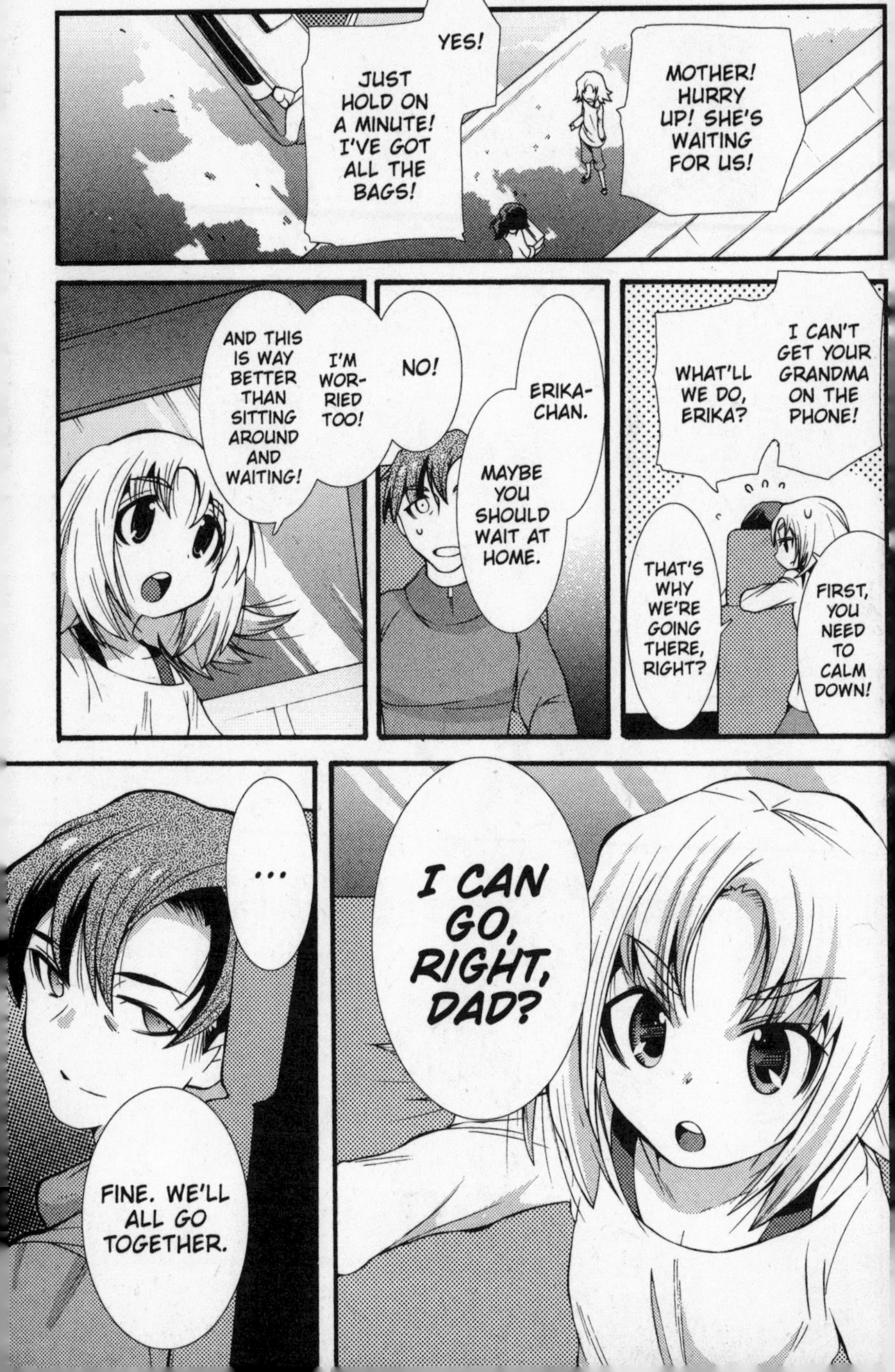
MOTHER! HURRY UP! SHE'S WAITING FOR US!
YES!
JUST HOLD ON A MINUTE! I'VE GOT ALL THE BAGS!
I CAN'T GET YOUR GRANDMA ON THE PHONE!
WHAT'LL WE DO, ERIKA?
FIRST, YOU NEED TO CALM DOWN!
THAT'S WHY WE'RE GOING THERE, RIGHT?
ERIKA-CHAN.
MAYBE YOU SHOULD WAIT AT HOME.
NO!
I'M WOR-RIED TOO!
AND THIS IS WAY BETTER THAN SITTING AROUND AND WAITING!
I CAN GO, RIGHT, DAD?
...
FINE. WE'LL ALL GO TOGETHER.

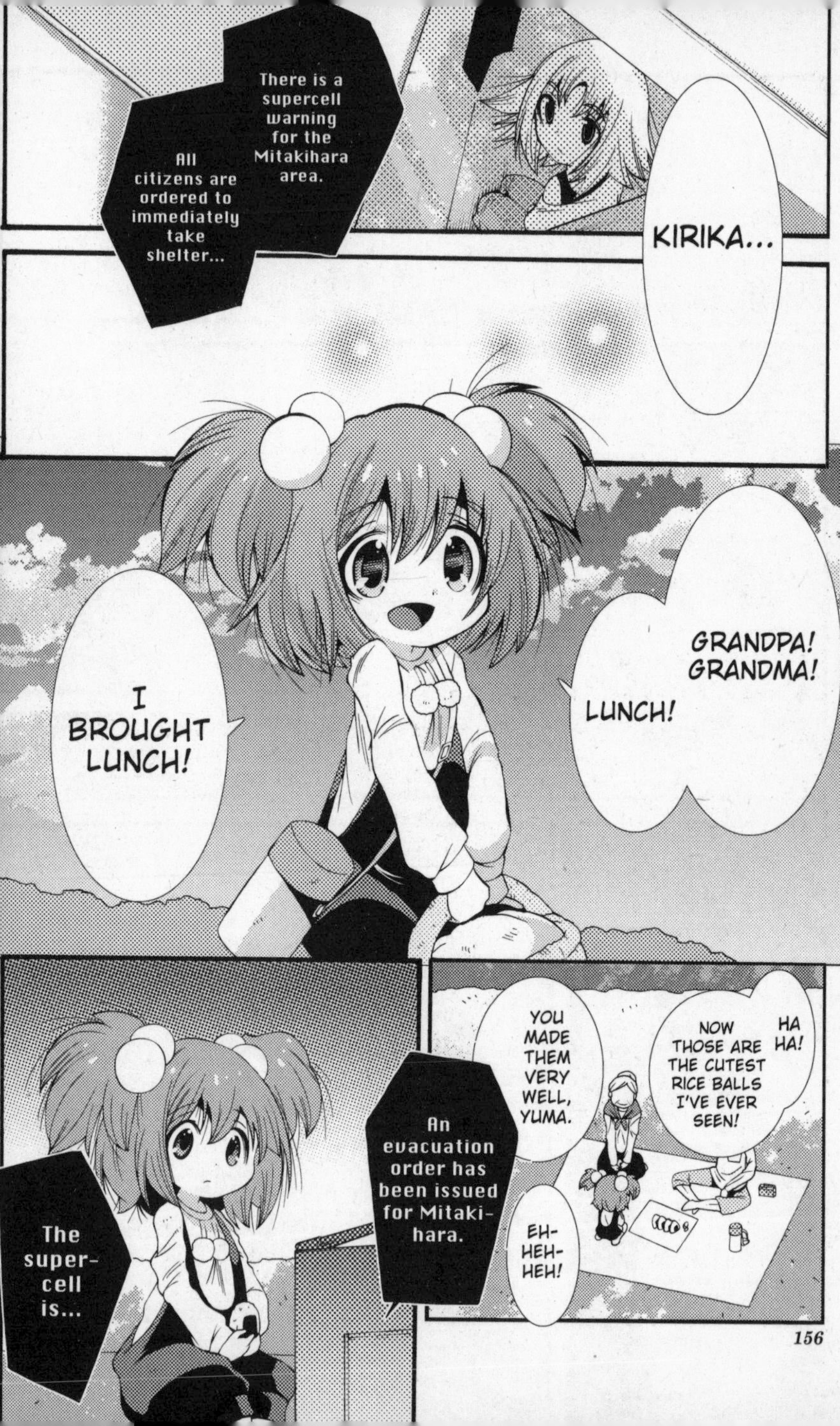
There is a supercell warning for the Mitakihara area.
All citizens are ordered to immediately take shelter...
KIRIKA...
GRANDPA! GRANDMA!
LUNCH!
I BROUGHT LUNCH!
NOW THOSE ARE THE CUTEST RICE BALLS I'VE EVER SEEN!
HA HA!
YOU MADE THEM VERY WELL, YUMA.
EH-HEH-HEH!
An evacuation order has been issued for Mitaki-hara.
The super-cell is...

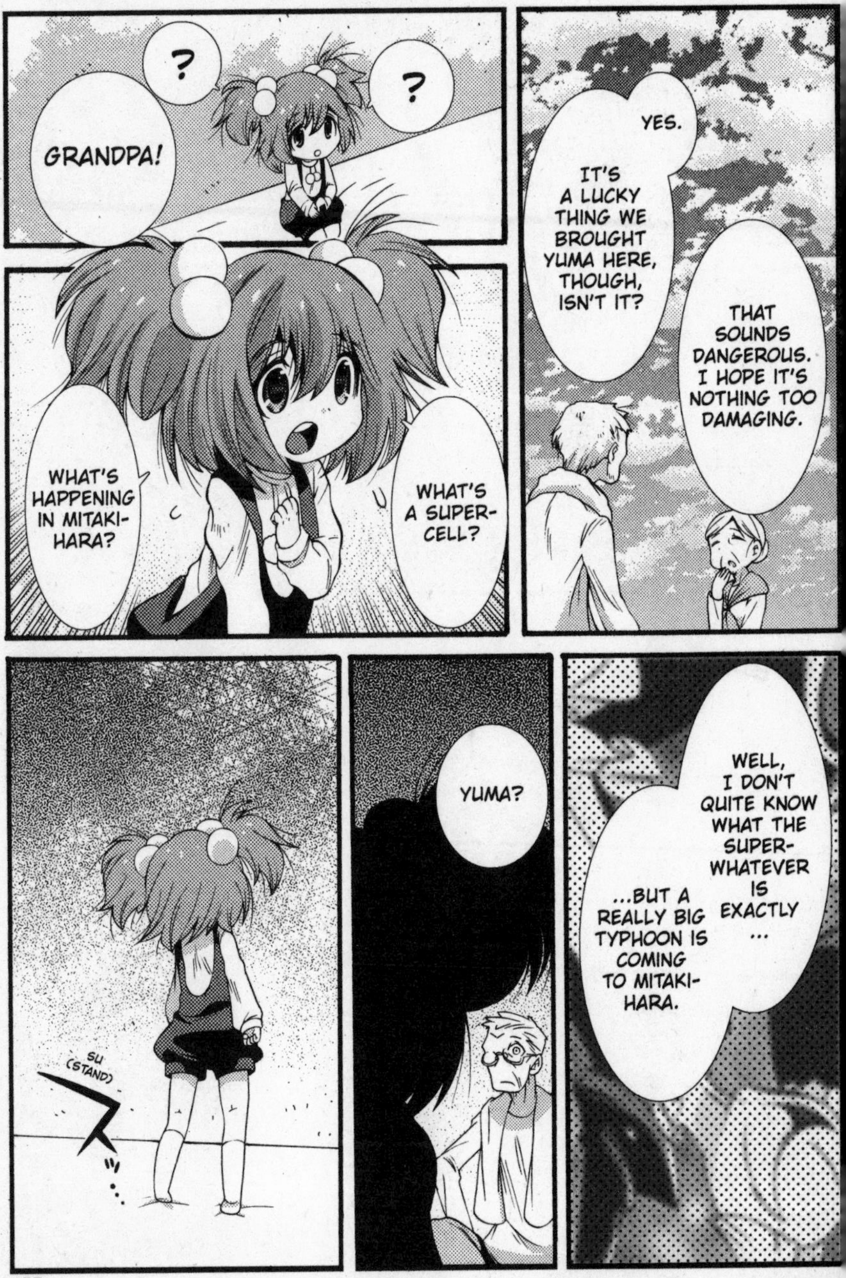
YES.
IT'S A LUCKY THING WE BROUGHT YUMA HERE, THOUGH, ISN'T IT?
THAT SOUNDS DANGEROUS. I HOPE IT'S NOTHING TOO DAMAGING.
?
?
GRANDPA!
WHAT'S A SUPER-CELL?
WHAT'S HAPPENING IN MITAKI-HARA?
WELL, I DON'T QUITE KNOW WHAT THE SUPER-WHATEVER IS EXACTLY...
...BUT A REALLY BIG TYPHOON IS COMING TO MITAKI-HARA.
YUMA?
SU (STAND)

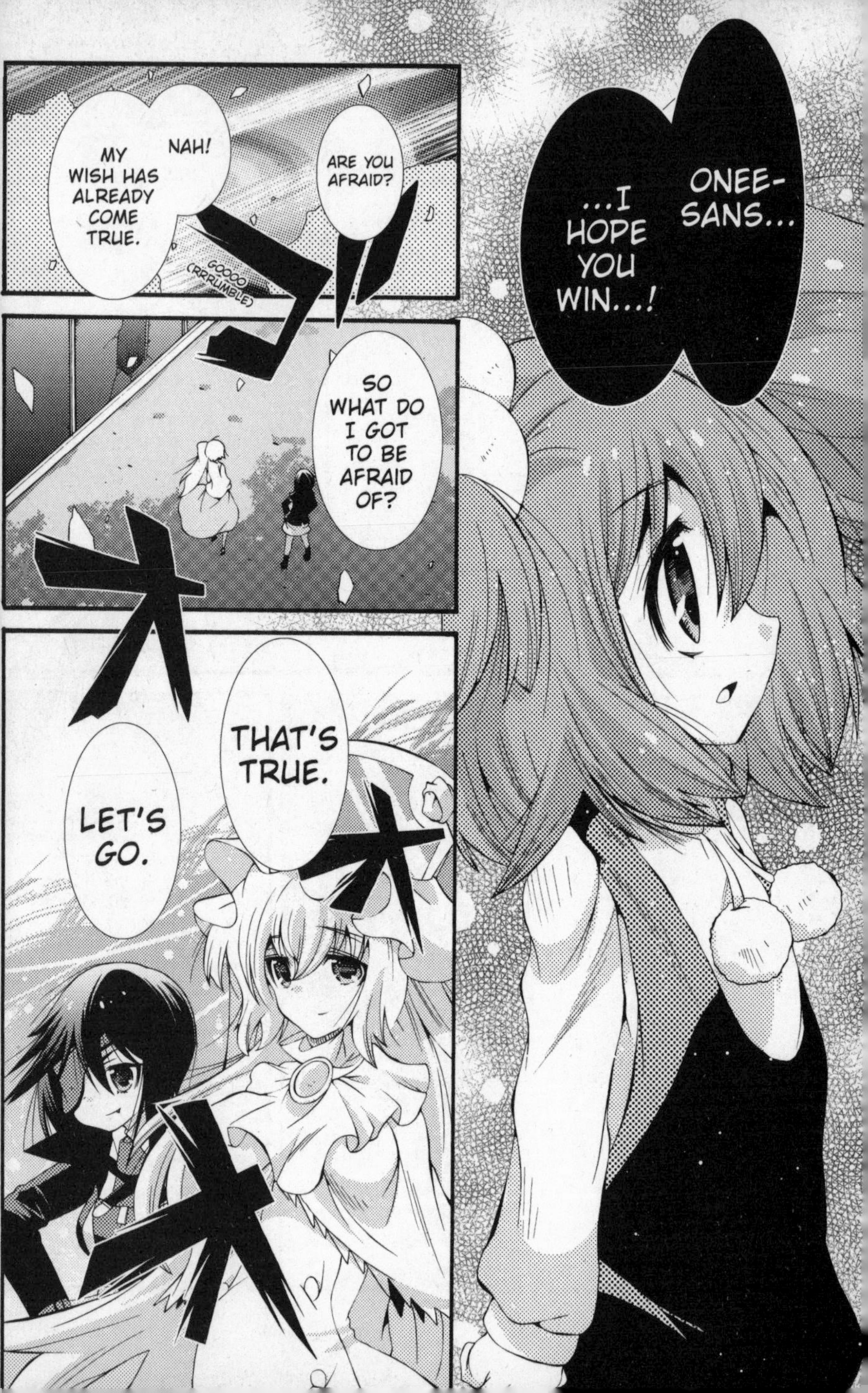
ONEE-SANS...
...I HOPE YOU WIN...!
ARE YOU AFRAID?
NAH!
MY WISH HAS ALREADY COME TRUE.
GOOOO (RRRUMBLE)
SO WHAT DO I GOT TO BE AFRAID OF?
THAT'S TRUE.
LET'S GO.

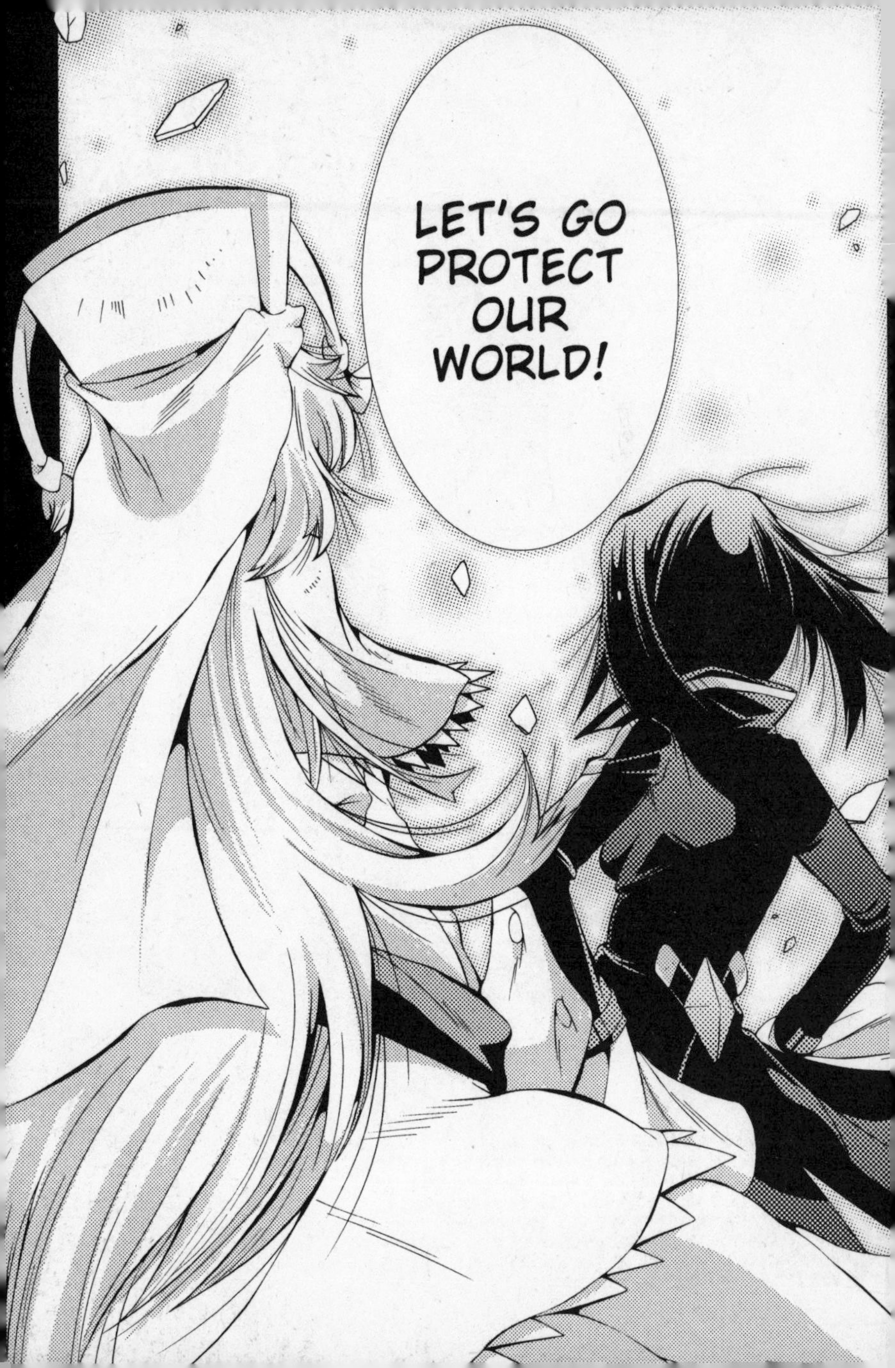
LET'S GO PROTECT OUR WORLD!

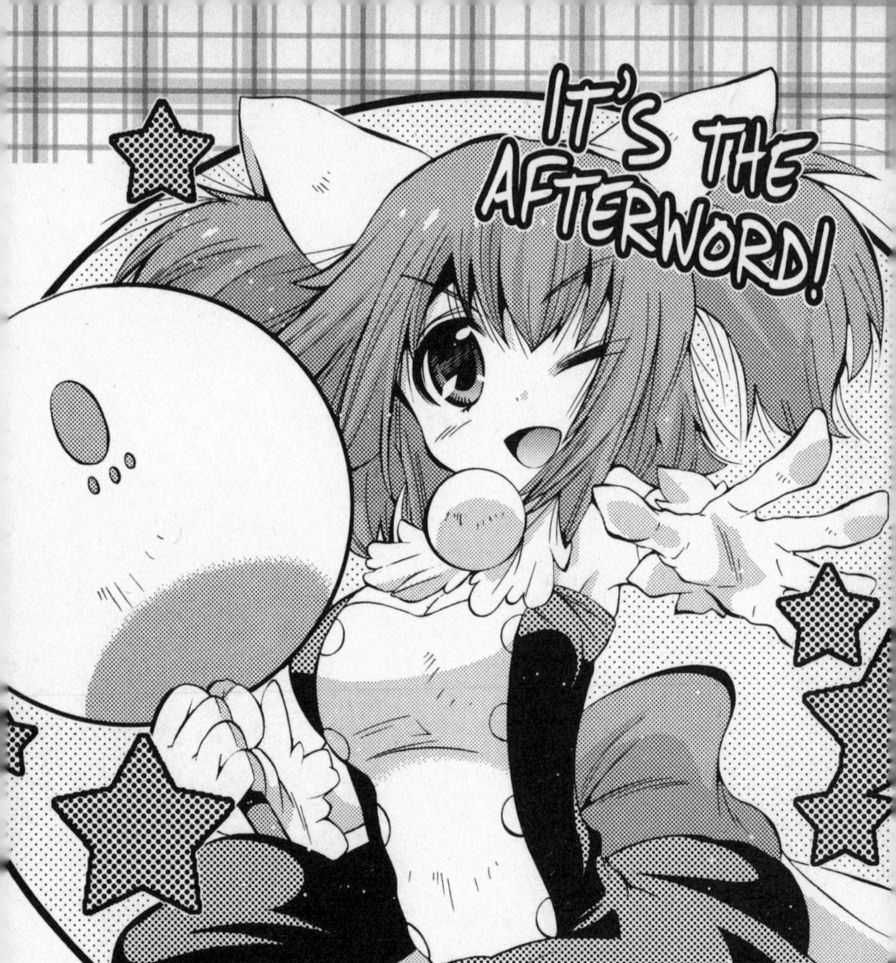
IT'S THE AFTERWORD!

THANK YOU SO MUCH FOR PICKING UP *PUELLA MAGI ORIKO ☆ MAGICA: EXTRA STORY*. WHEN I ACCEPTED THE ASSIGNMENT TO DRAW THE ORIGINAL ORIKO MANGA, I NEVER THOUGHT I'D BE INVOLVED WITH HER FOR THIS LONG. I'D LIKE TO EXPRESS MY THANKS TO THE READERS, EVERYONE WHO HAS SUPPORTED ME, AND ALL OF THE GOOD PEOPLE CONNECTED WITH *MADOKA☆MAGICA*!

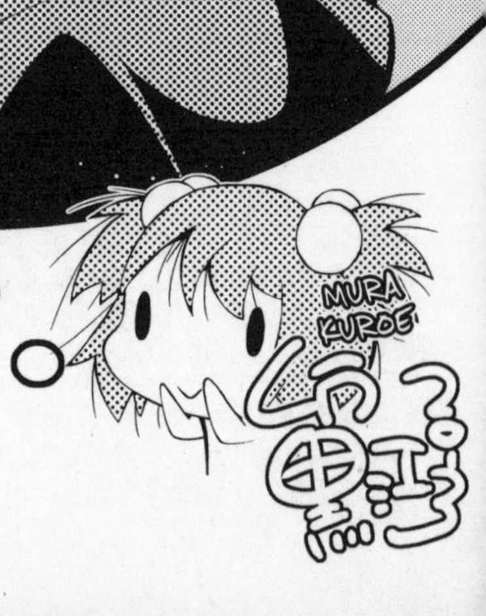
MURA KUROE